PRISON LIFE

Prison Life

Pain, Resistance, and Purpose

Ian O'Donnell

NEW YORK UNIVERSITY PRESS
New York

NEW YORK UNIVERSITY PRESS
New York
www.nyupress.org

© 2023 by New York University
All rights reserved

Please contact the Library of Congress for Cataloging-in-Publication data.
ISBN: 9781479816132 (hardback)
ISBN: 9781479816156 (paperback)
ISBN: 9781479816187 (library ebook)
ISBN: 9781479816163 (consumer ebook)

New York University Press books are printed on acid-free paper, and their binding materials are chosen for strength and durability. We strive to use environmentally responsible suppliers and materials to the greatest extent possible in publishing our books.

Manufactured in the United States of America

10 9 8 7 6 5 4 3 2 1

Also available as an ebook

Ar scáth a chéile a mhaireann na daoine.
(Irish proverb: "We live in each other's shadows")

Rather than being casualties of war, we realized we could be agents of change.
—Laurence McKeown, H Blocks, Northern Ireland

I'm the huevon Mexican, cell-taught, self-taught, the original writ-writer, chained up and locked down for a lifetime.
—David Ruiz, Eastham Unit, Texas

Before we had a code, the leader's strength mattered. Now there is a system, personalities matter less. It is more civilized.
—Chalew Gebino, Isir Bet, Ethiopia

The world outside is like another planet. I feel like I am trapped within a disease.
—Jack Powers, ADX Florence, Colorado

CONTENTS

Preface	xi
1. Twisting the Penal Kaleidoscope	1
2. H Blocks, Northern Ireland	31
3. Eastham Unit, Texas	82
4. Isir Bet, Ethiopia	127
5. ADX Florence, Colorado	171
6. Carceral Contours	220
Acknowledgments	259
References	261
Index	271
About the Author	287

PREFACE

This book had an unusual gestation. It began with an enterprising priest, continued with field trips to Ethiopia and Texas, looped back to a distant memory of a visit to an institution that has since been largely demolished, and culminated—after much reading, revision, and cogitation—in what follows.

First, the beginning. I had written a book about how men and women cope with prolonged isolation—*Prisoners, Solitude, and Time* (published in 2014 by Oxford University Press)—which my university used to promote its graduate programs in criminology via posters on buses and trains. One of these was seen by Paddy Moran, a Spiritan missionary, as he boarded a bus outside Dublin airport having traveled from Addis Ababa. Father Moran invited me to Ethiopia to advise on possible regime improvements in a prison he had taken a close interest in for several years. I accepted his invitation and, during the summer of 2016, spent a week in the Southern Nations, Nationalities, and Peoples' Region of this beautiful country. I was struck by the extreme sociability of prison life, the porous nature of the prison, and the hands-off nature of the relationship with staff. Despite the crowding and the poor conditions, the prison was a safe place where people spent their time constructively. The contrast with the supermax confinement that I had examined for *Prisoners, Solitude, and Time* could not have been greater.

This got me thinking about integration (high in Ethiopia but low in the supermax) and regulation (high in the supermax but low in Ethiopia). I began reflecting on these dimensions of prison life, visited Ethiopia twice more, and started to mull over the kinds of institutions that might be located at other points along these two scales. I recalled a visit to the H Blocks in Northern Ireland I made as part of an official delegation in November 1999, a time when I had exited university life for a few years to become the first full-time executive director of the Irish Penal Reform Trust. The visit was made in the context of a maturing peace process and, at its conclusion, the spokesperson for the men with whom we met presented visitors with a postcard to keep as a memento. It was striking that the prisoners' organizational structure in what was one of the highest-security prisons in Europe was so well embedded as for it to be unremarkable that we would meet directly with its leaders, who would distribute souvenirs. This was a place where both integration and regulation were high and I decided to find out more by meeting some of the men who had been incarcerated there. A return visit to the sole remaining, derelict, H Block to reacquaint myself with its internal configuration proved impossible to arrange despite more than two and a half years of trying. Initially this was because there was no functioning executive in Northern Ireland, then the coronavirus pandemic intervened, and I was finally beaten by bureaucratic inertia.

When I turned my attention back to the supermax I decided to focus on the apotheosis of this development in the US, namely the administrative maximum facility in Florence, Colorado. My request to visit ADX Florence, like everyone else's in recent years, was denied, so I was limited to first-person accounts of life there, litigation, policy documents, investigative journalism, and the reports of occasional audits and inspections. (For what it is worth, I am not entirely unfamiliar with the operation of prolonged solitary confinement, having visited high-security facilities in several other states, including Pennsylvania, New York, Texas, Illinois, and Missouri.)

This left me one case to complete, a prison that was low in both integration and regulation. The building tenders in Texas had first come to my attention as a graduate student in Cambridge, so I read what I could find, reached out to people who knew how they had operated, and traveled to the Lone Star State so that I could explore the archives of the Texas Prison Museum and tour the Eastham Unit, where the litigation that eventually brought down the building tender system originated.

As is often the case with writing, the final product includes only a fraction of the material consulted during its preparation. To keep this book to manageable proportions I had to sharpen Occam's razor and wield it mercilessly. Having collated and considered a wide variety of information relating to prisons in Latin America, Africa, Southeast Asia, India, Europe, the US, and so forth I decided, in the interests of parsimony (and, hopefully, clarity), to limit my attention to the four case study institutions, and in each of them to focus on a single decade. The same approach was taken to the key concepts that illuminate the book. Greater minds than mine have grappled with ideas relating to power, authority, discipline, governance, legitimacy, order, and compliance. Rather than attempting a systematic review I have limited my attention to a small number of contributions that seemed particularly germane to the penal realm. By painting in broad brush strokes, I hope that I have not sacrificed too much in the way of shade or perspective. I have applied the same principle to referencing, opting for a pertinent sparsity in preference to a gratuitous plenitude.

The process that led to this book might be summarized as serendipity, followed by scholarly immersion, and underpinned by an enduring commitment to the necessity of comparativism and the virtues of eclecticism. It was driven by curiosity about the social world and is the culmination of an individual intellectual project, according to a timeframe that was deemed suitable to the task, and not following the dictates of any external funding agency. I hope that the end result is more than a collection of snapshots. There is nothing wrong with such an exercise, of course, as long as the theme, texture, contrast, and emphasis of each picture is of sufficient clarity. But I believe that a properly assembled collage is greater than the sum of its parts. If the reader comes to share this view, the book will have achieved its ambition.

1

Twisting the Penal Kaleidoscope

Much has been written over many years about the challenges of prison life. Dominant themes include the use of force, intergroup rivalries, identity transformation, the erosion of autonomy, the tyranny of the timetable, the security imperative, the attenuation of family and community ties, and the struggle to spend time gainfully. But these understandings are based on texts that tend to be limited to the Global North and, in particular, the Anglosphere. This geographical constraint results in scholarship that can be insufficiently ambitious, and there is much to be gained from broadening the focus. This book is an attempt to add some necessary nuance to debates about what Gresham Sykes famously described as "the society of captives" by drawing on an example from the Global South and another from among the smaller jurisdictions that tend to be neglected on the basis of superficial similarities with Britain and the US.

As will become clear, *Prison Life* takes issue with the contention that custodial institutions share "basic similarities which . . . override the variations of time, place, and purpose" (Sykes 1958: xiii). It is an exploration of difference rather than a search for points of similarity and overlap. While the fact of confinement may be constant, its form and texture are not. My challenge is to the external validity of Sykes's classic work. Rather than suggesting his analysis has become redundant with age, my argument is that it never had the universality sometimes attributed to it. Even when it was written, there was no good reason to believe that prisons in New Jersey (where he did his fieldwork) would be the same as those in Texas or other US states, let alone in other countries. Sykes's insightful and eloquent rendering of a prison was just that: a depiction of one prison, in one era, which differed in important aspects from other contemporaneous prisons.

There is much to be learned from obvious divergence as well as apparent convergence. The monotony of the cellular prison, where those in custody wear a uniform, eat food that is selected, prepared, and served to them, and follow a rigid timetable, is worlds away from the conviviality of a congregate environment where they provide their own clothes, cook their own meals, and devise their own daily routines. The tools we have devised to understand the one may be of limited value when it comes to interrogating the other and may need to be reengineered or even replaced. Their continuing value will depend on their capacity to adapt to changing circumstances.

Sparks et al. (1996: 301) remarked how "the continual tendency in prison studies to seek to show that there exists some essential and irreducible ideal type of The Prison is almost certainly misleading. . . . It is more productive and more sociologically sensitive to think of a spectrum of possible ordering relations of which 'actually existing' prisons in any given society accentuate certain features." I have not refined my argument to yield a single irreducible type. But nor have I limited myself to a single spectrum of possible relations. What is proposed is an invitation to think about prison life along two dimensions that help to classify (and to clarify) but enable us to move beyond classification (and clarification). They provide a background against which the nature of confinement can be interrogated. They involve a process of parsing and paring so that what is central becomes easily recognizable. The intention is to provide something that is intellectually fecund and strikes a balance between oversimplification and unmanageable complexity.

My thesis is that it may be fruitful to think of prisons according to the degree of integration (among prisoners) and the degree of regulation (in terms of the expansiveness of the rulebook and the number of correctional staff). Any prison can be positioned along these two axes, and the way they combine is the route to understanding prison life. This is an exercise in description rather than prescription, and to articulate it I propose to examine institutions for adult men that represent the extreme combinations of high and low integration and a surfeit or deficit of regulation. Focusing on just four cases provides an opportunity to probe deeply and to present a series of rounded accounts. Rather than offering ideal types with which a variety of prisons can be compared or attempting to identify representative members of a "class" of institutions, I have chosen concrete examples from three continents, each of which is examined on its own terms.

From Europe we have the H Blocks of Northern Ireland, a place where both integration and regulation were high. The focus is upon men living in wings controlled by the Irish Republican Army (IRA), who saw the actions that led to their incarceration as politically, rather than criminally, motivated and moved as one, in perpetual defiance of the authorities. Despite a plenitude of staff and a plethora of rules and regulations, as befits a maximum-security environment, they won so many concessions over time that their cells were never locked, the prison's punishment block was decommissioned, they lived communally, answered to their own command structures, and even created spaces where speaking English was not tolerated. (The focus throughout this book is exclusively upon the "provisional" IRA as opposed to the "official" IRA, from which it split in 1969 and which declared a ceasefire in 1972, or the "continuity" IRA, "real" IRA or "new" IRA, groupings that reflect further subdivisions in 1986, 1997, and 2012 respectively.)

From the United States I have selected one state facility and one federal penitentiary. The Eastham Unit in Texas is an example of the kind of life that can emerge when both integration and regulation are low. It housed a population that was riven by racial discord and sexual exploitation, exhausted by field labor, and overseen by a cohort of violent men known as building tenders (BTs), who had been selected by staff to exercise a supervisory and disciplinary role, despite a clear legal prohibition on prisoner involvement in such matters. By abdicating its responsibility, the state allowed an informal system that was to the detriment of most people in custody to become deeply embedded. In ADX Florence, Colorado, the country's most restrictive prison, integration is virtually impossible because the men incarcerated there exist in a state of prolonged solitary confinement. This is social life at its most pared back and impersonal, and it is overseen by a large guard force whose interactions with those under their watch are terse and tense. The rule book is compendious and applied rigidly and relentlessly, with little scope for discretion. A dearth of opportunities for meaningful engagement has predictably pernicious consequences for prisoners' mental health.

From Africa we have (the pseudonymous, for reasons that are explained in chapter 4) Isir Bet in southern Ethiopia. This was a vibrant place whose inhabitants lived according to a code of conduct that they had devised and then agreed to with management. There was little formal regulation and a high degree of integration as prisoners cooperated to create a context where it was possible for them to generate an income during their incarceration, both to ease the pains of confinement and to support their families at home. Relations with staff, who were few in number and largely preoccupied with perimeter security, were distant, but cordial, and a range of committees existed to arrange the day-to-day business of living, especially in the institution's crowded dormitories.

In each case study I concentrate on a decade that proved pivotal, ranging from 1972 to 1982 in the Eastham Unit (from the initiation of a legal challenge to the BT system to its eventual abolition), 1990 to 2000 in the H Blocks (from the republican prisoners' adoption of a written charter to the institution's closure), 2001 to 2011 in ADX Florence (when the detrimental consequences of prolonged isolation became increasingly obvious), and 2010 to 2020 in Isir Bet (from before the election by the prisoners of a charismatic chairman to a brief period of turbulence that occurred after his resignation, and beyond).

Penal Milieus

The prison cannot be fully understood outside the context within which it emerged. In the words of Jacobs (1977: 11), it must be considered as "an organization in action, in dynamic relationship with its political, moral, and institutional environments. At any point in time, various pressures and criss-crossing strains are evident; there is no inevitable or predetermined outcome." Carceral relations, in other words, reflect wider societal imperatives and disciplinary priorities (or, more pithily, we get the prisons we deserve). The H Blocks in Northern Ireland were a direct reflection of the external conditions they were built to tame and remained closely linked to them as another site for the republican struggle; they were generated by a warring state. In Texas, fiscally conservative governments shirked their responsibility. A combination of underspending, limited oversight, and a history of slave plantations created a setting where BTs were co-opted to impose the administration's will and took on the role of adjunct custodians.

ADX Florence is the outworking of a vengeful penality. In a society preoccupied by exaggerated fears and entrenched racial, ethnic, and economic differences, prisoners must be separated from the law-abiding citizenry and from each other, with particular opprobrium reserved for the so-called "worst of the worst," demeaning and totalizing shorthand for those who are believed to deserve prolonged isolation in fiercely austere conditions. (In the Eastham Unit, the state cared little and spent less whereas in ADX Florence, it cares less and spends more.) The social life of Isir Bet was shaped by the harsh realities of an impecunious East African country where, of necessity, the prisoner society filled the gaps. It was not so much that the state decided to stand back as that it was not in a position to step forward, lacking the wherewithal to provide more than the barest essentials. The interstitial prison is characteristic of the Global South.

The four prisons are touched upon throughout this introduction and treated in sequence in chapters 2 to 5. I begin with the H Blocks, where both integration and regulation were high, then move to the Eastham Unit, where each was low, before proceeding to Isir Bet, which was high on the former and low on the latter, and concluding with ADX Florence, which exhibits extreme regulation and barely discernible integration. Key themes are teased out in chapter 6. This process of gradual immersion is intended to acquaint the reader with the contours of very different prisoner societies so that by the end of the book they are equipped with the conceptual tools necessary to become penal cartographers, ready to reconnoiter new worlds and to rethink existing ones. Some might see this as akin to an exercise in "carceral geography" (e.g., Moran 2015) or "southern criminology" (e.g., Carrington et al. 2016), and there are parallels. However, as one who is uneasy about the trend toward increasing subspecialization and disciplinary fragmentation, and uncomfortable with labels, I prefer to proceed independently, drawing inspiration from a diversity of sources. (Ethiopia stands out among the countries examined as it was never a colony.)

In addition to putting each prison in context, I present a pen portrait of an individual whose story is emblematic of the institution. These comprise Laurence McKeown in the H Blocks, an IRA volunteer whose reading of Paulo Freire contributed to the creation of a commune underpinned by a written charter; David Ruiz in the Eastham Unit, a man of violence who learned that a well-composed writ could be more effective than a well-directed shiv and whose actions had consequences that were unprecedently impactful; Chalew Gebino in Isir Bet, a first-time prisoner who drafted, and gained acceptance for, a code that aimed to displace the personal with a set of bureaucratic arrangements from which everyone stood to benefit; and Jack Powers in ADX Florence, a man whose spectacular deterioration was matched only by the arc of his recovery.

Each of these four men was shaped by, and in turn shaped, the carceral world he was compelled to occupy. Their status as prisoners did not come to define them entirely, even during the period of their incarceration. Simultaneously they were thinkers, writers, innovators, and survivors. While a sample size of one can never hope to be representative in a narrow statistical sense, there is much to be gained by sifting an individual's experiences and reflections and using these as a lens through which to investigate larger theoretical and empirical questions (e.g., Maruna and Matravers 2007). By this means, the personal can be connected to the social in a way that is reciprocally illuminating. Perhaps it is time for penology to take a more emphatic idiographic turn, to place sense-making and interpretation at the center?

Prison Life is an attempt to confront the procrustean tendency in prison studies by casting the net wider to capture a greater variety of custodial experiences. My goal is to situate each of the prisons I have selected in its own geographical and temporal milieu. The case studies are theoretically derived in that they occupy extreme positions along two dimensions—integration and regulation—that are fundamental to the prison's social life. My purpose is to invite other scholars to think of any prison as occupying a specific place along these dimensions and then to pinpoint its coordinates.

Having described the process of case selection in the preface, it is appropriate at this point to say something about the sources upon which my analysis is based. These varied from institution to institution but included a mix of court filings, judicial pronouncements, archival searches, official reports, interviews, policy papers, administrative data, audits, inspections, first-person narratives, publications from nongovernmental organizations, journalistic accounts, student dissertations, memoirs, scholarly literature, and observations from site visits. The book is somewhat unusual in its use of photographs, drawings, biographical notes, and sociograms in addition to the graphs and tables that typically adorn the pages of academic treatises. These illustrations are intended to be elaborative rather than purely decorative, to bring to life the internal arrangements of the societies under examination, and to foreground the experiences of those who spent time within them. They took considerable time and effort to compile and will repay careful—and unhurried—viewing. Pause, please, and peruse. Methodologically, then, *Prison Life* is proudly eclectic.

Integration and Regulation

The schematic in figure 1.1 provides the conceptual foundation for what follows. "Integration" refers to cohesion and solidarity, shared norms, the degree of identification with, and attachment to, a recognizable and enduring group, the density and emotional intensity of relational ties, the complexity of networks. It requires the kind of mixing that allows observable formations to evolve. It is about embedded social bonds. Membership of a well-integrated prisoner society provides a buffer against environmental uncertainty; the price of support is affiliation. The highly integrated society benefits the captives but not necessarily the captors.

"Regulation," on the other hand, involves the externally formulated and imposed aspects of the regime, specifically the rule book, its clarity and ambition, the diligence with which it is enforced, and the staffing complement. These are the official demands that the prison makes of its occupants, constituting an exoskeleton for the prisoner body, a set of constraints that determines the direction and nature of travel. They are resisted to a greater or lesser extent everywhere. The highly regulated society benefits the captors but not necessarily the captives.

At one end of the spectrum (ADX Florence), regulation is incessant, unyielding, and intrusive while at the other (Isir Bet) it is intermittent and indifferent. Integration ranges from the deep and united (H Blocks) to the shallow and fragmented (Eastham Unit). Power relations play out against these various backgrounds. IRA prisoners in the H Blocks were resolute in their rejection of attempts to regulate their behavior through policies of criminalization and individualization. In defiance of prison

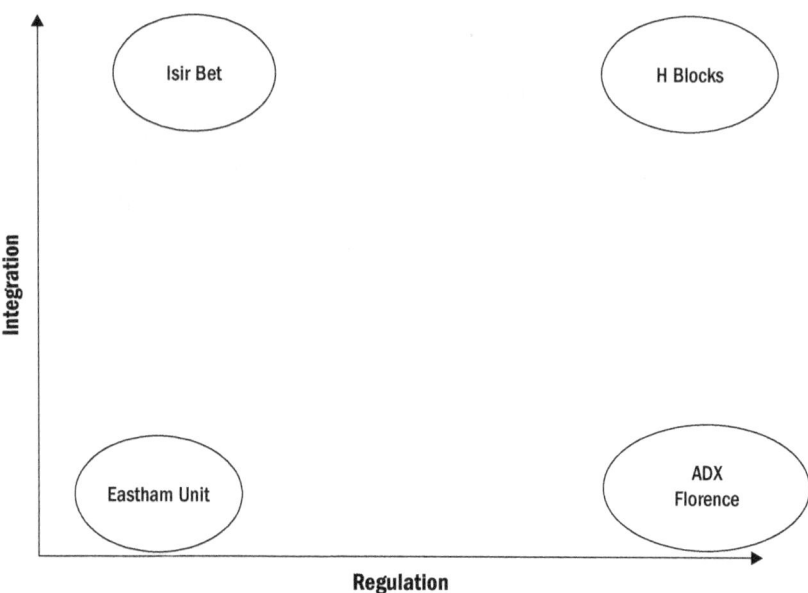

Figure 1.1. Plotting Prison Life.

management they wrote their own charter for daily life. In ADX Florence, there was little relational content to prisoners' lives. While they could spend years there, they were not in each other's presence long enough to form stable connections. The authorities did their utmost to deny them any opportunity for integration. They could not coordinate their activities, and meaningful engagement was seldom possible; this is society at its most attenuated.

The coercive power of the BTs in the Eastham Unit was difficult to resist effectively in-house, so the prisoners directed their efforts outside the prison walls, via litigation. The BT system was low in regulation (because there were few staff and the authorities delegated much control to selected prisoners, allowing them to carry weapons and use brutal violence with impunity) and low in integration (because the prisoners were divided). This system preceded (and possibly precluded) the emergence of gangs (at least those that were not underwritten by the administration). Isir Bet was something of a hybrid situation; the prison resembled the external community and operated according to the usual rules of commerce and congregation but was tightly compressed. As a result, the prisoners drew up detailed guidelines about how they might live at close quarters, perhaps for many years, while continuing to earn money and support their families.

The written constitutions that characterized the H Blocks and Isir Bet were not imposed on the prisoners. Rather, they originated from them, were endorsed by them, and became moral imperatives that they subscribed to and were obligated to promote. Everyone sacrificed a measure of personal autonomy in the interests of collective security and what was perceived as the public good. This process unfolded against a background of carceral regulation that was heavy-handed and fiercely resisted (H Blocks) or light of touch and largely irrelevant (Isir Bet). In these institutions, prisoners identified a need and then initiated a deliberative process to find a mutually satisfactory way of meeting it; governance was actively and far-sightedly brought about. In Isir Bet the document that emerged was approved by the prison's commander. In the H Blocks it was produced surreptitiously and sought no official imprimatur.

For those who chose to remain under the command of the IRA the tightness of social ties in the H Blocks did not become stifling, possibly because of the degree of autonomy that the self-governance structures allowed. The prisoners were united against what they saw as a common enemy and their solidarity was based on debate and discussion as well as the actions that had led to their confinement. They saw the prison as a site for the continuation of their struggle and benefited from staunch community supports. These protective factors prevented immersion from becoming submersion.

Discretion is important in creating an environment that is amenable to the give-and-take of human relations. Sometimes this requires rules to be ignored or selectively applied. This can be for reasons of morality, equity, natural justice, compassion, favoritism, or laziness. Or it can be utilitarian (in service of the smooth operation of the regime). Not in ADX Florence where rigid, and supposedly dispassionate, application was the order of the day and few aspects of prisoners' lives were not meticulously regimented. ADX Florence was the triumph of rational-legal authority, when discretion was entirely squeezed out and the rule book reigned supreme. It was the literal iron cage, a place where an exchange of blows might be the only type of human contact (sometimes being invited for this reason). This further desiccated a life that had already been stripped back so as to be almost unbearable where—grotesquely—even self-mutilation was viewed through a disciplinary lens.

Unlike in other prisons, there was no codependence of staff and prisoners at ADX Florence. Correctional officers did not need to compromise to stay in charge; the situational controls, and bodily restraints, to which prisoners were subjected were so tight that their subordination was never in doubt. The two groups did not get to know each other, meaning that the empathy gap remained wide and—as in the H Blocks—they responded to rigid stereotypes that could not be softened through familiarity. In the Eastham Unit the staff and prisoners came to know each other as workers and, while contact often involved assumed racial superiority and vicious subjugation, there were flashes of humor and humanity amid the hardship and degradation.

Governance

Recalling Sykes, Skarbek (2016: 845) argued: "While many of the basic characteristics of prisons are similar globally, the extent and form of informal inmate organization varies substantially." The task he set himself was to explain this variation, which he did by drawing upon governance theory. My perspective is somewhat different in that I am less persuaded by the extent to which "basic characteristics of prisons are similar globally." Apart from segregating their occupants by gender, reconstituting their spatiotemporal worlds, and seeking to prevent unauthorized egress, there seem to be more points of divergence than convergence as one extends the breadth of the analysis across countries and over time. Also, "basic characteristics" and "informal inmate organization" are often interdependent, with each influencing the other.

When I discuss regulation, it is specifically with reference to externally imposed frames of reference (i.e., legal governance). These emanate from the state (through its laws), the administration (through its policies), and prison staff (through their practices). Skarbek's focus is on (centralized and decentralized) extralegal governance and the conditions that promote or inhibit its emergence. Our interests therefore are overlapping and complementary rather than identical or oppositional. His argument is that "prison gangs form to provide extralegal governance when inmates have a demand for it and official governance mechanisms are ineffective or unavailable" (Skarbek 2014: 8). Gangs evolve as surrogates for decentralized governance mechanisms such as the (unwritten) inmate code and they have a stabilizing effect on a potentially anarchic environment. Many of them have detailed written constitutions and different grades of membership. They have a clear leadership structure, explicit goals, and sometimes are animated by an ideology. They did not exist in the US prior to the 1950s, and Skarbek's argument is that they were not necessary then because the prison population was smaller, and the inmate code governed behavior (for an early account of the code's parameters, see Clemmer 1940). Prisoners knew to keep a distance from staff, to do their own time, to not exploit their fellows, to keep their word, and to not relay information to the authorities. Individuals' reputations were known.

According to Skarbek (2014: 41): "The code became ineffective because there were more inmates, more violent offenders, more first-time inmates, and more young inmates. There was also a radical shift in the ethnic and racial background of inmates. Each of these demographic changes is associated with a weakening of decentralized governance mechanisms that rely on reputations." As the prison population became more heterogenous, that is to say, the inmate code became less effective and a state of anomie developed, accompanied by widespread violence. The governance vacuum ushered in by the diminution of the code was filled by centralized institutions such as gangs that were turned to for protection and order maintenance. Gangs mitigated conflict and enabled access to goods and services, usually prohibited ones. Businesses—including illegal prison-based ones—work better when the environment is stable and predictable. By standardizing their members' behavior with a view to reducing unwanted attention from guards, gangs provided the required measure of extralegal governance. They deepened and perpetuated racial divisions.

Some of my findings are inconsistent with Skarbek's theoretical predictions in that even in a prison where the authorities provide abundant governance the prisoners can still come up with their own centralized extralegal arrangements. In Northern Ireland, the state was strong, but its legitimacy was contested, and IRA members carried the struggle against it into the prison where they organized along military lines and answered to their own command structure rather than that of the prison. There was plenty of governance in the H Blocks, but the IRA men bucked against it and the authorities gradually ceded so much ground that, despite the framework of clear rules, a plenitude of staff, advanced surveillance systems, and strict curbs on association, they felt that it was a chaotic place controlled by the prisoners. While the quantity of legal governance was high, its acceptability to the prisoners was low. Given the inequality of arms, and the determination of the authorities to treat them as individual criminals, the prisoners' resolve was striking. They took what they deemed desirable from the generous available resources (e.g., access to education) and disregarded or destroyed the rest. Despite none of the conditions that promote centralization being evident, it was still a defining characteristic of daily life.

Extending Skarbek's analysis it might be argued that people in prison create centralized extralegal governance institutions when official governance is sufficient but rejected; what is necessary here is a high degree of integration (e.g., H Blocks). Or they do not necessarily create them when official governance is insufficient (e.g., the imposition of extralegal governance from above on a fractionalized prison population such as the Eastham Unit). Or they can create them in consultation with, and to supplement and operate alongside, official governance; here again a high degree of integration is required (e.g., Isir Bet). Self-governance, then, is likely to be found in a highly integrated prison population, regardless of the degree of legal governance. It is unlikely to emerge when integration is low, even if the governance gap is gapingly wide (Eastham Unit) or suffocatingly narrow (ADX Florence).

Skarbek argued that small numbers and low social distance allowed reputations to become established and the informal code to work effectively through mechanisms such as gossip, ostracization, and the threat of violence. Under these circumstances, governance theory suggests that informal rules will suffice and written constitutions will not emerge. Turnover is important too. In small, unstable prison populations people do not have time to establish, or burnish, reputations and to reap the associated rewards. The degree of daily interaction is another relevant factor. If prisoners are free to associate, they will get to know each other better than if they are only unlocked for short periods with a specific purpose (e.g., to collect food, take a shower, attend school, see the doctor). It is during unstructured periods of time that characters are formed and tested.

The scale was small in the H Blocks and in Isir Bet (if the dormitory is taken as the unit of analysis) and personalities were well-known, yet written constitutions still emerged along with sophisticated committee structures. Isir Bet was like a village and there was so much interaction that its inhabitants were well acquainted with each other. The wings of the H Blocks were claustrophobically compact, many of the men had been comrades outside, and their reputations preceded them (even though any formal rank they may have held did not accompany them into prison). Even when prison populations are small and stable, therefore, centralized governance arrangements can be found. But not always: the degree of regulation in ADX Florence is such that any moves in this direction are easily stifled. (In his later work, Skarbek [2020: 156] acknowledged that prisoner societies in Northern Ireland might buck the general trend.)

Legitimacy

Legitimacy is the perception that those who wield authority do so rightly. It is intertwined with my two organizing precepts rather than standing alone and needs to be added to give a subjective sense of life in a particular captive society. Integration and regulation are objective measures. But we need to take account of legitimacy to get a sense of how life *feels* for the prisoner. This adds a third dimension to my carceral geometry.

Sparks argued that the problem of legitimacy in the penal realm is generally overlooked or, at best, addressed obliquely and this is to the detriment of obtaining an adequately subtle appreciation of the intricacies of life in captivity. To make good this deficit its "practical, theoretical, and normative dimensions need to be much more carefully and patiently examined" (1994: 14). Just as Sparks found the concept of legitimacy to be a useful tool for analyzing the role of the private sector in

> **Box 1.1. Right Relations. From Beetham (1991: 16–20).**
> Power is legitimate to the extent that:
>   i. it is legally valid, conforming to established rules; these may be written or unwritten (absence constitutes "illegitimacy")
>   ii. these rules can be justified by reference to shared beliefs and values (absence constitutes a "legitimacy deficit")
>   iii. consent has been expressed by the subordinate party and they feel morally obligated to comply (absence constitutes "delegitimation")

corrections, so too I find it helpful as an organizing idea for the various manifestations of prison life detailed in the chapters that follow.

Legitimacy entails a claim to justified authority by a dominant group and the approach to its interrogation taken by Beetham (1991) can be applied with profit to the prison setting. By this account, power is legitimate to the extent that it displays the distinct characteristics summarized in box 1.1. There is a peculiar asymmetry—and inelegance—to this formulation in that legitimacy has three levels but the absence of each has its own name. (More recently, Beetham [2013: 20] has labeled the three levels as legality, normative justifiability, and legitimation.)

The first level of legitimacy, which concerns legal validity, ranges from informal conventions and customary practices to detailed legal codes. The second level, which addresses shared beliefs and values, has several components. The source of authority from which power is derived must be valid, those who hold power must be competent to do so, and they must serve the common interest rather than simply prosecuting their own agenda. This does not assume a static uniformity of beliefs across a society but rather that among the competing and shifting priorities there are some that would be generally shared between dominant and subordinate groups. The third level involves consent. What is important here are the actions of subordinate groups that indicate their consent to the power relations within which they exist. These actions may be motivated by self-interest, but even so they "have a subjectively binding force" (Beetham 1991: 18). (There is a question, of course, about whether consent can ever be freely given in an environment, like the prison, where people are coercively confined.)

Following Beetham, legitimacy is present to a greater or lesser extent in any set of power relations, wherever the institution under examination lies along the axes of integration and regulation. It is not a single quality that is either present or absent and its assessment requires a holistic, and dynamic, appraisal. As he put it: "Although I have presented the different components of legitimacy as separable elements for purposes of analysis, for any given structure of power it is the ensemble that is important, and the internal connections between them" (1991: 98). Beetham's criteria are rarely fulfilled completely or, indeed, entirely absent. Even at ADX Florence the first element of the definition is satisfied in that the regime conforms to established rules. While it may be immoral and inhumane, it is legal; the right to rule does not coexist with right rule.

In Isir Bet the claim to legitimacy rested on the election of the prisoners' leaders by the entire community and their endorsement by the prison's commander, whose ultimate authority was not contested. In the H Blocks, the arrangements were flatter, communal, and consensual but underpinned by sworn allegiance to an illegal army whose members demonstrated blithe disregard (and sometimes murderous disdain) for the staff of the Northern Ireland Prison Service. It was accepted that if there was a collision of interests at any stage, the requirements of the paramilitary command structure would take precedence over those of the commune. In the Eastham Unit, the BTs' (tenuous) claim to legitimacy lay in their appointment by the authorities. In ADX Florence no individual or group could wield authority—legitimate or otherwise—over their fellows on account of the fractured society they found themselves in, which was based on isolation and encompassing, uncompromising control. The staff at ADX Florence cared little about how the prisoners viewed the legitimacy of their treatment.

The first aspect of legitimate power can usually be assumed present in prisons. But not always. The BT system endured for many years despite a sizable legitimacy deficit (it was racist to its core) and its regular delegitimation through, for example, self-mutilation and writ writing. It was only when the courts deemed it to be unconstitutional that it finally crumbled. This noncompliance with the law made it illegitimate; the power holders had gone too far and breached the rules that were supposed to constrain their behavior. The subordinate party successfully sought legal redress. As we will see in chapter 5, the same applied to aspects of the regime in ADX Florence when it came to the treatment of mentally ill prisoners and litigation forced change upon the Federal Bureau of Prisons (BOP).

All three of Beetham's conditions were present in the highly integrated and poorly regulated society of Isir Bet. This is what I call triple-ply legitimacy; it is strong and likely to retain its shape even when significant pressure is applied. As far as the prisoners were concerned, the same was true in the H Blocks for their charter (but only the first when it came to the prison's official rules). The poorly integrated and poorly regulated Eastham Unit displayed none. The very existence of BTs contravened the law—the rules were broken to facilitate the BT system—and those who were not favored by the authorities were cowed into submission rather than agreeing to their subordination. The BTs were certainly not serving the interests of the general population. This explains why, when the system was overturned, chaos replaced it for a time (see chapter 3). The highly regulated and poorly integrated world of ADX Florence satisfied only the first level.

There is another consideration: the rules must be applied fairly and with respect to the inherent dignity of the person if the legitimacy of the power arrangements is to be sustained. In Isir Bet it is possible that the legitimacy of the prisoners' code, and the level of adherence to it, were enhanced because the legal environment outside the prison, especially the system of prosecution, conviction, and punishment, was widely perceived to be manipulable by those with financial or political resources. Ethiopia's history was for the law to serve the purposes of the emperor, or the Derg and its successors, rather than the people. The prisoners may have had more trust in their own arrangements than in the law of the land, which they had learned to their cost was open to selective enforcement. Most of them benefited from the code; the same was not the case when it came to the state's laws. Furthermore, it is possible that the code's legitimacy was enhanced because it was recognized by the prison authorities, with whom the prisoners' leadership team communicated openly on matters of mutual importance. The IRA charter, by contrast, derived its legitimacy from its repudiation of the official emphases on criminalization and individualization.

If the acquisition of power contravenes the rules, it is illegitimate. This is how IRA men in Northern Ireland's H Blocks viewed the staff who treated them as common criminals according to the prison rules rather than as prisoners of war (POWs). Also, the BT system was illegitimate because Texas law stated unambiguously that prisoners could not be involved in supervisory or disciplinary roles. Yet it was routinely breached. Indeed, the system's survival depended on it being breached. If the rules do not correspond with generally held beliefs about the source of authority or the goals of government, there is a legitimacy deficit. Where the subordinates withhold their consent, we are in the realm of delegitimation.

Changing Direction

It may be analytically fruitful to introduce a directional aspect to considerations of legitimacy—vertical versus horizontal—to allow for the possibility that a regime can simultaneously be legitimate and nonlegitimate. For my purposes, vertical legitimacy is the social contract between captives and captors and the degree to which the authority of the latter is accepted. (This relates to regulation.) Horizontal legitimacy concerns the community of prisoners, the extent to which it is cohesive or fractured, inclusionary or exclusionary, impartial or partisan. (This relates to integration.) When we fold legitimacy into the analysis, we get a rounded sense of prison life from both the organizational and the experiential perspective.

For example, the highly regulated and highly integrated society of the H Blocks satisfied all three of Beetham's levels of legitimacy shown in box 1.1 if the focus remains on the prisoners' internal arrangements (horizontal perspective) but only the first if a vertical perspective is adopted. IRA members, who saw themselves as POWs, accepted that the state they were fighting would do whatever it could to take—and keep—them out of circulation. However, it was not the criminal justice state that they recognized but rather the military state. Viewed vertically, the official perspective was that the communal arrangements put in place by republican activists in the H Blocks betokened a catastrophic failure to implement the rules. But when viewed horizontally, by the prisoners who devised the regime, the view was that it constituted a spectacular success. Where the legitimacy gap is greatest, in other words, can be a matter of perspective.

Prisoners in the H Blocks and Isir Bet consented to be governed by those of their peers whom they selected to hold office. In the H Blocks this did not extend to those who held them captive and they demonstrated their dissatisfaction through a rolling series of protests, all of which were intended to delegitimate the authorities. During the years of the BT system, horizontal legitimacy was fatally compromised and as a result the prisoners felt anxious and unsafe (even the BTs had to remain on guard for fear of retaliation from those over whom they wielded authority). The vertical dimension was tenuously present—although it was brutal, it was ever thus—until the courts ruled that the system operated in defiance of the law.

Both horizontal and vertical components need to be incontrovertibly present—as in Isir Bet—to maximize the likelihood of a flourishing social life that finds favor with all concerned. If neither exist, stability is uncertain and must rely on fear and force rather than consent and compliance.

As currently constituted, ADX Florence can never be fully legitimate because of an absence of shared beliefs and consent. Neither component is meaningfully present, from the prisoners' perspective. Of course, life along these lines can be lawfully perpetuated but not without exacting a colossal price in human and financial terms. As in Northern Ireland in the 1990s, the energy, resources, and coercion required to sustain the system (with all the associated human consequences in terms of anger and alienation) is so out of proportion to the penal aims of incapacitation and rehabilitation that huge commitment is required to keep on failing. To prevent single-ply legitimacy, where only the first level of Beetham's definition is satisfied, from warping and splintering requires a costly and incessant effort.

If the horizontal and vertical components exist in tension, as will often be the case, then it makes sense to think of legitimacy as something that can ebb and flow, affecting life differently in accordance with the prevailing balance. It can be diminished, challenged, lost, renegotiated, rebuilt.

It is seldom entirely absent or unambiguously present. It is a work in progress, a palimpsest. As well as being relational, legitimacy is performative and the entity claiming it must demonstrate that it continues to earn it through, for example, commitment to shared ideals, enabling participation in decision-making, providing services, or maintaining security.

Legitimacy is realized in action, and Beetham (1991: 20) described how it "may be eroded, contested or incomplete; and judgements about it are usually judgements of degree, rather than all-or-nothing." McNeill and Robinson (2012: 117) view it as "dynamic" or "liquid." For Bottoms and Tankebe (2012: 129), it is "dialogic" and thus, "legitimacy should not be viewed as a single transaction; it is more like a perpetual discussion, in which the content of power-holders' later claims will be affected by the nature of the audience response." The power holders are usually staff but may be prisoner representatives and how they view, and use, the authority vested in them shapes the ongoing dialogue.

In ADX Florence and the Eastham Unit the conversation was entirely one-sided until, through litigation, the prisoners forced the authorities to listen to—and act upon—their expressed grievances. The intervention of the courts was required to introduce some flow to a situation that had long been stagnant. In the H Blocks the IRA erected its own legitimacy structures and, rather than dialogue, there was an argument where each side was deaf to the entreaties of the other. In Isir Bet there was a closer approximation to the dialogic model in that a code that claimed legitimacy was produced after extensive debate, and it remained open to contestation and revision. It was designed to be a living document that could be amended to reflect changing circumstances; the possibility of further iterations existed. Consent is never final and must be renegotiated from time to time.

Power

Prison power is inherently problematic (see Edgar et al. 2003: 160–84). Those subjected to its exercise are constrained (sometimes humanely, sometimes abusively), perhaps humiliated, and their life chances and bodily integrity may be jeopardized. Those who wield it differ as to the enthusiasm with which it is pursued. As a result, Beetham (1991: 3) claimed that all systems of power relations seek legitimation and "societies will seek to subject it to justifiable rules, and the powerful themselves will seek to secure consent to their power from at least the most important among their subordinates." This is in the interests of efficiency and longevity. Legitimacy cultivates order and stable, enduring relations. Coercion and unresponsive regulation on the other hand require eternal vigilance, and face a continuing risk of retaliation and unpredictability, all of which are costly in terms of resources and human consequences.

Beetham argued that it was rare for the powerful to have no interest in legitimacy. He gave slavery as one example of indifference, although it probably satisfied the first element of his definition in that it was legal and for a time perhaps the second in that it was approved of widely. It would be going too far to offer penal systems as another example; even in the case of ADX Florence it is important for the BOP to feel that it is operating within the law, however narrowly that may be defined and however at odds it may be with considerations of decency. This is single-ply legitimacy and, as mentioned above, the apparatus required to bolster and sustain it is sizable.

In ADX Florence, power relations are peculiarly asymmetric (prisoners have little influence over staff or their peers), and the authorities are peculiarly careless as to the consequences of such an imbalance (there is little need to strive for legitimacy because the prison can be run without the consent of the prisoners). There are no meaningful social relations between those who wield power and those who are subjected to it. Indeed, how could there be when the latter group are characterized as the worst of the worst, a label that implies incorrigibility and reduces them to irredeemable ciphers? In ADX Florence the gulf is widest between the rules, norms, and expectations of consent that pertain within the prison and shape its social life, and the sensibilities of the wider society within which it is located. In the latter, consent is cherished while in the former it is redundant. This distance is perhaps narrowest in Isir Bet where, alone among my case studies, the legitimacy deficit is not so burdensome that it weighs down the entire prison experience.

ADX Florence is a striking exception to the general rule, as expressed by Sparks and Bottoms (1995: 53), that "it is precisely because the formal powers of the custodians are largely non-legitimate from the prisoners' point of view that the former must strain after a *modus vivendi* acceptable to the captive." A frictionless workday is guaranteed when prisoners are isolated as severely as they are in this fortress of solitary confinement. Under these circumstances of persistent non-contact, the pressure to ignore, or underenforce, the rules recedes. There is no ebb and flow, no negotiation, no turning a blind eye, no trading off, no balancing of competing imperatives, no letting things slide. Life is less dialogic and consensual than elsewhere. It is not necessary for staff to elicit the consent of the prisoners to retain control. This is a one-sided affair where compromise and discretion are absent and the staff view invariably prevails. This is custody without concession, imprisonment untouched by realpolitik, an inescapable monologue rather than a dialogue (however lopsided).

When staff and prisoners are in regular contact, power relations are more diffuse and the former take care not to overstep the mark too regularly because reprisals are always possible. This is not a pressing concern at ADX Florence either in the prison, where the opportunities for an effective attack are limited or, indeed, outside. Given its remote location, few prisoners will have supporters living in the vicinity, and the tightness of the regime and the restrictions on communication make it unlikely they would have the wherewithal to gather intelligence on, and then target, a correctional officer at home. A patient prisoner might wait until after his release to exact retribution, but many are serving such long sentences that they will die in custody or be so decrepit upon sentence expiration that any threat they pose is negligible.

In the Eastham Unit, the staff cultivated a subset of incarcerated men with whom they recognized the importance of maintaining good relations, mutual understanding, and loyalty. They could reward their favorites, coerce the reluctant, and win respect through their work ethic, steadfastness, and courage (even if they were simultaneously feared and loathed). They did not need to seek legitimation from the entire population of prisoners so long as the bond with their proxies was solid. In the H Blocks the authorities' search for legitimation with IRA prisoners was doomed from the outset, given the political and penological chasm separating the sides. Republican activists never sought the kinds of approval or rewards that staff could dispense, disrespected and undermined their captors at every opportunity, accepted the staff's right to keep them incarcerated (just as it was their duty to attempt to escape), and tenaciously fought any attempts to criminalize them. Despite being backed by the state, supported by the British Army, and present in large numbers, the staff in the H Blocks seldom felt in control, no matter how vital, and noble, they viewed their calling. Their power was constantly challenged and often found wanting.

Echoing Beetham, Sparks (1994: 15) observed that legitimate power relations benefited all parties: "Only legitimate social arrangements generate commitments towards compliance on moral rather than just expedient grounds. Meanwhile, the need for legitimation constrains the actions of the powerful." The harshness of life on the Eastham Unit shows how the dampening effect of this constraint is sometimes modest.

In Isir Bet, the prisoners' elected leaders believed in their moral right to exercise power. They had a dedicated office where they could store records, host meetings, and prepare various edicts to be stamped with the office seal, printed, and posted around the compound. In a cramped environment where competition for space was fierce, to set aside a room for the executive committee, rather than allowing it to be used as a shop, workspace, or place of recreation, said a great deal about how they were viewed and how they viewed themselves. In addition, the staff were seen as legitimate, although they were so few in number and had such a low level of daily contact that the prisoners' code was the usual basis for rewards and sanctions.

My case studies add some shade to discussions of legitimacy and power distributions (among prisoners and between the keepers and the kept) because I am not only examining the acceptance, by prisoners, of the authority of their custodians, but also their acceptance of the authority of their peers. Sometimes the latter is underpinned by the institution (Eastham Unit and Isir Bet). Sometimes it is underpinned by an external body (the IRA in the H Blocks). Sometimes prisoners play virtually no role in each other's lives (ADX Florence).

Compliance

Coercion is omnipresent in prison life. It is why people can be held against their will and forced to toe the line in a place not of their choosing for a period of time determined by others. It governs interactions with staff, their surrogates, and other prisoners. Order in prison can result from the threat, or exercise, of force, but it would be an exaggeration to suggest that it is predicated upon prisoners being (brow) beaten into submission. Every use of violence by staff has the potential to undermine legitimacy. Was it lawful? Was it fair and proportionate? Did it serve the interests of the wider prison community? If prisoners are to accept the necessity of force it must be properly, and sparingly, applied. It cannot be viewed as retaliation.

Sometimes order is normative, arising from shared values, beliefs, and priorities; prisoners strive to generate consensus and to do what is right. They take advantage of whatever opportunities are on offer and work hard to build better lives. Sometimes it is prudential; prisoners comply because they have calculated it is in their (economic and security) interests to do so (this does not apply in ADX Florence, where prisoners are stripped of autonomy and the only decisions they can make with reasonably swift and predictable outcomes are ones that worsen their predicament). Of course, self-interest is not always restrained and can veer into cynical opportunism. Consent can be tactical and deference insincere. But so too instrumental actions repeated over time can become the basis for normative compliance as beliefs and behaviors are aligned.

Carrabine (2005: 903) described how rule-following can flow from "the dull compulsion of prison rituals" (drawing on Marx's view of how the dull compulsion of economic relations copper-fastens the worker's subjugation) as opposed to coercion, rational choice, or normative compliance. (Prisoners have demonstrated through the behavior that led to their incarceration that they are either poor calculators or weakly influenced by the likely consequences of their actions.) Sometimes the daily grind of getting up and carrying on precludes much in the way of reflection and critique. Unchanging routines provide scaffolding for the day and allow immersion in the present without too much thought. They make life foreseeable and allow it to be continually reproduced. There is consolation to be found in the accompanying predictability (O'Donnell 2014: 198–200). Often, in prison, the unexamined life is the one worth living and compliance reflects thoughtless conformity; prisoners follow the rules because they waymark the path of least resistance. The pressure to go along with the majority is enormous. Group processes are important and deviation requires the kind of courage and stubbornness that many either lack or choose not to deploy. There is a qualitative difference between compliance rooted in (passive) resignation and that which is won through (active) normative commitment.

When the structural constraints and power relations that govern daily life are viewed as inevitable, resistance is futile. Carrabine (2005: 905) related this to Durkheim's notion of fatalism, distinguishing between fatalism rooted in ritual rather than belief. In the former there is an acceptance that things cannot be altered (the system may lack legitimacy, but it will always beat the individual malcontent; suffering is unavoidable in prison), whereas in the latter the individual accepts the legitimacy of their subordination (why resist something that is deserved?). In either case—and the line between them will not always be clearly defined—it is appreciated that there is an inevitability about the situation and how it will play out. Carrabine adds another helpful layer to our understanding of the factors underpinning prison order and encourages us to think seriously about how rituals and routines are a part of the picture. When it comes to understanding compliance, "dull compulsion" is as necessary as coercion, calculation, and consensus.

Dull compulsion differs from learned helplessness. An individual can always decide to buck the routine even though it is easier to go along with it. They know they are acquiescing to something that they could act upon, even if their actions are unlikely to make much of a difference. Their agency is depleted but not entirely denuded. However, in a situation of learned helplessness they do not think that their actions make any difference. Past experience has instilled a sense of powerlessness and they do not act even when they could do so effectively. They have lost the sense that they can do anything to impact the world around them. In the first scenario there is a decision not to act and this becomes routinized, although action remains a distal possibility. In the second, there is no decision to be made as all action is seen as quintessentially pointless; nothing is done to attempt to alter an aversive environment.

Carrabine (2005: 908) made the additional point that interruptions to order are sometimes ways of breaking the tedious monotony of prison life, referring to "the libidinal attractions of transgressing order in prison, with its deadening routines and daily inevitability." Even in a legitimate and well-ordered prison the monotony is sometimes broken through noncompliance for the purposes of diversion and novelty (or, no doubt, irritation). Prisoners can choose to live dangerously, to resist strategically, to subvert the regime. These are all expressions of agency, creative acts of defiance, ways of staying afloat in a world that threatens to overwhelm. Now we must add carnival to dull compulsion, coercion, calculation, and consensus.

These intentional disruptions of the routine are very different from the major jolts that I describe in the following chapters which result from legitimacy deficits developing into delegitimation (e.g., the tumult that followed the creation of a League of Communist Republicans in the H Blocks; what became known as the "war years" in Texas prisons when the number of gang murders escalated suddenly; and a riot that followed the failure of anticipated pardons to materialize in Isir Bet). Beetham (1991: 205) described the breakdown of order as a developmental process whereby "legitimacy deficits develop into delegitimation and then illegality." This process moved to the final stage in the Eastham Unit when the courts deemed treatment there to be unconstitutional.

Prisoners comply for different reasons depending on the time and place, and we must look quizzically at any explanation that overemphasizes a single one of them at the expense of the others. Carrabine (2005) is not arguing that an analysis of legitimacy has no place but rather that it must jostle for ascendancy with other factors, some of them perhaps more mundane but no less significant for that. The balance between the various factors can shift, find a new equilibrium, and then shift again.

The BTs were invested with a great deal of power by the administration, but they lacked moral authority and ruled through fear and force. This was very different from the prisoner leaders in Isir Bet who were elected by their peers and confirmed in post by the prison's commander. In Isir Bet, compliance was normative. In the Eastham Unit, it was through gritted teeth. In the H Blocks, it was withheld. In ADX Florence, it was neither necessary nor sought; as previously noted, this is a prison run without the need for prisoner consent.

Relationships between captors and captives ranged from nonexistent to hostile. In none of the institutions examined was there evidence of engagement that could be seen as meaningful, sustained, or deep. (But is this ever truly possible in a place where one group is holding the other captive, even if relationships develop that are mutually respectful, trusting, and enduring?)

The prison staff in the H Blocks felt that they were doing a dangerous and legitimate job, but the prisoners saw them as part of the enemy's security apparatus to be destroyed at any opportunity (initially) or as an irrelevance (eventually). The legality of the arrangements in Isir Bet was never in doubt as the code was agreed to with the prison administration. The legality of the arrangements in the Eastham Unit was certainly questionable and led to a constitutional challenge. Until the system was dismantled, the BTs were confident that their actions would be supported by the prison administration even if viewed as abhorrent and not legitimate by those who bore the brunt of them. They felt that they were morally entitled to act in the way they did even if such a view was not shared by the other prisoners, who grudgingly accepted that this was the way order had always been maintained but could not accept that it was right. Compliance was ruthlessly manipulated rather than normative.

People can retain a belief in, and loyalty to, a criminal justice system that deprived them of their liberty so long as they feel that correct procedures were followed and they were treated fairly, decently, and respectfully. Procedural fairness is defined by neutral protocols administered by trustworthy authorities that are mindful of individuals' dignity and rights (e.g., Tyler and Jackson 2013). This could never be the case in the Eastham Unit (where the BT system was constructed on a foundation of preferential treatment and fear), the H Blocks (where the rules were seen as designed to advance a strategy of criminalization), or ADX Florence (where the characterization of prisoners as the worst of the worst was inherently disrespectful). Only at Isir Bet (or among IRA prisoners in their communes, ignoring the wider prison and its priorities) did normative compliance merge with procedural justice.

For Beetham, the extent to which a system of power relations was legitimate (across his three levels) determined the degree of moral compliance that in turn promoted order and stability. There was more at issue here than a simple calculation of potential costs and benefits. As he put it: "This normative status derives from the character of a legitimate power relationship as legally valid, justifiable according to shared norms and beliefs, and confirmed through actions expressing consent" (1991: 38). A regime that is unconcerned about legitimate power (or dialoguing about same) can function in an orderly fashion but only at a huge cost (both in terms of the required regulatory resources and the psychological impact on those subjected to it). A highly integrated prisoner society is likely to encapsulate Beetham's three levels of legitimacy in that there will be evidence of legal validity, shared values, and consent. A highly regulated one may persist even when the latter two levels are largely absent. Given that they are established by the state under a clear legal framework, it will be rare for a prison not to fulfill the first level of legitimacy. But the Eastham Unit failed to do so (for all of its occupants) and ADX Florence fell short too (when it came to the treatment of a subset of mentally ill offenders).

To summarize the discussion thus far, order is negotiated among prisoners and between prisoners and staff. This happens to varying degrees according to how integrated the prisoners are and how rule-bound and plentiful the staff. Only a prison whose interior arrangements are legitimate will generate compliance that is normatively derived. Legitimacy promotes voluntary compliance at the individual level and this in turn contributes to social order and stability. But order can also exist in the absence of legitimacy (e.g., coercion, self-interest, habit, helpless resignation).

Conclusion

This book offers a comparative case study analysis. By limiting the sample size to four I hope to offer descriptions that are sufficiently well elaborated for the reader to gain a sense of the institutions and their contexts and to be able to juxtapose them in various ways to garner fresh insights. I do not wish to impose a single, rigid set of meanings on the material; each case study says something about the others and different readings are possible. The title of this chapter uses the image of a kaleidoscope—it is not just a question of closer examination but an openness to the unfolding of (potentially surprising) new patterns.

Each of the following four chapters opens with an epigraph capturing the official purpose of the establishment during the period of interest and then probes the degree of difference between stated aims and the dynamics of carceral life. The gap between official rhetoric and penal practice was narrow in Isir Bet and wide in ADX Florence, the

H Blocks and the Eastham Unit. I will examine how order is generated and maintained and what happens when it is threatened. Other themes to be explored include the variety of organizational forms (from the rigidly hierarchical with clear role definitions to the emphatically flat, where no prisoner has dominion over another); the status of prisoners and the nature of their relationships with staff and the outside world; threats to the body and the mind; and how prison life is influenced by written constitutions that can displace central tenets of the inmate code.

The pen portraits that complement the chapters are chronicles of endurance. Laurence McKeown joined the IRA, aged seventeen, at the height of the conflict in Northern Ireland. He received five life sentences from a court he refused to recognize and his early years of incarceration were characterized by protest, culminating in a ten-week hunger strike. He was instrumental in creating a social life for republican prisoners that was rooted in contestation and debate, communal in nature, and energetically political. He was one of the lead authors of the charter that underpinned these arrangements. In the early stages of his custodial career David Ruiz was an angry man. He did fearsome damage, slashing those around him as well as his own body. Over time his weapon of choice became the writ. The litigation that bore his name (*Ruiz v. Estelle*) cost the state of Texas a fortune and ushered in wide-scale reforms. Ruiz was released but offended on parole, was reimprisoned, and spent the last two decades of his life in administrative segregation.

Chalew Gebino spent much of the first part of his sentence in leg irons in an Ethiopian prison. To his surprise and distress, his sentence was increased on appeal. Resolving not to falter he established himself as a successful artist and entrepreneur, was elected by the prisoners as their chairman, and drafted a governance code for the prison. Jack Powers was brutalized by his experience of incarceration in the BOP. Having witnessed the murder of his friend and lent his support to the prosecution of the perpetrators he found himself isolated and under threat. His response was to escape. Soon recaptured, his situation became even more intolerable with his transfer to the most restrictive facility in the federal system where, held in prolonged solitary confinement, he engaged in a war of attrition against his own body. Powers was a plaintiff in litigation that led to a major overhaul in the assessment and treatment of mentally ill prisoners (*Cunningham v. Federal Bureau of Prisons*). He regained his composure and dedicated his life to writing and reflection.

I conclude the book by bringing together the theoretical considerations outlined throughout this chapter with the findings from the various case studies and individual biographies to propose a three-step approach to appreciating the social life of the prison. This is an attempt to show how individuals are molded by, and in return can mold, the institution that holds them, just as the prison is shaped by, as well as shaping, the society within which it is found. To understand one, we need a sense of the other.

Postscript: Gender (or the Lack Thereof)

My analysis—like the society of captives itself—is gendered (with gender framed in a binary fashion). While the carceral churn of women and girls is greater than ever, more than nine out of ten incarcerated persons worldwide are male, so it is not surprising that men's concerns dominate.

The H Blocks held no women. Female republicans were jailed elsewhere, and they too saw prison as a theater of war where doing time was characterized by a sustained pattern of resistance (Corcoran 2006). ADX Florence holds no women. A special housing unit at the Federal Medical Center Carswell in Fort Worth, Texas, caters, among others, to the handful of females who require high security custody (Federal Bureau of Prisons 2021a). The Eastham Unit was exclusively for men. From the scant available literature, it would appear that female prisoners in Texas—known as "key girls"—provided support services without which the system could not have functioned. However, the extent to which they held dominion over the others was not pronounced. Two women testified during *Ruiz v. Estelle* and in his summation of their evidence Chase (2020: 322) noted "the absence of carceral violence" in their accounts of prison life. In Isir Bet, women had their own dormitories in a separate part of the compound, sometimes accompanied by their children. Their lives were more cramped than the men's and they had fewer opportunities to prosper.

The dimensions of integration and regulation might align differently in a female world. The same goes for deliberations of legitimacy and compliance, power and dominance. A sequel to this book could look with profit at the social geometry of women's prisons. A further refinement would be to extend the analysis to test its ability to accommodate nonbinary, intersex, and transgender perspectives. Or, indeed, to apply it to other sites of coercive confinement (O'Donnell and O'Sullivan 2020). These are tasks for another day.

2

H Blocks, Northern Ireland

To treat prisoners as individuals regardless of their religious beliefs or political opinions; and to offer them the opportunity to serve their sentences free from paramilitary influence.
—Northern Ireland Office, 1989, *Report on the Work of the Northern Ireland Prison Service 1988/89*, p. 4

The Northern Ireland Prison Service (NIPS) outlined its aims and objectives for the first time in its annual report for 1988/89. The fourth of five stated objectives stands as the epigraph to this chapter. As will become clear, the "opportunity" it offered was neither sought nor availed of and the implication that "paramilitary influence" was a baleful external force that prisoners may have wished to be protected from was woefully off target. The republican activists who are the focus of this case study freely chose—and actively strove—to live according to their own principles and priorities, key among which was a desire to be seen as POWs who would not have been incarcerated had the political situation not demanded that they take up arms. The name of the institution where they served their time was contested. Officially it was Her Majesty's Prison Maze, but no self-respecting political prisoner would refer to it as such; for them it was the Long Kesh camp or simply the Kesh. For convenience—and the avoidance of controversy—I refer to it by reference to the shape of its famous cell blocks.

The formal objective of the NIPS may have emphasized individualization of treatment, but the prisoner society was characterized by the creation of a charter that set out the men's aspirations for a comradely but critical collective existence, the publication of a quarterly magazine and the occasional collection of poetry, the cultivation of the Irish language, and the enthusiastic pursuit of educational opportunities. As the architect of the charter, Laurence McKeown (see pen portrait), recalled: "Rather than being casualties of war, we realized we could be agents of change." The decade under examination in this case study extends from the adoption of the charter in 1990 to the prison's closure in 2000, a period that has attracted little academic interest. By this time, after a lengthy and determined struggle, the prisoners had won a great deal of autonomy. They wore their own clothes, engaged minimally with staff, decided how to spend their time, and responded to self-defined organizational imperatives.

Laurence McKeown (b. 1956), Educationalist

Laurence McKeown grew up in Randalstown, a rural area in Northern Ireland, in a home without electricity, indoor sanitation, or a telephone. He enjoyed what he described as "a very idyllic, peaceful upbringing" (cited in Reinisch 2017: 226). Aged seventeen, he joined the Irish Republican Army and three years later was arrested for IRA membership, causing explosions, and carrying out a gun attack on a police patrol. He was remanded in custody to Crumlin Road Gaol in Belfast.

Convicted in April 1977 by a court he refused to recognize, he received five life sentences and was transferred to the H Blocks where, like many other republicans, he refused to wear the prison uniform. Soon after his arrival, as he sat naked and alone in his cell, he picked up the only permitted reading material, the Bible, later recalling: "The pages fell open at the Book of Sirach and I read, 'Gold must be tested in the heat of the furnace' (or words to that effect) . . . those words were like manna to me. I felt as if a friend had slapped me on the shoulder, shaken hands with me, hugged me tightly. I gathered my blanket around me and surveyed my surroundings in a new light" (McKeown 1996: 44).

In March 1978, McKeown joined the no wash protest and for three years lived in an excrement-covered cell without access to television, radio, reading materials, or association. The only times he was allowed out were to attend Sunday Mass on the wing or to accept the monthly visit permitted to prisoners who would don the uniform for it. In June 1981, McKeown became a hunger striker. By the time he began refusing food, four prisoners had already died; six more were to follow. He lapsed into a coma on the sixty-ninth day, and the following day his mother authorized medical intervention to revive him. Had she not acted he would have been the eleventh man to die. Not long afterward the hunger strike was called off.

McKeown recalled: "Often the prison experience was a brutal one, but my memories of it also contain moments of the most intense feelings of love and comradeship, of exhilaration, of creativity, of achievement" (cited in Sharoni 2001: 106). The prison cell became a crucible for ingenuity and imparted lessons about the limits of human resilience. Rather than being crushed by the experience McKeown was tempered by it, emerging different but stronger, bent into a new shape and ready to direct his life along a new trajectory.

The protest years caused the participants to look inward, to reflect deeply, to challenge received wisdom and authority, and to formulate a new approach to education. They became self-taught critical thinkers. These lessons were hard won and not soon forgotten. McKeown (2001: 71) summarized the process as follows: "A critical approach to education plus a cooperative as opposed to competitive regard for the pursuit of knowledge was cultivated which radically altered our outlook upon the world and the struggle we were involved in. Most significantly, however, not having access to books, we began to look critically at the orthodox republican values and beliefs we had held up until then. We also began to 're-interpret' the content of academic studies we had pursued earlier in life."

McKeown enrolled with the Open University in 1984 and this was a transformative experience: "It was like all I had ever wished for. It gave a structure and coherence to my scattered political thoughts and understanding of the world at that time" (McKeown 2020: 182). After his release in 1992, he completed a doctorate at Queen's University Belfast, with the uncompromising title "Unrepentant Fenian Bastards: The Social Construction of an Irish Republican Prisoner Community." He has since written several plays, the most recent of which, "Something in the Air," inspired by the fiftieth anniversary of the burning by a Protestant mob of Catholic homes on Belfast's Bombay Street, premiered in May 2019. He remains alive to the power of reinterpretation and used a blanket from the H Blocks to create a variety of fashion items, including a scarf, bow tie, and waistcoat. With the aid of a tailor, a garment of last resort became a piece of elegant attire.

According to Gormally et al. (1993: 54), there existed "a de facto recognition of the paramilitary command structures through which the authorities negotiate and manage the prison." By the mid-1990s the prison governor was meeting regularly with the prisoners' leaders. Indeed, Her

TABLE 2.1. A Concise Chronology of Carceral Conflict

Date	Event
August 9, 1971	Introduction of internment without trial. Internees held in Nissen huts on a former military airfield where they wear their own clothes, do not work, and are segregated by affiliation. Known as Long Kesh Detention Centre, the compound is patrolled by British soldiers. According to Ryder (2000: 86), anyone who entered in the early 1970s "would easily have been forgiven for thinking they had stepped back some thirty years into a Second World War POW camp."
March 30, 1972	Direct rule imposed in response to escalating violence and instability in Northern Ireland. Long Kesh begins to receive men convicted of politically motivated offences and is formally renamed Her Majesty's Prison Maze.
June 19, 1972	After a hunger strike in Belfast prison, "special category" status is conceded to those convicted of politically motivated offences, who are distinguished from "ordinary decent criminals."
March 1, 1976	Special category status is withdrawn. Perpetrator of any offence committed after this date dealt with as a common criminal and sent to newly constructed H Blocks. Existing special category prisoners remain in the compound, where they continue to organize their own affairs, but their numbers are never augmented.
September 14, 1976	Kieran Nugent becomes first republican to be sentenced since withdrawal of special category status. Given three years' imprisonment for hijacking a van, he refuses to wear the prison uniform offered to him, stating that the staff would have to "nail it to his back." Like hundreds who follow he is escorted, naked, to his cell where he wraps himself in his blanket.
March 17, 1978	The "blanket men" refuse to leave their cells and the following day, the "no wash" protest begins. Without an opportunity to visit the ablutions area to empty their chamber pots, prisoners smear the contents on walls and ceilings of cells.
July 30, 1978	Tomás Ó Fiaich, head of the Catholic Church in Ireland, visits H Blocks and declares afterwards: "I was shocked at the inhuman conditions.... One would hardly allow an animal to remain in such conditions.... The nearest approach to that I have seen was the spectacle of hundreds of homeless people living in sewer pipes in the slums of Calcutta. The stench and filth in some of the cells, with the remains of rotten food and human excreta scattered around the walls was almost unbearable. In two of them I was unable to speak for fear of vomiting."
October 27, 1980	Hunger strike begins with seven men declining food simultaneously. Ends after 53 days with no loss of life.
March 1, 1981	On fifth anniversary of withdrawal of special category status a second hunger strike begins. Prisoners demand right to wear their own clothes; not to do prison work; to free association; to one visit, one letter, and one parcel per week; and to restoration of lost remission.
March 2, 1981	No wash protest ends so that focus is exclusively on hunger strike and associated five demands. Four hundred and eleven men ask to be moved to clean cells. They still refuse to work or wear prison uniforms.
October 3, 1981	Second hunger strike ends after deaths of ten prisoners, the first of whom—Bobby Sands—had been elected a Member of Parliament in the UK. Blanket protest is wound up by end of month.

TABLE 2.1. (*cont.*)

November 1, 1982	Prisoners end no work protest. Their attitude had been one of sloth, sabotage, and subterfuge, operating at a glacial pace, destroying expensive machinery, producing nothing of value, and stealing material from the workshops.
September 25, 1983	Mass escape of 38 IRA prisoners from H Blocks.
June 5, 1988	The 92 men still in compound are moved to H Blocks, where they retain all their special category privileges.
September 18, 1991	The seven special category prisoners still in custody, occupying a block built for 100 are transferred to a pre-release scheme.

Majesty's Chief Inspector of Prisons for England and Wales (1998: 171) reported that the governor of the H Blocks had come up with his own bespoke mission statement and recommended that this be formally adopted as a more accurate and honest account of the prison's role. It began with a frank acknowledgment: "This prison serves the community by holding prisoners who have been committed by the courts for acts of terrorism and other crimes linked to paramilitary organisations. We will operate a secure, safe and humane regime which recognises the individual and the organisation to which he . . . claims allegiance." This dual recognition was an operational necessity.

Table 2.1 is a potted history of the Northern Ireland conflict as it played out in the prisons. It ends at the beginning of my period of interest, by which time the blanket and no wash protests and the hunger strikes, about which so much has been written (for a recent survey, see McConville 2021), had concluded; the Long Kesh compound, which predated the construction of the H Blocks, was shut; the "special category" era was finally over; and the peace process was soon to get underway.

Ceaseless Strife

The intensity of the prison protest was related to the intensity of the conflict in the community. Both were more extreme in the early years of what became euphemistically known as the "Troubles." Figure 2.1 shows the estimated death toll between 1969 and 1999. A number of the 3,497 killings took place outside Northern Ireland, with 115 recorded in the Republic of Ireland, 125 in Britain, and 18 elsewhere in Europe. The

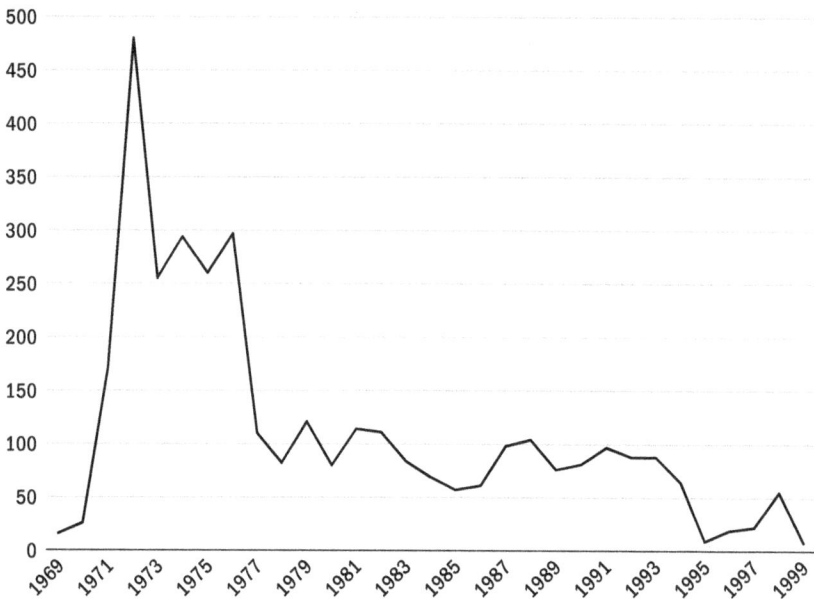

Figure 2.1. Deaths Related to Northern Ireland Conflict, 1969–99. Compiled from Sutton (2020).

organizations responsible for the deaths are summarized in figure 2.2. The IRA, which sought to sever the link with Britain and to unify the island of Ireland, made the largest contribution, being responsible for 1,705 fatalities, almost half of the total.

IRA operatives were dispersed across several high-security establishments in England, where they were in a small minority among nonpolitical prisoners and faced substantial hurdles maintaining family ties and a semblance of organizational coherence. They were repatriated during the 1990s and if their place of origin was Northern Ireland they likely completed their time in the H Blocks. They were present as well in the Irish Republic, particularly in Portlaoise Prison, which in 2022 continued to hold a small number of dissident republicans.

During the protest years (see timeline in table 2.1), the staff were in control in the conforming wings (where different factions coexisted and enjoyed the benefits of compliance with the prison rules) and in the nonconforming wings (where prisoners were locked down and meaningful engagement was minimal). It was when this phase in the prison's history ended that a concerted effort was made by republicans to undermine the regime, frustrate the ability of staff to apply the rules, and weaken the formal apparatus of control by superimposing their own command structures. This was done in a sustained and strategic way that left staff dismayed, disenchanted, and disengaged. When republicans reorganized after the protest years, they endeavored to create an environment that was shaped by their priorities, namely to escape, to deny the legitimacy of staff power, and to live as politically engaged, segregated communities. The staff role was pared back to a bare minimum and, by the early 1990s, rule enforcement was haphazard at best.

McKane (2008: 138) admitted that, in the aftermath of the hunger strikes, "there is little doubt that Special Category Status was achieved

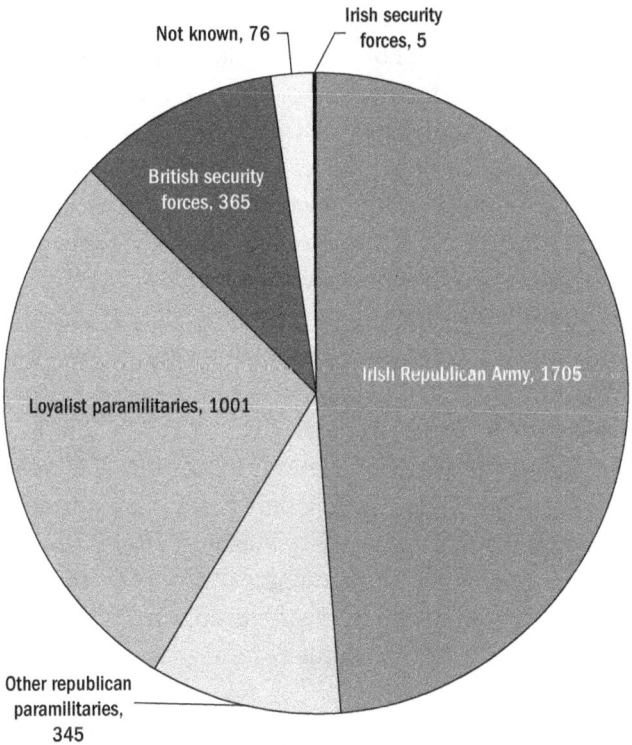

Figure 2.2. Thirty Years of Bloodshed: Number of Killings and Organizations Responsible, 1969–99. Compiled from Sutton (2020).

by the prisoners in everything but name. It was a total reversal of prison policy." This alarmed McKane, who worked as a prison officer in the H Blocks and saw the men in his charge as evil, sadistic, sectarian killers. By his account, the regime became less restrictive and prison officers who "were perceived to be too authoritative and over-zealous were moved out of the blocks to run visits and other off beat areas of the jail" (p. 157). Their replacements were "weak, subservient men" (p. 158). When the authorities decided to segregate the prisoners according to paramilitary affiliation, staff morale plummeted and "the security of the prison gradually drifted into a languid state" (p. 158). Achieving segregation was critically important as it meant that the prisoners could embed and solidify their own organizational imperatives, internal discipline, and approach to community living without the distraction of loyalist adversaries on the same wings.

The prisoner society of interest in this chapter comprises republican activists on wings controlled by the IRA. Not all had been convicted of membership of a proscribed organization, even if their status as IRA volunteers was obvious, and some were sympathizers who had provided material support or intelligence. They shared the political goal of a united Ireland and believed in physical force as an acceptable means to this end. Whatever the basis of their incarceration their allegiance to the IRA was unambiguous. These men sought a way to ensure that they could live together in harmony while not losing sight of the paramilitary organization under which they operated. They decided to live communally, to create a revolutionary society within the prison (if they could not do it there, what hope would they have outside?), to become articulate in the language of political theory (and, indeed, in Ireland's first official language). They were not the only paramilitary group in the H Blocks, as table 2.2 shows, but they were the most numerous and the best organized. Members of the other groupings, most of them loyalists who had resorted to violence to preserve the union with Britain and reckoned that they too deserved the status of combatants, benefited from the concessions won by the IRA.

Content to proceed carefully and strategically, IRA operatives pursued their goals incrementally but with unwavering focus. Each victory prepared the ground for the next offensive. This was

TABLE 2.2. Composition of H Blocks, March 1998

Republican		
Irish Republican Army	213	(41%)
Irish National Liberation Army	30	(6%)
Loyalist		
Ulster Volunteer Force	99	(19%)
Ulster Defence Association	97	(18%)
Loyalist Volunteer Force	27	(5%)
Ulster Freedom Fighters	23	(4%)
Other/not known	36	(7%)
Total	525	

Source: Her Majesty's Chief Inspector of Prisons for England and Wales (1998: 40, where the Ulster Volunteer Force is incorrectly described as the Ulster Defence Force).

methodical, attritional, painstaking work. They gained a concession, consolidated their position, then pressed ahead. Campbell et al. (1994: 266) described how, in its early days, the prison protest was "more instinctive than analytical." The refusal to wear a prison uniform led to the blanket protest; the refusal to leave cells to slop out led to the no wash protest, and so on (see table 2.1). Over time, analysis displaced instinct and by the beginning of the decade of interest every move was planned, executed, reviewed, refined, and aligned with other moves. The prisoners were patient and over a short number of years created conditions that would have been unimaginable at any high security prison in Britain. The way they lived was an emphatic renunciation of the authorities' formal refusal to acknowledge that they were anything but common criminals. After 1990 there were no conforming prisoners left in the H Blocks, making the prison system's statement of aims and objectives that had just been published seem excessively optimistic, even delusional.

There were eight flat-roofed, single-story H Blocks, made of reinforced concrete and grouped into three "phases" according to when they became operational. Each phase was enclosed by a twenty-foot concrete wall and separated from the others by a series of gates, movement through which was controlled by an officer in a watchtower supported

Figure 2.3. Incarceration, to the Letter. Credit: *Irish Eye*/Alamy.

by a colleague stationed on the ground. Within the phase each H Block was surrounded by an eighteen-foot metal fence. Soldiers from the British Army patrolled the perimeter and surrounding area to prevent an attack from outside. Military planes flew over the site using infrared photography to search for any evidence of tunneling. Figure 2.3 gives an aerial view of the complex.

Each of a block's four wings was designed to accommodate twenty-five men in individual cells measuring nine feet by seven feet, six inches. They had a single window, fitted with four concrete bars that blocked out some of the natural light. There was a dining hall/recreation area, a hobbies room, a small gym, and a shower/toilet area (there was no sanitation in the cells). Each wing was like a self-contained prison. Classrooms were available on each side of the block and were shared by two wings. Each wing had its own exercise yard large enough for a game of five-a-side football. The crossbar of the H (known, despite its lack of curvature, as the "circle") was an administration area where the control room and staff mess were located along with a medical room and offices for the governor and principal prison officer.

The group that oversaw the body of IRA-affiliated prisoners was known as the camp staff. It comprised an Officer Commanding (OC), an adjutant who liaised with block and wing OCs on administrative matters, an intelligence officer who coordinated his efforts with the IRA on the outside, and a vice-OC with responsibility for security, including escape planning. An additional vice-OC post was created in 1985, with responsibility for education, bringing the camp staff to five. The camp OC was appointed by the IRA's army council (he was the official point of contact with the movement outside) and he filled the other staff positions of adjutant, intelligence officer, and vice-OCs. As figure 2.4 shows, IRA prisoners looked for authority to their own command structures (inside) and the army council (outside). The prison's administrative apparatus was irrelevant as a source of moral authority.

Antecedents

In the early days of republican imprisonment in the 1970s, men who had broken under interrogation were ostracized and they exercised and took their meals separately (McKeown 2001: 50). They were "suspended volunteers," second-class citizens in this echelon society. McKeown (1998:

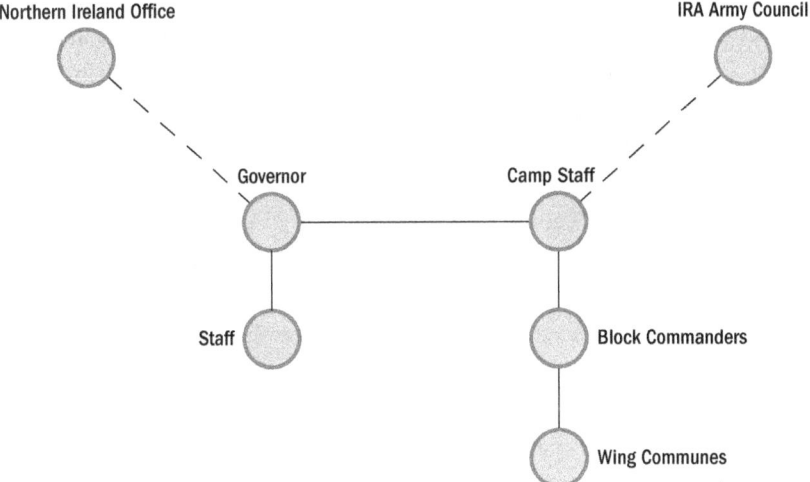

Figure 2.4. Never the Twain Shall Meet.

132) explained how there was a "rigid categorisation" between suspended and cleared volunteers, with only the latter having access to certain communications from the republican movement and being allowed to take a position on the camp staff.

The discipline in the compound that preceded the H Blocks (see table 2.1) brooked no dissent. It was based on hierarchy rather than comradeship. It was imposed rather than invited. There were kit inspections, physical drills, parades, and compulsory lectures. But while military hierarchies might be sustainable in the short term—previous IRA campaigns had resulted in fewer, and shorter, jailings—they cannot endure for sentences that extend into decades, and republican prisoners needed to come up with new arrangements that would be flexible enough to deal with unprecedently long terms of incarceration, many of which were for life. This meant that the community had to adapt and change. A strict hierarchy with a multiplicity of defined roles (and, often, little competition to fill them) was not sustainable over the long run.

The protest years, from the opening of the H Blocks until the early 1980s, had been a time of introspection, questioning, and debate and those who participated developed a thirst for a model of education that was egalitarian and provocative rather than returning to the compulsory lectures of the past, which were regarded by many as a (tedious but necessary) chore rather than an opportunity for self-development and critique. What emerged over time was the displacement of a didactic approach with a cooperative one; prisoners were encouraged by their peers, rather than berated by their commanders. The emphasis was on "the concepts of democracy, communal responsibility, a revolutionary discipline, open discussion, self and mutual criticism, social analysis and accountability" (McKeown 1998: 257). The prison system strove to treat prisoners as individuals. The prisoners resisted this strenuously, appreciating the power of a collective approach.

Traditional structures and hierarchies were broken down. A more questioning ethos emerged and the organization's reactionary, Catholic ideology was greatly diluted. The hard line between suspended and cleared volunteers was erased. It seemed absurd to deny a man who had been on the blanket and no wash protests, and whose courage and commitment had been amply demonstrated, from occupying any official role simply because he had given way under police interrogation as a terrified teenager, several years previously.

This was a bottom-up process. Wing committees were established. The wing OC was more akin to a committee chairman. In the words of McKeown: "A new value system was being consciously put in place which stressed mutual co-operation and re-enforcement for the betterment of all" (p. 251). The protest years led to a flattening of hierarchies. It did not matter what rank an individual may have held outside, how long a sentence they had received, or their renown as an activist; after spending several years unwashed, unshaven, wearing nothing but a blanket, all barriers with similarly situated peers were broken down.

The blanket and no wash protests and hunger strikes radicalized the prisoners, forged a deep level of solidarity among those who had participated, and equipped them with a good understanding of how the prison regime worked, all the better to undermine it going forward. They had a profound influence on the experiment in communal living that followed. The reconfiguration of prison life had major implications for republican activism more generally. The radical change that occurred in the H Blocks shaped the movement, in both its political and military guises.

McKeown (2020) recalled that men who were not taking part in education were only allowed to receive works of fiction from their families (limited to two books per month). Nonfiction was reserved for conforming prisoners who were engaging with the teachers. As IRA members refused to do prison work they were denied access to educational facilities at the time. The prohibition on nonfiction was easily circumvented as the men's families simply purchased the titles they requested and replaced the covers with those of popular novels. Apparently, this was enough to deceive the prison censor. McKeown recalled: "One of the books we received in such a manner was *Pedagogy of the oppressed* by Paulo Freire and it was to have a major influence on us, not only in terms of how we viewed education and subsequently structured our own political education programme, but on how we developed our structures of command to become less hierarchical and more inclusive and collective" (p. 181). The prisoners were struck by Freire's argument that learners were active, striving, creative agents rather than the passive recipients of knowledge that was delivered to them by experts to be uncritically absorbed for later regurgitation. They appreciated the revolutionary potential of the educational process to become "a focal point in the battles against Britain that would be staged within prison walls" (Dana and McMonagle 1997: 68).

Freire's model was democratic, comradely, and participatory and, as such, diametrically at odds with the rigid command structure of the IRA. The challenge for those who found Freire's ideas appealing was to reorganize their lives so that they were aligned with the revolutionary doctrines they were discussing. A program of political development and education was designed by the prisoners and became the subject of intense debate. A new, flatter structure was promoted.

As the communes evolved, the principle that positions of responsibility were the preserve of IRA volunteers was diluted. By the time the process had been fully elaborated it was not essential for a wing, or even a block, OC to have been a sworn member of the IRA. It was decided that wing maintenance, handicrafts, sports, education, and so forth would be distinguished from escape planning, internal security, and intelligence gathering. The latter activities would remain the preserve of the IRA and so the intelligence officer would, of necessity, be an IRA volunteer. But the other roles could be discharged equally effectively by members of the republican community who had not been directly involved in the military campaign outside or had been aligned with the Irish National Liberation Army (INLA), a small and volatile paramilitary group (Ó Mocháin 2011: 84–85). This deepened the pool of potential leadership candidates. There was a degree of flexibility about who assumed positions of authority and individual circumstances were taken fully into account. There was no point foisting responsibility onto one who was reluctant to bear it.

Decision-making was dispersed and distinct spheres of deliberation were created. The communal life that the prisoners designed did not conflict with the imperative to escape and to outmaneuver the enemy at every opportunity. All action was underpinned by the shared understanding that IRA supporters were part of a bigger movement from which sustenance was derived and to which loyalty was owed. The internal changes that culminated in the communal and self-governing life of the 1990s did not rupture the overall chain of command within the institution or the relationship with the movement on the outside. While they had a great deal of freedom to decide how they lived and what form of resistance to mount from within the prison, they remained accountable to their leadership. The consensual nature of their lives was underpinned by the coercive power of the group to which they owed allegiance.

League of Communist Republicans

The League of Communist Republicans (LCR) was formed in November 1986 when Sinn Féin, the IRA's political wing, reversed its longstanding policy on abstentionism, deciding that members who were elected to Dáil Éireann (the Irish parliament) would henceforth take their seats. The LCR was led by Tommy McKearney, a senior activist and former hunger striker. It objected to electoral politics, feeling that to embrace them required too many compromises to the revolutionary struggle that was their raison d'être. The group was fearful of adopting a reformist agenda that would inevitably condemn it to slide into irrelevance. It believed in the need to establish, along Leninist lines, a vanguard party of the working class that would drive an anti-imperialist movement on a national scale.

According to O'Ruairc (2001), an initial nucleus of about five enthusiasts soon grew to a steady state of between twenty and twenty-five members, scattered across seven of the eight H Blocks. They were mostly from rural areas. Communication and organization were difficult on account of the lack of a community support structure and the antipathy, or even hostility, of their fellow prisoners. From early 1987 the LCR put in place a small support base outside the prison, comprising around two dozen friends, relatives, and sympathizers. But when this group attempted to mobilize support it came under pressure from the wider republican movement, with an edict from the IRA describing its organizers as "counter-revolutionaries . . . offering assistance to the enemy" (p. 4).

The LCR's members were orthodox Marxist-Leninists who had arrived at the view that both the armed struggle and the electoral politics of Sinn Féin were unhelpful diversions from the task of creating an all-island revolutionary democratic government under the control of workers and small farmers. Its program, written by McKearney, envisioned an Irish state that could guarantee its citizens work at an acceptable wage, a home suitable to their needs, an education to the highest level compatible with their ability, comprehensive healthcare, and access to divorce, contraception, and abortion. There would be separation of church and state, and meaningful equality between the sexes.

Much of the LCR's energy was devoted to the production of a magazine, *Congress 86* (inspired by the short-lived Republican Congress of 1934, when a group of left-wing agitators broke away from the IRA). The first issue appeared in June 1987 and thirteen more were published between then and 1991 with a print run of between five hundred and one thousand copies per issue (O'Ruairc 2001: 3). The material for the newsletter was smuggled out of the H Blocks, it was edited, typeset, and printed, and then copies were sent into the prison where they were read and discussed. This was a prison environment characterized by curiosity and an openness to ideas, nurtured by men who had endured a great deal of isolation and deprivation during the protest years. The creation of the LCR and its newsletter are good examples of the institution's fervid intellectual atmosphere.

Congress 86 was the first journal produced by the prisoners that served as a forum for debate. It was innovative in that it was by prisoners for prisoners. Given the paucity of resources, small number of members, and limited readership it is impressive that so many issues could be compiled. It was an earnest, text-heavy publication. The first installment set the tone with articles on the role of the vanguard, dialectical materialism, sectarianism, and a range of economic matters. There was a sprinkling of photographs of Lenin and clenched-fist salutes. The second carried the strapline "For a Workers' and Small Farmers' Republic" (League of Communist Republicans 1988: 9). Many articles in subsequent issues dealt with theoretical aspects of Marxism and republicanism or strategic concerns around how best to organize a revolutionary movement. Later issues were written entirely by McKearney (O'Ruairc 2001: 9).

For more than a year, LCR members lived alongside men who remained strongly committed to the organization they had left, and relations were frosty, but never descended into an exchange of blows. In 1988 they moved as a whole to a wing of their own in H Block 6 and then on to HMP Maghaberry, which had recently opened (McKeown 1998: 279–80). When they relocated to Maghaberry, which offered enhanced conditions and facilities for conforming prisoners, they were accommodated in different parts of the institution and this depleted their cohesiveness and sapped their energy.

The collapse of communism in Eastern Europe was a body blow to the organization. According to O'Ruairc (2001: 9): "It is no coincidence that the last issue of the LCR journal appeared in December 1991, the same month that the Soviet Union came to an official end. With communism gone, it was extremely difficult to argue in Ireland that it provided a better socio-economic organization of society, and that made the LCR redundant." The LCR dwindled to the point of near irrelevance after the last issue of its magazine was published and it disintegrated further as people were released and tried to survive as atheistic communists; ideological purity was difficult to maintain in a conservative country and some had moved far from their origins. The absence of a political structure with which prisoners could have engaged post-release had they wished to remain involved contributed further to the LCR's demise. The League became extinct when McKearney was released in 1994.

The establishment of the LCR resulted from—and precipitated—a crisis of legitimacy (see box 1.1). The sequence here was of a legitimacy deficit when the policy on abstentionism was changed, developing into delegitimation, a split, and the transfer of a group of prisoners who could no longer accept the communal life that their peers enjoyed, seeing it as something of a distraction from an ideological project that required unwavering commitment. After the LCR there were no further schisms among IRA prisoners.

Building an Integrated Community

Unlike members of other prisoner societies, republicans in the H Blocks had much in common apart from their incarceration. They came from small, tight-knit communities. Many hailed from families with a tradition of insurrection. They were homogeneous in terms of race (all white), gender (all male), religion (overwhelmingly Roman Catholic), and social group (predominantly working-class), tended to be young, and were serving very long sentences. They held a shared view of political ends and means. They were supporters of an illegal army and had a common enemy in the security forces of the United Kingdom, whose presence in Northern Ireland they wished to terminate. The risks they took were high, both for themselves and their families, with death or incarceration being very real hazards. Regardless of how their motivations might have been viewed by others they were—as Irish republicans so often are—bonded by sacrifice.

They benefited from the kind of support networks—families, political parties, nongovernmental organizations, political representatives—that could mobilize national and international opinion behind the drama of their struggle. They appreciated the power of collective action in a way that prisoners elsewhere did not. They were highly integrated before they were imprisoned. Songs were written to celebrate them. People took to the streets to campaign on their behalf. Their prison time was a badge of honor and they appeared proud, unbroken, and defiant when released. Those who desired to dissociate themselves from militant republicanism, or who regretted the consequences of their actions (whether for others or themselves), moved on, generally without much fuss.

IRA volunteers saw their imprisonment as an extension of their activities outside. According to Dana and McMonagle (1997: 70–71), "being in prison does not mean that the British government has defeated them. Their work just takes on a different form and operates within a different context." While they may have had age, race, gender, and social class in common with what are described in Ireland as ODCs (ordinary decent criminals), their motivation, family circumstances, and history of criminality were very different. They also differed in that they were not characterized by high levels of mental illness, self-harm, and drug use. Their minds were intact and the degree of solidarity they enjoyed was a buffer against psychological disintegration. For the ODC a term of imprisonment was an interruption (or perhaps the termination) of a criminal career. For the IRA man it offered a new theater of activity in which the operation of the "British war machine" could be opposed and disrupted.

The prisoners resisted by vying for control of their spatiotemporal world and preparing themselves intellectually to continue the struggle for national unification and self-determination when released, sometimes by becoming involved in electoral politics. The case study in this chapter is of a prison where both integration and regulation were high (figure 1.1), although during the period under examination, the staff came to despair of ever being able to enforce those aspects of the rules that pertained to relationships with prisoners.

As the program of political education developed, a new consensus emerged among the men and there was discussion around how best to share the limited available resources. Wing communes emerged as initial anxiety (what about those who would contribute little and take much?) and hostility (why should nonsmokers subsidize smokers?) were gradually overcome. Everyone contributed their weekly pay. Several orderlies were officially assigned to every wing and were nominally responsible for janitorial duties. The role of the orderly was collectivized and the wages paid by the prison for cleaning, organizing laundry, and distributing food were pooled. A list was drawn up of what was required in the way of stamps, confectionary (for consumption on the wing or for sharing with visitors), and so forth. The total cost was calculated and if the combined wages were insufficient each member was asked to contribute an equal share of the difference from their personal account. Outside prison the quartermaster looked after arms and explosives. Inside, he was in charge of biscuits and teabags.

Some people withdrew from the commune and there was no penalty for so doing. But most accepted that this was the fairest way of achieving access to the widest range of items for the greatest number of people. The prisoners merged their resources to purchase books and to create a welfare fund that allowed discretionary payments to be made, on application, to those whose domestic circumstances were particularly straitened. The commune was an important way of redistributing resources so that men whose families could not support them were not disadvantaged.

The communes were partly utopian and partly pragmatic. Dana and McMonagle (1997: 69) described how "everything is shared as equally as possible, including the general maintenance of the wings, food received in parcels, postage stamps, and the use of the television and other items. For these men, living as political prisoners means the 'community' always comes before personal gain.... Regardless of one's position outside, in the H-Blocks no one is considered more or less important than another, and each man is obligated to contribute to the best of his abilities." Even the staff recognized the communes that

McKane (2008: 184) disparagingly referred to as "Socialist, collective-type, shopping systems."

The evolution of the commune took time and there were internal differences to be surmounted. Sometimes these involved ideological disputes, sometimes there were personality clashes or tussles between regional groupings (e.g., urban against rural), sometimes there were competing priorities (not everyone wished to share their limited resources, at least initially). When these conflicts were resolved, a unique society emerged, where the prisoners were in control, their focus was on political education (as well as attempting to escape), and they were involved in the push for peace in Northern Ireland.

Ryder (2000: 321) recounted how a prison that "had so authoritatively been a university of terrorism in the past . . . was now proving to be a forceful powerhouse of peace." He described the educational journey of the prisoners as generating "a more thoughtful, visionary and pragmatic brand of republicanism. . . . This was based on some extraordinary soul-searching debate about the failings of their campaign, and a willingness to evaluate cherished republican ideals and beliefs and adapt them to a more modern context" (p. 290). This political evolution was critical to the peace process that gathered momentum during the 1990s, eventually leading to a cessation of paramilitary activity in Northern Ireland. Incarcerated republicans influenced developments on the outside. Just as prisons are shaped by the society in which they are located, so too can they sometimes shape that society in return. Indeed, the expedited release of qualifying prisoners was integral to the Good Friday Agreement, which was approved in 1998 by an overwhelming majority on each side of the border in Ireland (McEvoy 1999).

The Armalite and ballot box strategy, which involved the republican movement's furtherance of both the armed struggle and electoral politics, had pivoted strongly toward the latter. This was not an acknowledgment that physical force was a regrettable failure but more a clear-eyed determination that politics was war by other means. These men had an intellectual framework that made sense of whence they had come and where they were headed. They were characterized by unwavering determination coupled with an esprit de corps that was buoyed by the solidarity shown during the protest years. It was this shared experience of not buckling under the most intense pressure that convinced them of the power of the collective over the individual. (It took the writ writers in the Eastham Unit to show the potential of joint action, but the prisoners remained divided and it was left to the courts to drive change.)

The 1990s, the period of interest in this chapter, was a time of penal realpolitik. It resulted from a pragmatic and sober assessment by prison management and its political masters in the Northern Ireland Office (NIO) of how best to adapt to a prisoner bloc that had proven to be largely immovable. McEvoy (2001: 311) described the regime at this time as "perhaps better viewed as a reluctant acceptance of the reality of the prisoners' power base rather than an unprincipled series of capitulations." I would put this slightly differently: it was a series of capitulations based on political rather than penological principles. The ideological conflict between the parties remained intense, but a modus vivendi had been found.

IRA prisoners were determined to resist the policy of criminalization and to craft their own way of life, despite huge obstacles to so doing in what was one of Europe's most secure prisons. They pushed back against the imposition of a regime that was at odds with their view of the world. This defiance was ferocious, took a variety of forms inside and outside the prison, and was sustained for decades. They faced a fragmented, disillusioned, and anxious staff whose solidarity had been dented when they saw prisoners wearing their own clothes, associating freely on wings where they were segregated by faction, and refusing to deal with them directly, choosing for all communications to be via their OC.

Staff knew that decisions regarding the treatment of prisoners were often political rather than operational and this increased their uncertainty about where authority lay and what support there would be for rigorous rule enforcement. Many individual staff members felt vulnerable in the face of such concerted, coordinated—and relentless—intractability. They seldom felt recognized either from above (by their superiors) or below (by those in their charge) contributing to a low level of what Bottoms and Tankebe (2012: 151) described as "self-legitimacy." If understanding and backup were to be found anywhere it was among their similarly situated peers. The uniform they chose to wear in Her Majesty's service seemed to render them invisible to management when at work, while at the same time enhancing their vulnerability to attack when at home.

An Iron Fist in an Iron Glove

If the prisoners felt that they were making insufficient progress they could call on their organization outside for assistance and sometimes this involved lethal violence. The shootings of an assistant governor outside his house in 1984 and a senior prison officer the following year as he left Sunday Mass had a chilling effect on their colleagues' willingness to enforce discipline thereafter. This was reinforced in 1988 when a car bomb killed the vice-chairman of the Prison Officers' Association. (This was the penultimate killing of a staff member by the IRA, with one more occurring in 1989.) These men were singled out because they were viewed as playing a key role in the criminalization policy and favoring a stern approach to prison discipline. Their deaths were personal. By contrast, when the IRA killed prison staff previously it had gone for the easy marks; they were targeted for what they represented rather than anything they might have done. A minority worked at the H Blocks and some had no direct contact with prisoners. Most died during the height of the prison protests between 1976 and 1981.

McEvoy (2001: 118) described a chilling incident in 1990 when a van carrying a policeman and four prison officers was stopped at an IRA checkpoint. Two of the prison officers managed to flee. The other two, who worked at the H Blocks, were released having been told that the situation in the prison was not currently a cause of concern to the republican movement. The policeman was shot dead.

The message to staff was clear: adopt a hands-off approach if you wish to remain safe from attack. These killings had the intended impact, inhibiting some officers' desire to enforce the rules. This was consolidated by the lack of support that they received from the NIPS. In the report of an inspection carried out in 1998, the staff were identified as the "real victims" on account of "many of the normal Prison Rules being inoperable and Prison Service Headquarters not being as understanding or supportive as one would wish" (Her Majesty's Chief Inspector of Prisons for England and Wales 1998: 4). The chief inspector expressed his "admiration and sympathy for the vast majority of the staff, who have been 'piggies in the middle,' between unsupportive management and implacably opposed prisoners, for so long" (p. 6). He acknowledged that operational issues were often trumped by political ones and that this had a cumulatively devastating effect on staff morale. "Inevitably," he wrote, "because of the nature of the intense unrest that has beset Northern Ireland society in the past thirty troubled years, much of the current situation in the Maze results from ministerial decisions, made for political reasons, over which civil servants and prison staff have had little or no control" (p. 172).

Working in the H Blocks took an emotional toll on staff and one of its deputy governors estimated that more than fifty took their own lives (Murtagh 2018: 23), often with the handguns issued to them for personal protection. This was considerably more than were assassinated for their service (twenty-eight between the ending of special category status in 1976 and the closure of the H Blocks in 2000). Many others were wounded or narrowly escaped injury. Writing in the third person, Murtagh described how, when he worked at the prison between 1980 and 1988, "there were numerous foiled attempts and two failed attempts to murder him, a foiled plan to kidnap family members and an unsuccessful attempt to murder his wife" (p. 23). He reckoned that more than two thousand prison staff were attacked and injured by prisoners (p. 776). This is a considerable toll of human suffering and exceeds the harsh treatment inflicted on prisoners by staff.

The predation, domination, and sexual violence that punctuate—and exacerbate—life in other prisons were not found on the IRA wings of Northern Ireland's H Blocks in the 1990s. Prisoners there did not fear for their bodily integrity.

The prison officers' world was a small and intimate one. They knew each other and identified with colleagues in the police and army (where some served as reservists). When one of them was shot or blown up it was not an abstract feeling of dread that descended but real sadness and anger at the murder of a friend, someone who was perceived to be taking the same risks for the same honorable purpose. Funeral services were packed with mourners. These killings communicated with brutal efficiency a message to the survivors who wished to avoid a similar fate. They knew it was not simply a question of seeking a transfer out of the H Blocks (soft targets at other prisons were ambushed), or of taking extra precautions at home (sometimes neighbors, or colleagues, facilitated attacks), or of speaking out (some of those who went public placed themselves firmly in the crosshairs), or of being a coreligionist (some of the murdered prison officers were Roman Catholics), or even of retiring (some of those killed had left the service). The message was clear: if you want to live, keep quiet and do not interfere. If you insist on doing your job, your safety cannot be guaranteed.

Murtagh described the prisoners as "common criminals" (p. 26), "thugs" (p. 226), and members of a "murder gang" (p. 214) or "murder squad" (p. 307). For him, they were terrorists for whom politics was used as a flag of convenience to cover heinous acts of criminality. Even so, he acknowledged their "discipline, determination and strategic skills" (p. 265). In a similar vein, Longwell (1998: 191) described the nature of the prisoners' protest in the 1990s as "patient, relentless, perpetual." They were unflinching in their determination to live according to the dictates of the republican movement rather than the rules of what they perceived as a non-legitimate administration. As far as the prisoners were concerned there was no basis for compliance with the prison rules. Coercion had failed and their value system was in direct opposition to that of the NIPS. In any event, those who calculated that it was in their interests to abide by the prison rules in order to expedite their release, or who no longer wished to be under IRA control, had moved on.

Political Education and the Frelimo Documents

Some prisoners enrolled in an Open University course in what was known at the time as Third World studies as part of which they learned about the war waged in Mozambique by Frelimo (Frente de Libertação de Moçambique), the nationalist movement that became the country's ruling political party. As they began to write up their own education program they were aware that any documentation relating to the IRA or Irish republicanism would be difficult to conceal if it was circulated as widely as intended (the point was to introduce a common approach across every IRA wing) and that it would be confiscated by the authorities if discovered. Consequently, they prepared their materials substituting "Frelimo" for "IRA," "Mozambique" for "Ireland," and "Frelimo prisoners" for "IRA prisoners." This ruse succeeded and the documentation moved freely across the prison without attracting unwanted attention. These documents set the direction of political education within the institution and constituted a sophisticated account of attempts to imbue prisoners with a spirit of praxis; to influence the movement outside (eventually); and to live as revolutionaries during their incarceration rather than seeing this as a role to defer until release.

The Charter for Frelimo Communities was put together in 1988/89 (McKeown 1998: 311) after the turbulent period referred to above when experienced activists disaffiliated from the movement, the League of Communist Republicans was formed, and a sizable group departed the H Blocks for the integrated regime at Maghaberry. O'Ruairc (2001: 2) estimated that between eighty and a hundred men resigned, amounting to about one in five of those on IRA wings in the H Blocks at the time, although some rejoined later. The community was strong enough by this stage to withstand these shocks and the disaffection never resulted in more than harsh words.

However, the exodus of a significant cohort of long-standing members precipitated a period of reflection on what an association of republican prisoners should look like, what values should underpin it, and what should be the rights and responsibilities of those who opted to be part of it. A ten-paragraph charter resulted from a long process of discussion, negotiation, and review in which every prisoner participated. It was the culmination of the process of generating the Frelimo documents, setting out a vision of comradely coexistence based on egalitarianism and an ethos of debate and constructive criticism. It was drawn up while Laurence McKeown, shown in figure 2.5 posing in the block exercise yard several years before he turned his attention to constitution building, was vice-OC for education. The charter was formally adopted early in 1990. It is reproduced in full in box 2.1.

The charter set out the minimum expectations of life on the IRA wings. Anyone accepted by the republican movement onto a wing they controlled agreed to abide by it (para. 1). There was an emphasis on progressive values, socialism, and consensus. The charter made clear that the right of residence was conditional on continuing compliance (para. 9). Besides, there was no doubt that the communes were subordinate to the organizational requirements of the IRA in the prison as a whole (para. 10). This was a contract underwritten by the IRA and security considerations remained paramount.

The camp staff dealt with the prison administration and the republican activists on the wings went about their business largely without any

Figure 2.5. Laurence McKeown in 1983. Credit: Taken with smuggled camera by volunteer photographer.

Box 2.1. Charter for Frelimo Communities

1. All sentenced for Frelimo related actions have automatic right to Frelimo communities. Non-political offenders (or those not connected with Frelimo) who seek to reside in Frelimo communities must make a request to the camp leadership. Each case will be considered on its own merits, giving particular consideration to the activities of the individual within our communities outside. No one in Frelimo communities has the automatic right to remain there indefinitely (see para. 9).
2. Frelimo communities guarantee the right of the individual to:
   a. Freedom and protection from physical abuse or harassment, intimidation, bullying, discrimination, slander or sustained verbal abuse.
   b. Live and practice his religious beliefs (equally conscious of the wishes of non-believers).
   c. His own sexual orientation.
3. Our living conditions are safeguarded primarily by our willingness (and the prison authorities' recognition of such) to defend our communities by whatever means necessary. This means unified action, directed and controlled at all times in a disciplined manner. It requires the willingness of all to participate in providing that unity and strength. At all times the leadership will give careful consideration to special cases or particular circumstances.
4. Everyone in Frelimo communities is encouraged to develop their personal and intellectual abilities to their fullest potential and to place these at the service of the community. Personal attacks on people, malicious gossip or slander will not be tolerated. It is the duty of all to combat this.
5. The promotion of socialist ideals and values is given the utmost importance. The distribution or promotion of pornography, sexually abusive literature, fascist, racist or other anti-people literature is contrary to such ideals and in total opposition to the values promoted by Frelimo.
6. Each community has firmly established structures through which everyone can voice their opinion and contribute to the decision-making process. Everyone is encouraged to participate. If an individual feels, for whatever reason, that these structures are not working on his behalf he

can appeal to the appointed leadership at the community level. If still not satisfied he can then, via the local leadership, make an appeal to the leadership of the prison camp. The decision reached by the camp leadership will be final and binding.

7. All those in Frelimo communities have responsibility for the continued well-being of the whole community. This entails various obligations concerning general maintenance and assisting in efforts to better living conditions (see para. 3).

8. The smooth running of Frelimo communities depends greatly upon our communication system. As recent discussions have pointed out communication takes many forms. Generally we can define it as the passing on of knowledge which is essential to our continued well-being and development. This can take the form of either verbal or written material. All have a crucial role to play in this.

9. Anyone acting contrary to the interests and well-being of Frelimo communities will be approached regarding their behavior. If their destructive attitude and activity persist (and it is known that there are no personal problems or other such factors which could be the cause of this) the community as a body will confront the individual(s), point out how their behavior is endangering the community and ask them to desist. The camp leadership will be made aware of all such approaches and their outcome. If the activities are sustained and are regarded by the camp leadership as intolerable the individual(s) will be told there is no longer a place within the Frelimo community for him/them.

10. Frelimo communities exist under the guidance and protection of Frelimo itself. Its interests and the pursuit of its objectives override all other considerations. Whilst every attempt will be made to complement Army and civilian needs/requirements, contradictions will occasionally arise. Where such does occur the Army needs will be explained (if feasible). Ultimately, Army considerations will outweigh all others. In all such instances Frelimo is the final arbiter.

meaningful engagement with prison officers. The commune coexisted with a command-and-control structure. Over time this seems to have become a comfortable set of arrangements for those who decided to remain under it. In any case, anyone who was hostile to the idea that the IRA would exert such control over their daily lives could always apply to transfer out of the H Blocks, so it was the willing who remained.

Despite the protection offered by the charter (para. 2), this was an environment characterized by little openness around sexual orientation, where gay men led an anxious and hidden existence (Rolston and McKeown 2017).

Transgressions were dealt with at local level if possible but could be escalated if breaches were persistent or more serious. This would result in a more formal intervention involving a member of the camp staff or "the possibility of details of the transgression being read out on every republican wing in the jail in an attempt to reassert the primacy of communal thinking" (Ó Mocháin 2011: 94). The ultimate sanction was expulsion and this was used sparingly.

In 1994 it was discovered that drugs and pornography were in circulation. The men involved were lying in bed all day, openly smoking cannabis, and not contributing to wing activity. This was divisive and negatively impacting morale. The incident was dealt with under the charter's provisions. Four men were expelled from the prison, one of whom was allowed back later. The expulsions were not just on account of the prohibited nature of the contraband, the adverse implications of its use for security, and the objectification of women, but also because this was a deliberate snub to the camp staff. As the punishment block had been shut down the administration had no choice but to comply with the prisoners' decisions regarding disciplinary matters. The way the problem was dealt with strengthened the sense of discipline and collective resolve and refocused minds on the development of a positive and progressive way of life. Ó Mocháin (2011: 109) noted that in 1993, before they had their own designated wings, three members of the INLA were expelled from IRA wings for refusing to cooperate with IRA structures.

In any other prison in Britain or Ireland in the 1990s cannabis consumption was so prevalent as to hardly merit comment. Her Majesty's Chief Inspector of Prisons for England and Wales (1998: 27) noted the absence of pornography and graffiti on cell walls in the H Blocks, which was in "marked contrast" to other institutions inspected. He also commented on how well maintained the small cells were, painted or wallpapered according to the occupant's taste and often with matching curtains. Communal areas were adorned with murals (see Rolston 2013). As artistic representations of what was important to the prisoners and their connection to past struggles, these were another creative form of resistance. They reminded anyone passing—especially staff—of the historical nature of the IRA's campaign and the lineage of the men who joined it. (The prisoners were not teetotal, and the IRA army council permitted alcohol consumption a couple of times a year such as to celebrate Christmas and Easter or on August 9 to mark the anniversary of the introduction of internment without trial. The men drank what they had managed to stockpile after 8 p.m., when staff went off duty.)

At a fundamental level IRA prisoners accepted the inevitability of the detention, by an enemy power, of POWs, but would never accept the language of criminality. There was a world of difference between being held at the Long Kesh camp, where his predecessors had been recognized as political prisoners and accorded special category status at the outset of the Troubles (see table 2.1) and again—in all but name—after the protest years, and being treated like a common criminal at HMP Maze. To conform would require accepting an identity that could not be squared with that of republican activist. The IRA's mission was to thwart the system, to undermine its inevitability, to make outcomes uncertain, to superimpose an alternative set of arrangements. Clearly there was comfort and strength to be drawn from an identity that emphasized heroic self-sacrifice and struggle against the odds and downplayed the grubbiness and violence of actions where civilians, rather than members of any of the warring groups, were so often disfigured or killed.

A Point of Order

Among the Frelimo documents were meticulous accounts of wing *coiste* (committee) structures, summarized as follows by Ó Mocháin (2011: 131):

> (1) the task of the group leader was to "create a learning environment" among members of the study group, and ensure that discussions were

productive and inclusive; (2) one member had to ensure that educational resources were available to the wing; (3) another was to promote academic education throughout the community; (4) one person was responsible for promoting cultural activities, including the Irish language; and (5) one member maintained the wing commune, and organized entertainment such as sports days, concerts and dramas. This document . . . provided guidelines for the smooth conduct of coiste meetings and outlined a detailed assessment process on a twice yearly basis, with monthly reports to be sent to the vice OC for education.

The purpose of the *coiste* was to coordinate the various activities of the wing community; membership was open to all, and the emphasis was on participation and collective decision-making. The degree to which this marked a departure from the hierarchies of the past is captured by the observation, from a prisoner who had been instrumental in their establishment, that "in the carrying-out of all wing activities . . . we learn to be conscious and purposeful activists rather than passive followers of instructions" (O'Hagan 1991: 8). He continued:

> What we have consciously tried to establish in our prison community is a culture wherein individual initiative and creativity are encouraged and harnessed towards the collective good. We have sought to develop democratic structures in which the worth of each person is recognised and where mutual and comradely support is offered in order to build individual confidence. If we have learned one lesson over the years, it is that rigid hierarchical structures stifle initiative and retard the progress of all. (p. 9)

Reading lists were prepared and prisoners were expected to take notes on, and be ready to discuss, the texts shown in table 2.3, in the specified order, in study groups of six to eight people. The first list was made up of fiction that addressed issues of working-class culture, capitalist exploitation, and imperialism. The second comprised historical and political works, putting the Irish situation in context and describing revolutionary struggles in other countries. The third was a comprehensive introduction to Marxist-Leninist thought. Even for those whose intellectual range had proven to be elastic, this must have stretched them almost

TABLE 2.3. Revolutionary Reading

List 1

Robert Tressell	*The Ragged Trousered Philanthropists*
Patrick MacGill	*Children of the Dead End / The Rat-Pit / Moleskin Joe*
James Plunkett	*Strumpet City*
John Steinbeck	*The Grapes of Wrath*
Ernie O'Malley	*On Another Man's Wound / The Singing Flame*
Brendan Behan	*Borstal Boy*
Liam O'Flaherty	*Famine*
David Yallop	*In God's Name*
George Orwell	*Animal Farm*

List 2

Michael Farrell	*Northern Ireland: The Orange State*
David Reed	*Ireland: The Key to the British Revolution*
Kevin Kelley	*The Longest War*
Margaret Ward	*Unmanageable Revolutionaries*
Liz Curtis	*Ireland: The Propaganda War*
Bernadette Devlin	*The Price of My Soul*
Eamonn McCann	*War and an Irish Town*
Eileen Fairweather, Roisin McDonough and Melanie McFadyean	*Only the Rivers Run Free*
Bobby Sands	*One Day in My Life*
Tim Pat Coogan	*On the Blanket*
Margaret Randall	*Sandino's Daughters*
John Gerassi	*Venceremos! The Speeches and Writings of Ernesto Che Guevara*
John Reed	*Insurgent Mexico*

List 3

James and Grace Lee Boggs	*Revolution and Evolution in the Twentieth Century*
Ernest Mandel	*Introduction to Marxism*
Maurice Cornforth	*Materialism and the Dialectical Method / Historical Materialism / The Theory of Knowledge*
Vladimir Lenin	*What Is to Be Done? / Two Tactics of Social-Democracy in the Democratic Revolution / Imperialism: The Highest Stage of Capitalism / The State and Revolution / "Left-Wing" Communism: An Infantile Disorder*
Peter Berresford Ellis	*James Connolly: Selected Writings*
David McLellan	*Karl Marx: Selected Writings*

to breaking point, but—as evidenced by the emergence of the League of Communist Republicans—a few became diehard converts.

Many of the prisoners lacked much formal education and the aim was to educate them politically in a way that would promote harmony and consensus on the wing, and beyond. Education was both a means to an end and an end in itself. For the prisoner who was open to the possibilities it offered, this could be a route to personal and political transformation as well as a highly effective stratagem for filling the day with constructive activity and investing a difficult situation with meaning. Over time, the lists of required reading became less prescriptive and the syllabus less tightly controlled. (Of course, giving prisoners reading lists is a direct attempt to shape their thoughts and behaviors, even if the methodology is Freirean rather than militaristic. There is the additional problem of autodidacticism in that an absence of external guidance can lead to the selection of a program of reading exclusively in support of one's preconceptions.)

As well as being introduced to the charter, new arrivals were provided with documents that set out some basic points about the wings and how they operated, together with an account of the evolution of the communes and how the autonomy enjoyed by prisoners was hard won and should not be taken for granted. Complacency had begun to set in by the 1990s, so the camp staff drew up a formal induction process for newcomers, especially those who had not previously been incarcerated, so that they would not lose sight of the sacrifices that had been made to win them the freedoms they currently enjoyed. Ó Mocháin (2011: 268) observed that "prisoners active in the 1976–1981 protest period featured in every IRA camp staff up to the closure of the H-Blocks in 2000." Some of them had been released and recaptured. These were men whose commitment had been tested and not found wanting. They were well regarded.

A compulsory jail history program took place over a five- or six-week period and gave new prisoners an insight into the protest years, the mass escape of thirty-eight prisoners in 1983, and the place of the prison in the overall republican struggle. This was about internalizing—and reinforcing—the identity of the republican POW. Nothing was beyond the pale and one of the first questions the newcomers were asked to consider was whether the hunger strikes, in which ten of their comrades died in 1981, had been worthwhile. They were encouraged to adopt a reflective and interrogative approach to their situation. There was significant pressure to abide by the communal existence on offer.

Life on the wings was characterized by solidarity, peer education, and connectedness with Irish republicanism's long struggle, which is intimately tied up with death and imprisonment. There was a high level of mutual support and a feeling that this was a stage in an individual's life just as much as it was a phase in the fight for independence. Those who would not fit could always move on, so the life described in this chapter was that enjoyed by the group of republican prisoners who refused to conform and served out their time in the H Blocks.

The Charter for Frelimo Communities differed from the Isir Bet governance code in one crucial respect: it was designed not only to facilitate harmonious life inside the institution but to have a transformative effect outside when the men who had lived by its tenets were released. It was about building a new society within and without the prison and modeling the latter on the former. It entailed a process of conscientization. It was political as well as pragmatic. It was not delimited. The way that the critically aware prisoner engaged with the authorities was continued—and promoted—post-release. Another major point of contrast is that the Isir Bet code was agreed to with the prison administration prior to implementation, and harmonized with its priorities, whereas the Charter for Frelimo Communities was created by a group that rejected the legitimacy of the prison rules and resisted—to the death, if necessary—the policy of criminalization. Serious breaches of the Isir Bet code were referred to the prison administration, whereas what emerged in the H Blocks was an entirely parallel set of arrangements.

Party Politics

A Sinn Féin *cumann* (political party branch) was established in the prison in 1990 (Ó Mocháin 2011: 142). It demanded—and eventually received—the right to be represented and to vote at the *Ard Fheis* (annual party conference) (McKeown 2001: 248). The *cumann* met regularly on the wings to hold debates and to propose motions for discussion at the *Ard Fheis*. It became the locus of much of the political palaver on the wing, giving a more formal structure to the culture of critique that had existed for so long. (It is difficult—even fanciful?—to conceive of the Republicans or Democrats organizing a caucus in ADX Florence or the Eastham Unit.)

During the 1990s the prisoners became more fully engaged in conventional education with prison teachers and the Open University, where they could complete a wide range of undergraduate and postgraduate programs. This shifted the focus from peer learning and widened the spread of subjects covered:

> As well as the perennials of Irish history, economics and political ideologies, short courses were provided on counselling skills, a course was organised on parenting skills and child centred play, and several local academics presented aspects of their research. Individuals had access to creative-writing, music theory and song writing, storytelling, sign language and basic literacy teaching classes. On the back of a drama course two separate blocks undertook to produce and perform a lengthy production based on the theories of Augusto Boal, a radical theatre theorist. From a skills and training point of view, courses were provided in fish fly-tying, in the coaching of football, and a number of republican prisoners completed a yoga teacher-training course lasting two years in total, which also involved a process of temporary release to attend examinations in Dublin in early 1998. (Ó Mocháin 2011: 152)

This was quite a shift from Marxist-Leninist orthodoxies, but the impulse was the same; the prisoners continued to pursue their desire for the kind of developmental opportunities that would enhance their ability to play effective roles in their communities post-release, as politically aware critical thinkers. The fall of the Berlin Wall had shaken the confidence of all but the most fervent believers in the utopian possibilities of communism. The reorientation of political education was toward Ireland and away from abstract theoretical issues; it was about praxis, and realizing a republican vision through incremental steps forward, followed by consolidation and periodic review. It was a disciplined march toward a new Ireland.

The IRA communes were vibrant places. The impetus behind them was not about creating an easy social life, although this ensued, but rather about utilizing the prison experience to further political goals.

As McKeown (2001: 148) expressed it: "For all involved in the political education process within the jail it was not simply about the learning of new concepts and theories. It was also about the acquiring of new values and the construction of a new society."

Not all prisoners wished to embrace the commune (but everyone benefited from the harmony and enhanced sense of solidarity that it prompted). Some were content to relax, train in the gym, watch television, do handicrafts, and wait to be released, feeling that they had played their part. The ethos was communal and political and educationally oriented, but there was space for people to structure their day according to their own whims or preferences. Nor did the emphasis on discourse appeal to everyone. Some felt that they had joined a guerrilla army and not a debating society. They did not wish to spend their evenings discussing colonialism or Freirean pedagogy. But the creation of the position of vice-OC for education emphasized the value that the republican movement placed on its supporters developing their critical faculties and becoming articulate in political theory; "struggle" and "education" became synonyms.

These developments added to the despair of those trying to run the prison as a prison, only the most willfully myopic of whom could maintain the pretense that the men in their custody were no different from the thieves, robbers, and murderers to be found in other high security prisons across the United Kingdom. The uncompromising declaration by Margaret Thatcher (1981), prime minister of the UK between 1979 and 1990, that as far as the activities of the IRA were concerned "Crime is crime is crime: it is not political, it is crime" had become completely hollow.

Conditions and Conditioning

Murtagh (2018: 668) described prisoners' leaders issuing orders to staff, and by 1994, the situation had deteriorated, from his perspective as a senior manager, to the point where they "were telling the staff where and when they could search on the wing. On occasions the search team was refused entry." The administration was required to give advance notice of any proposed search and the camp staff would decide on the level of compliance. Combined with inadequate supervision, dangerously low morale, and "some officers showing classic symptoms of Stockholm

Syndrome" (p. 632), the balance of power was tilted decisively in favor of the prisoners.

There was a high degree of consensus among the men on IRA wings, and the degree of conflict with staff depended on their strategic priorities at the time; sometimes the threat of lethal violence was deployed, other times "friendly" repartee was preferred. There was no such thing as idle chat. This was banter with a very specific purpose, namely staff conditioning.

Alan Longwell was an assistant governor from 1995 until the prison closed in 2000, having served in a similar capacity between 1988 and 1992. He described the conditioning process in some detail, including how weak and pliable staff were cultivated by prisoners who applauded the good working relationship that existed to ensure they remained in place. Stricter or more resilient staff were moved on when management were informed that their safety could not be guaranteed. In this way the prisoners shaped work rosters. IRA men were demanding, assertive, and unbiddable. They eroded staff confidence and wrested control away, leaving them listless and unsure. As one officer described the routine, he would draw "a line in the sand every morning and the next day come into work, rub the line out and move it back another foot or so" (cited in Longwell 1998: 10).

Longwell described how a lengthy memorandum on "counter-conditioning" prepared by a governor described republican prisoners as acting with "noticeable solidarity in pursuit of clearly thought-out objectives. To achieve these goals they continually attempt to 'shape' the behavior and attitudes of all ranks of staff by rewarding 'good' responses and punishing 'wrong' responses" (p. 234). One of the staff who had been on the receiving end of this treatment recounted how himself and his colleagues were undermined in two ways. The prison's senior management was preoccupied with appeasing the prisoners, and the latter were exploiting this laxity to keep the pressure on the frontline workers with whom they were in daily contact (McKane 2008). Why would the staff jeopardize their safety for a leadership that did not support them and in a context where political developments outside the prison seemed to dictate the pace of change inside?

Another retired governor, William McKee (2009), wrote an account of his experiences in the H Blocks. He was frank about the extent of the conditioning, the fact that wings became "no go" areas for staff, that prisoner consent was required for any change to the regime, that if the prisoners were unhappy with a decision made by the administration the governor could expect to be summoned before them to give an account of himself. He was similarly explicit about the toll that working in such an environment took on the mental health and family life of an officer who was attempting to be diligent in the discharge of his duties.

In late 1993 the IRA prisoners pushed, successfully, for access to the classroom and gym during daytime lockup. In March 1994, daytime lockup was abandoned. The next fight was for access to the yard during the day; again this was won. Then attention turned to ending nighttime lockup. The 1994 football World Cup allowed the prisoners to force this issue. They argued that the time difference between Ireland and the US (where the tournament was being staged) meant that many matches would be televised after they had been secured in their cells for the night. (An ancillary argument was that they needed twenty-four-hour access to sanitation and that slopping out was an abuse of their human rights.) As a result, the prisoners refused to accept lockup during the World Cup. When the competition finished they agreed to be shut in at night for two weeks on condition that this requirement was abolished thereafter. In addition, they were permitted access to the yards from 7:30 a.m., two yards were combined and a running track was created around them, and OCs and other men with block roles were allowed to move throughout all four wings of their block.

The camp OC was given permission to move around the entire complex to explain what had been agreed to. This gave the prisoners total control of their living arrangements, round the clock, from August 1, 1994 (Murtagh 2018: 691). It was a watershed moment and marked the official end of the criminalization policy that had been resisted since 1976. It was special category status, or more, in all but name. The following day, staff were withdrawn from the wings. They remained on duty at wing entrances, in the administrative "circle" in the bar of the H, and when providing escorts to the visiting area and the hospital. The prisoners then lobbied for the removal of the secure barriers that separated the wings on each side of the H. This was approved and meant that the staff were now confined to the circle.

The punishment block was closed and the prisoners' leadership were expected to take responsibility for internal disciplinary matters

(McKeown 2001: 199). Murtagh (2018: 698) was aghast: "To any experienced prison professional this [agreement of prison authorities to close punishment block] was an incredible surrender of control on the last bastion of discipline in the prison and in empowering convicted criminals to formally exercise power in enforcing discipline, and probably unlawful." It is difficult to imagine such a move being made in any other maximum-security prison and it says a great deal about the tension that existed between the NIO (with its eye on political developments more generally) and the NIPS (which was prevented from operating anything approximating an appropriate regime for the hardened criminals they believed to be in their custody). I would agree with the assessment of Gormally et al. (1993: 125) that what transpired in the H Blocks during the period of interest reflected a "policy of organized hypocrisy."

These changes were not happening in a vacuum. Political developments clashed with operational imperatives and the NIO had no desire to impede the former. This is why the sociogram for this chapter (figure 2.4) includes a dotted line to this external entity. The degree of outside involvement, and even interference, is unusual. Most of the concessions were won before the IRA declared a complete cessation of military operations on August 31, 1994. The impending ceasefire must have contributed to the decision to grant twenty-four-hour unlock. As the staff had withdrawn from the wings, head counts became difficult to complete, so a practice evolved of "assumed roll-checks (guessed numbers) and incredibly this was accepted in a high-security prison" (Murtagh 2018: 695). The prison officer walking along the wings checking that everyone was where they should be (figure 2.6) had become a thing of the past.

Murtagh (2018: 25) described the prison as "completely out of control" in the 1990s; this was the "most difficult period" (p. 644), when it had "descended into a complete state of anomie" (p. 662). As far as the prisoners were concerned the opposite was true and what was seen as chaotic by the authorities was viewed as orderly by them. But these are two sides of the same coin. Over the years, the prisoners wrested control from the staff, leaving the latter uncertain about how to respond (and whether they would be supported if they intervened to enforce the rules). What appeared to be an anarchic situation to a conscientious staff member—cells never locked, no direct communication with the

Figure 2.6. All Present and Correct? An Abandoned Practice. Credit: PA Photos.

men supposedly in their charge, no meaningful disciplinary apparatus—was precisely the kind of self-governance that the prisoners desired. Returning to the question of legitimacy, its horizontal aspect was strong for the prisoners while its vertical component was nonexistent. The prisoners viewed their own arrangements as embracing all three levels of Beetham's model (see box 1.1); this was triple-ply legitimacy. But they saw the regime imposed by the NIPS as satisfying only the first: it conformed to established written rules, but these were not derived from shared beliefs and values and there was no moral obligation to comply with them.

In January 1995 the IRA presented its "conditions document" to the prison management (Longwell 1998: 192 and appendix G). This built on written proposals that had been put forward in 1988, and while acknowledging that there had been some progress, expressed concern about the "pace and degree of change in many areas." The document extended to five typewritten pages and listed a dozen areas where the authors believed there was "absolutely no logical reason why the following requests cannot be acted upon with the minimum of fuss." The areas identified as requiring rapid remedial action were: (1) a right to compassionate parole; (2) abolition of the red book policy (a classification used for men deemed to be especially high risk); (3) provision of telephone facilities on wings; (4) conjugal visits; (5) artificial insemination for those who wished to start, or augment, families; (6) enhanced education; (7) handicrafts workshop; (8) access to clothing, the prison shop, and parcels from families; (9) better wages; (10) cooking facilities on the wings; (11) increased access to the gym and football pitches; and (12) an end to the censorship of correspondence.

This was a well-thought-out document written with confidence by a group that expected its demands to be met. As well as setting a clear program for the next phase of the struggle and pressuring the prison administration, it gave the prisoners a unity of purpose, binding them tightly together in terms of shared objectives. The IRA was setting the agenda (literally), defining what constituted meaningful change, and specifying the pace at which management should move. It must have been exhausting dealing with such a concerted effort day in day out, and it is easy to appreciate why the response of the administration was often to yield and then to capitulate in the face of what McEvoy (2001: 136) characterized as "the tyranny of relentlessly reasoned argument." The prison authorities were worn down by IRA discipline and intransigence.

When prisoners are highly integrated (and supported by armed comrades outside) they can break down the staff through a combination of co-option, fear, and attrition. Staff felt it was not worth the aggravation to fight all the time with a group who were in a prison from which unauthorized egress was thought to be impossible. But their acquiescence and the creation of an easygoing atmosphere on the wings created the circumstances for major security breaches.

Exploiting Perceived Weakness

Longwell (1998: 22) described: "By 1997 the prisoners had so much control over the staff that they were able to dig a tunnel from a cell . . . with the luxury of not having to hide or dispose of the tunnel debris . . . in the knowledge that staff would not be disturbing them." Ryder (2000: 327) reported that the tunnel was thirty-two meters long and a subsequent search of the wing found "two cells packed to the ceilings with 25 tonnes of rubble and spoil." He continued: "The most worrying aspect of the affair, from the security point of view, was that 95 inmates in the block had been able to improvise tools, chip their way through several inches of concrete and hardfill, drop a seven-foot shaft and dig and dispose of the spoil for weeks on end without a single prison officer spotting anything suspicious" (p. 327). A dog handler on night patrol on March 23 noticed subsidence and the following morning the partially collapsed tunnel was found.

The existence of the tunnel was a cause of major embarrassment for the authorities. It showed that, however relaxed the regime may have become, the men in the H Blocks still saw themselves as POWs whose first duty was to escape. (The ceasefire that had been declared in August 1994 ended in February 1996. It was reinstated in July 1997 and has endured since.)

McKane (2008: 228) described 1997 as the prison's "darkest year." As well as the discovery of a tunnel, Liam Averill escaped on December 10 dressed as a woman after a Christmas party for prisoners and their families. The party involved bouncy castles for the children, three-legged races, professional clowns, and karaoke singing. (It is well-nigh impossible to imagine the domestic or foreign terrorists being held at ADX Florence being permitted such jollities). His absence was only noticed when it was brought to the attention of staff by the OC of his block when the party was over, the guests had left, and the men were back on the wings. Finally, Billy Wright, a notorious loyalist leader known as "King Rat," was shot dead by INLA prisoners (who had yet to declare a ceasefire) on December 27 as he sat in a prison van waiting to be taken from his wing to the visitors' complex. From the perspective of the staff working there, according to McKane, the prison was in a state of "total chaos" (p. 236).

When he visited in 1998, Her Majesty's Chief Inspector of Prisons for England and Wales described a tense atmosphere, with a lack of clarity as to the boundaries of acceptable conduct. Relations between republican prisoners and staff were superficially cordial, comprising "a strange mixture of polite friendliness tinged with apprehension . . . the presence of both Officers and prison managers was seen by prisoners as an irritating irrelevance, and one that was only endured for the benefits that could be extracted from the system" (p. 48). "The conditioning of staff was constant" (p. 51) in that demands and complaints were interspersed with banter. Staff did what they could to avoid conflict both to ease their workday and to reduce the risk of direct action at home against themselves or their families. Prisoners were not searched, head counts were seldom thorough, wing shakedowns were permitted only by prior agreement with the OC. The inspector's conclusion was unequivocal: "In any prison other than the Maze, the way in which prisoners were able to determine their own lives, and force staff into a largely subservient role, would, unquestionably, be wholly unacceptable . . . successive governments had been unwilling to fully challenge the paramilitary influence in the Maze, because of consequences in the community" (p. 185).

The IRA prisoners knew that by manipulating social relations with staff they could tilt the balance of power further in their favor, regardless of the prevailing rules and management structures. Sometimes this involved ignoring staff. Sometimes it involved seemingly affable relations. Sometimes it involved verbal abuse and threats of violence. Sometimes it involved petitioning the NIO or challenging decisions in the courts. This made the imposition of sanctions for indiscipline cumbersome and fraught, and rendered outcomes uncertain. It sapped the energy and resolve of the staff who were trying to maintain order by applying the prison rules. It was impossible to deal with a collective using prison rules and procedures that were expressly designed for individuals. Longwell (1998: 196) described how republican prisoners "move and act, as one." They were a group, not a crowd.

IRA prisoners created an environment that endured over time, that could accommodate new arrivals, that operated according to a well-articulated set of principles and norms, where roles and relationships were clear, and where a measure of personal autonomy was willingly surrendered in the interests of group solidarity. Not only did they succeed in shaping their own environment, but they influenced the occupational world of their captors and even the wider society. Their impact ranged deep and wide. Longwell (1998: 203–4) viewed them as terrorists who were "dedicated, skilled, clever, resilient, determined and, where necessary, ruthless . . . they gather information, plan and ultimately take action. They resist the efforts of the Crown Forces in the wider society, similarly they resist the efforts of prison staff within the confines of the prison."

The prisoners' resolve was stiffened by their ideology (a firm allegiance to the ideal of an all-island socialist republic), camaraderie, sense of history, and knowledge of support outside the prison walls. They were sustained by the motif of martyrdom, the idea that they were suffering so that others might ultimately enjoy the prize of Irish freedom. They sloughed off a degree of regulation that in other circumstances could have been crushing.

The peace process that unfolded in Northern Ireland during the 1990s made the prison even more porous. Future president of South Africa Cyril Ramaphosa visited the H Blocks with an African National Congress deputation in April 1998; IRA women were brought from Maghaberry for this event (McKeown 2001: 216). Mo Mowlam visited in January 1998 when she was secretary of state for Northern Ireland. I was part of a delegation in November 1999, and the postcard I was presented with by the prisoners' spokesperson is reproduced as figure 2.7. The dramatic image hearkened back to a struggle—the blanket protest, when republicans refused to wear the convict uniform—that had concluded almost twenty years previously. The use of the Irish language in the title (which translates to "The Spirit of Freedom, H Blocks, Long Kesh") and the quotation from Bobby Sands (the first hunger striker to die in 1981) are further indications of priorities and perceived continuities. The postcard captures much that the prisoners held dear and that defined their struggle.

The last batch of qualifying IRA prisoners was released en masse on July 28, 2000, and shortly afterward the prison was closed for good. All that remains is one derelict block. My desire to make a return visit to reacquaint myself with its layout could not be facilitated in the first instance because there was no functioning executive in Northern Ireland. Ironically, it was easier to visit a high-security prison in the late 1990s when it held "dangerous terrorists" than it was to visit a vacant site twenty years later when the same individuals were now in government but had reached a political impasse with unionists. When business eventually resumed at the Northern Ireland Assembly, my plans were thwarted by the closures and travel restrictions resulting from the COVID-19 pandemic. When these restrictions eased, bureaucratic inertia could not be overcome, so having first applied to visit in March 2019, I accepted defeat thirty-two months later. (The physical force tradition has not been extinguished and small numbers of activists, aligned with a variety of

Figure 2.7. The Spirit of Freedom (artist unknown). "I am now in H-block, where I refuse to change to suit the people who oppress, torture and imprison me, and who wish to dehumanize me . . . I have been stripped of my clothes and locked in a dirty empty cell where I have been starved, beaten and tortured . . . I remain what I am, a political prisoner of war, and no one can change that." Bobby Sands.

dissident republican groups, continue to appear before the courts and, when incarcerated in Maghaberry, to lobby for political status.)

Literature of Confinement and the Language Revival

An Glór Gafa/The Captive Voice was a magazine published several times a year, its content generated entirely by republican prisoners wherever they were held. Most of the contributing authors and artists were based in Ireland, north and south, but some were in Britain and Europe and one who featured regularly (Joe Doherty) was in the US; his lengthy extradition fight and eventual return to the H Blocks was covered in the magazine's pages. The first issue appeared in the autumn of 1989 and the content was varied and interesting, ranging from poetry and short stories to political commentaries on a range of subjects including women's issues, the environment, international affairs, and emigration, as well as crosswords, quizzes, book reviews, and cartoon strips. There were occasional articles written in the Irish language (accompanied by a vigorous debate about whether an English translation should be supplied—those in favor felt it would assist potential readers who lacked fluency but wished to improve; those against felt that this would consolidate the view that everything Irish had to have an English reference point). It was supposed to be a quarterly publication, but there were never more than three issues in a year (McKeown 2001: 185).

The artwork in figure 2.8 (the cover of the Winter 1996 issue) portrays traditional music, drama, writing, and sport all sprouting from the fertile culture of a H Block, which is beginning to crack as a consequence of this internal vibrancy. The drab gray of the prison and its environs contrasts starkly with its colorful outputs. The magazine's final issue appeared in 1999 and the following year the last prisoners were released. According to Campbell (1991: 15), each issue of *An Glór Gafa* sold over seven thousand copies. This gives some indication of the level of community support for, and interest in, republican prisoners. Indeed, they even have their own membership organization, the Felons' Club, a popular restaurant and music venue located in West Belfast.

It is difficult to imagine magazines of such range, frequency, and appeal emerging from the other prisoner societies examined in this book. In Isir Bet, prisoners did not have a common purpose to the same degree

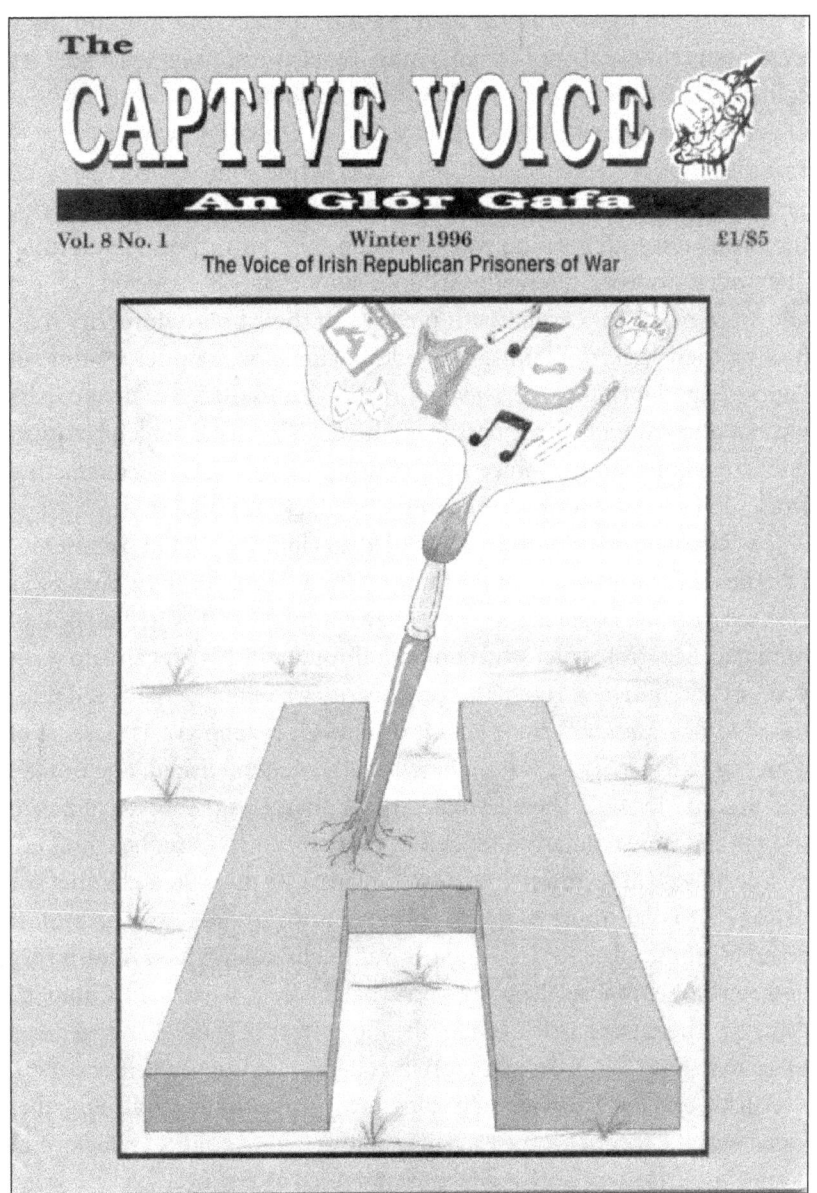

Figure 2.8. Writing Is Fighting. Credit: Sinn Féin POW Department. Art by Mickey Doherty.

and needed to make a living. Additionally, literacy was low and there were many different spoken languages. By virtue of their strict solitary confinement, the men held in ADX Florence could not sit down together to debate and discuss content, make editorial decisions, arrange printing and distribution, and consider feedback. While some of the men who served time at the Eastham Unit wrote memoirs and others wrote writs, there was not much in the way of fiction, poetry, or political writing. They were too worn out by the arduous labor that was expected of them and were more concerned with preserving their bodily integrity than honing their literary talents. There are forums for prisoner writing, of course (e.g., *Journal of Prisoners on Prisons*), and there are newspapers written and edited by prisoners (e.g., the *Echo* in Texas, which has been published continuously since 1928), but the volume of copy emanating from such a small group of men in the H Blocks is remarkable.

The prisoners surreptitiously recorded an album in 1991 to commemorate the tenth anniversary of the hunger strike. *Music from the Blocks* was spirited outside, copied, and sold. They compiled and edited a book of reminiscences from men who had been through the blanket and no wash protests and hunger strikes. This oral history was smuggled out and published as *Nor Meekly Serve My Time* (Campbell et al. 1994). Two issues of a poetry journal, *Scairt Amach* (shout out), were published, one in 1989 and another in 1991. These emerged from poetry workshops that began in 1988 and were regularly attended by over fifty men (Campbell 1991: 12).

Iris Bheag (little magazine) was intended to provide a channel for prisoners to contribute to the development of Sinn Féin. Not as professionally produced as *An Glór Gafa*, it was published between August 1987 and September 1990 as the party's "internal theoretical journal" (Campbell 1991: 15). There were articles about the movement in general and women's place in it, Sinn Féin's organization in colleges and universities, abortion, socialism, and legal developments. It was to be a monthly publication that would act as a forum for the exchange of ideas about political policies and strategies. Prisoners were deliberately targeted as potential contributors. Their submissions tended to be theoretical and left-wing and had little in common with the concerns of grassroots members, many of whom must have been baffled by the issues addressed and the language used. Over time the volume of prisoner contributions diminished.

All of these publications were preceded—and possibly provoked—by *Congress 86*, the newsletter of the League of Communist Republicans. In a lengthy survey of writing by Irish republican prisoners, Whalen (2007) failed to mention *Congress 86*. Perhaps this was because it was an anachronism after the collapse of the Soviet Union and any ripples it may have caused had long since faded. Perhaps it was because its originators had detached themselves from the mainstream of IRA prisoners. Whatever the reason, it would appear to have been effaced from the dominant narrative.

By the mid-1990s the prisoners wore their own clothes, did no prison work, were never locked into their cells, were deeply involved in education, and lived on entirely segregated wings. Now they aspired to immerse themselves more deeply in the Irish-language tradition. The next item on the agenda was the creation of a Gaeltacht within the prison, an area where the use of the English language would be forbidden.

Ryder (2000: 301) noted that an Irish-speaking censor was appointed in April 1987 to scrutinize the increasing volume of Irish-language material requested by prisoners. Mac Giolla Chríost (2012: 117) referred to a letter from a prisoner to an *Irish Times* columnist in 1987 requesting an Irish-language edition of *The Communist Manifesto*. Ironically, the letter making the request was written in English because the ban on correspondence through Irish remained in place, although "suitable" books were allowed. Mac Cormaic (1991: 19) gave 1986 as the year when prisoners won the right to be allowed to receive Irish-language books but noted that any incoming texts had to be reviewed by the censor and this could delay their arrival in the prison by a year or two. As always, victories were hard-fought and came about slowly.

The Irish-speaking area of the prison was called Gaeltacht na Fuiseoige (Gaeltacht of the lark) (see figure 2.9), a tribute to Bobby Sands, whose pen name was "the lark" (Mac Giolla Chríost 2012: 91). Gaeltacht na Fuiseoige was established on one wing in May 1995 with twenty-four Irish-language enthusiasts selected by the camp staff (Ó Mocháin 2011: 148). This rekindled interest in the language throughout the prison and soon there was a waiting list to join. The following year the Gaeltacht expanded to embrace a second wing in a different block.

Each Gaeltacht wing had three or four men who were fluent Irish speakers. They brought the mid-level speakers up to speed and they in

Figure 2.9. The Irish Language in Captivity. Credit: Bill Rolston.

turn brought on the beginners. The emphasis was on the spoken language and it was up to the individual to hone their grammatical skills if they were so minded. It was a full-immersion environment with everyone studying, debating, and socializing through the medium of Irish. There was a class every day and an event each evening. It was compulsory to speak Irish in any of the public areas of the wing, but if an individual needed to communicate something that exceeded his linguistic ability he could do this in a private area like his cell. There was no tolerance for anyone who relapsed into English. It was a boon when Teilifís na Gaeilge, an Irish-medium television service, began transmission in October 1996. Prisoners remained in the Gaeltacht until they were released and then a space became available for the next person on the waiting list. The Irish-language wings continued to thrive until the prison shut.

During the protest years of the late 1970s and early 1980s the prisoners taught each other Irish. This was partly patriotic (a way to signal identity in an environment where there were few other possibilities for so doing), partly a political statement, and partly a way of rendering shouted communications unintelligible to the guards (although Ryder [2000: 252] suggested that some officers had a better grasp of the language than they pretended). The longer the protest endured, the more the men needed intellectual stimulation and learning Irish was a part of this. Many burnished their language skills, benefiting from the fluency of their bilingual comrades. By Mac Cormaic's (1991: 18) estimate there were only a couple of Irish speakers in the H Blocks at the beginning of the blanket protest, but by the time it was wound up there were around three hundred of them (see also Mac Ionnrachtaigh 2013).

There was a diminution in interest when the protests ended. When it was revived it was an extension of the community into the prison, emphasizing the porosity of the prison walls, the connections between inside and out, and satisfying the prisoners' desire for learning. It was something that extended beyond the prison rather than something that was used to combat the prison. It moved from being a tool for coping with the pains of imprisonment to being a way of life that would continue post-release. When the protests ended, the prisoners had much more to occupy themselves with and learning Irish from their peers was less of a priority. It took some determination to reprioritize the language in the face of so many competing demands, but this was done with the usual determination and was a great success. The Gaeltacht wings show how language had been weaponized (O'Hearn 2009: 511) and then became normalized as the trajectory of the prison struggle shifted.

The social life of the H Blocks was what the prisoners wished the outside world would look like; it was not a reflection of it.

Coda

When prisoners share a political perspective that leads them to challenge the legitimacy of their confinement and are part of an organization that supports this contention, their carceral lives are likely to involve deliberation, contestation, and resistance. IRA members were by no means unique in this regard. Writing about the opponents of apartheid in South Africa who were held in maximum security on Robben Island (also in H Blocks, but most of them in communal cells), Buntman (2003: 237) noted their desire to "dilute, circumvent, or eliminate" the power of the prison authorities. They did this by drawing up their own code of conduct, putting the needs of the community ahead of those of its individual members, acting collectively, making education central, designing an induction process for new arrivals, and manipulating relations with the prison guards. As in Northern Ireland, the life that they created "coexisted with or, at best, displaced, the regime's coercive apparatus" (p. 266). The prison became another front in the struggle for racial equality and justice.

3

Eastham Unit, Texas

An inmate in the custody of the Texas Department of Corrections ... may not act in a supervisory or administrative capacity over other inmates [and] ... may not administer disciplinary action over another inmate.
—House Bill 1056, enacted by 63rd Texas Legislature, May 19, 1973

The state of Texas purchased the 12,970-acre Eastham farm in 1915 (having previously leased the land) and a maximum-security building was constructed on it in 1919. This was where prisoners picked cotton until their fingers bled for fear of a thrashing with "the bat," where the state exploited the labor of its captives, where the echoes of the slave plantation rang loud, and where the Texas Prison Rodeo originated. According to Perkinson (2010: 42), while there are many types of prison and jail in Texas, "if any unit stands for the rest," it is Eastham. It is one of the most famous prisons in the Lone Star State, the place where Bonnie Parker and Clyde Barrow helped several accomplices to shoot their way to freedom in January 1934. Barrow had previously served time there and hated it, cutting off two of his toes to avoid the brutal field labor that was mandatory unless a man happened to be injured or ill. His self-harm was far from exceptional. Prisoners deliberately infected themselves with lye and kerosene, cut off digits, and sliced their Achilles tendons (a practice known as "heel stringing"), so that they could be relieved of the unrelenting and backbreaking toil.

That such extreme action would be taken to escape its rigors speaks volumes about the odious nature of the work regime. This was self-mutilation as a form of communication, using the body as a site of resistance. There is a direct parallel with Jack Powers in ADX Florence, who also severed his Achilles tendon to draw attention to his predicament. (In Greek mythology Achilles's only weak spot was his heel; when this was punctured with an arrow he died. For prisoners, the reverse was true in that their entire bodies were vulnerable, but they could regain a measure of control by lacerating their heels.) It is also analogous to the hunger strikes in the H Blocks that preceded the evolution of a communal life and the attempts by Muslims held in ADX Florence to refuse food. These are methods of fighting back that transcend time and place. When prisoners lose control over everything but their bodies, they use flesh and blood, and skin and bone, to signal their concerns and to assert their capacity to contribute to, and even control, a dialogue that would otherwise be emphatically one-sided.

Press (1986: 48) described the Eastham Unit as "a symbol for America's prisons" and his *Newsweek* cover story about the institution (see figure 3.1) recounted how it had its own way of doing things, consisting of "one part head knocking, one part line toeing, and two parts hard laboring." The prison ran on unquestioning obedience and exhausting labor. When he heard that he would be serving time there, the initial thought of Bobby Delgado (2007: 170) was: "The word Eastham was a cuss word."

I have chosen this institution as an example of what prison life can be like when regulation is low, the state having abdicated its responsibility by refusing to make adequate resources available. But so too was integration low. The fissures in the prisoner society were deep. Divided by race, ethnicity, place of origin, and language, the men sent there were worked so hard and for so long that organizing themselves was a luxury they could scarcely afford; it was sleep and survival that motivated them when not at labor.

A defining characteristic of the Eastham Unit, like other Texas prisons, was the cultivation of a hand-picked cohort of prisoners—the building tenders (BTs)—to oversee the others. They were depended upon for gathering intelligence and enforcing discipline. Through a combination of fear and force, the BTs made life predictable. Their presence further divided an already riven society. The staff did not hand matters entirely over to the prisoners. But the degree to which they applied the (largely customary) rules was greatly diminished because they could rely upon the BTs to do battle for them. Regulation was low, not entirely absent. The prison is noteworthy because it was the location for a legal challenge by David Ruiz and others that transformed prisons right across the state.

Figure 3.1. Still Making the Headlines. Credit: *Newsweek*.

The reference decade in this chapter extends from the submission of Ruiz's petition in 1972 to the abolition of the BT system in 1982.

A Hierarchy of Force

Marquart and Crouch (1985: 562–64) described the organization of the BT system at the Eastham Unit. A head tender was assigned to each cell block or dormitory. He was expected to preempt or quell any disturbance, to mediate and settle disputes among those in his charge, and to act as a conduit to staff, passing on information relating to contraband or threats to security. They were prison-wise, aggressive men serving long sentences, who tended to be older than average.

Beneath the head BTs were rank-and-file BTs, three to five of whom were generally assigned to a cell block or dormitory. They delivered messages from staff, kept a count of who was where, explained how things worked to newcomers, broke up fights, protected correctional staff, and referred matters to the head BT as required. They disciplined men who failed to conform; sometimes this involved a beating, sometimes a transfer to another cell block. There was no rule book for BTs, no document that set out their roles and responsibilities. The building major gave new BTs an orientation and their head BT completed the formalities. The head BT created a roster to ensure that there was always sufficient manpower available to control their area.

The average prisoner had no say in who would become a BT, but other BTs often made recommendations for the warden's consideration. The warden's choices were reviewed by the State Classification Committee. These were "the only jobs assigned to inmates in the TDC [Texas Department of Corrections] system which require approval by the Classification Committee" (*Ruiz v. Estelle* 1295). The committee members had their own preferences, and one of those involved in the selection process at the Eastham Unit stated: "I've got a personal bias. I happen to like murderers and armed robbers. They have a great deal of esteem in the inmate social system . . . they tend to be a more aggressive and a more dynamic kind of individual" (cited in Marquart and Crouch 1985: 566).

The goal was to identify men who were tough but not predatory, not the kind in the words of George Beto, a former director of the TDC, "who would rape a snake through a brick wall" (cited in DiIulio 1987a: 113). An experienced warden recalled that, when it came to selecting BTs, size and physicality were primary concerns: "If you chose a little sissy, it wasn't any use in puttin' him in as a building tender, 'cause the rest of 'em'd whip him, you see" (cited in Chase 2020: 111). Another selected as a BT a man who had been sentenced to death for a double murder but whose sentence had been commuted to life imprisonment. He was said to have burnished his credentials as someone not to be trifled with by killing three other prisoners during more than a quarter century of incarceration.

On a third tier were "runners, strikers, or hitmen" who were selected by BTs rather than appointed by staff. They acted as block janitors, sweeping and delivering supplies to the cells, tasks that they carried out at the end of the day when they had completed their officially assigned work in the prison or the fields. This kept them in close contact with the ordinary prisoners about whose activities and intentions they informed the BTs. They acted as a reserve force that could be called upon in a crisis. Sometimes runners had been friends with BTs outside prison, sometimes they were their sexual partners within the institution. Either way, their loyalty was not in doubt. The number of runners varied from cell block to cell block and from dormitory to dormitory, with some having three or four and others eight or nine. The runners did not engage directly with officers but passed information up the line so that the head BT could filter incoming reports and communicate as appropriate with a senior staff member such as a captain or major.

The modern Eastham Unit is a telephone-pole design the spine of which is a hallway, "almost one-quarter of a mile long, measuring 16 feet wide by 12 feet high" (Marquart and Crouch 1985: 559) with cell blocks on each side (see figure 3.2 for an aerial shot from 1985). "Turnkeys" manned the seven large, barred gates along the hallway. These gates acted as riot barricades that could be locked shut to prevent any disruption from spreading. The turnkeys slammed the gates to alert the BTs that their attention was required to quell a disturbance (Delgado 2007: 188). They locked and unlocked cell doors, assisted with counts, and controlled pedestrian traffic along the central corridor. According to Marquart and Crouch (1985: 565), "the block guards and turnkeys worked elbow to elbow and assisted one another so much that only their

Figure 3.2. Bird's-Eye View of a Texas Institution. Credit: Texas Department of Criminal Justice.

respective uniforms separated them." When not on duty in the corridor the turnkeys helped the BTs to manage the block. They were more powerful than junior correctional officers. Because they worked in the hallway, they picked up a great deal of intelligence about what was going on outside the cell blocks, the movement of contraband, and who was in cahoots with whom.

Finally, there were bookkeepers who provided clerical services to the prison's various departments, such as the kitchen, laundry, or farm. The most influential of all were the clerks who worked in the major's office processing information relating to counts, job allocations, and disciplinary violations. According to Crouch and Marquart (1989: 107): "The major's head bookkeeper was typically the most influential inmate within the population." This was because of his (often decisive) role when it came to designating accommodation. While a strong physical presence was a prerequisite for BTs and turnkeys, bookkeepers required a

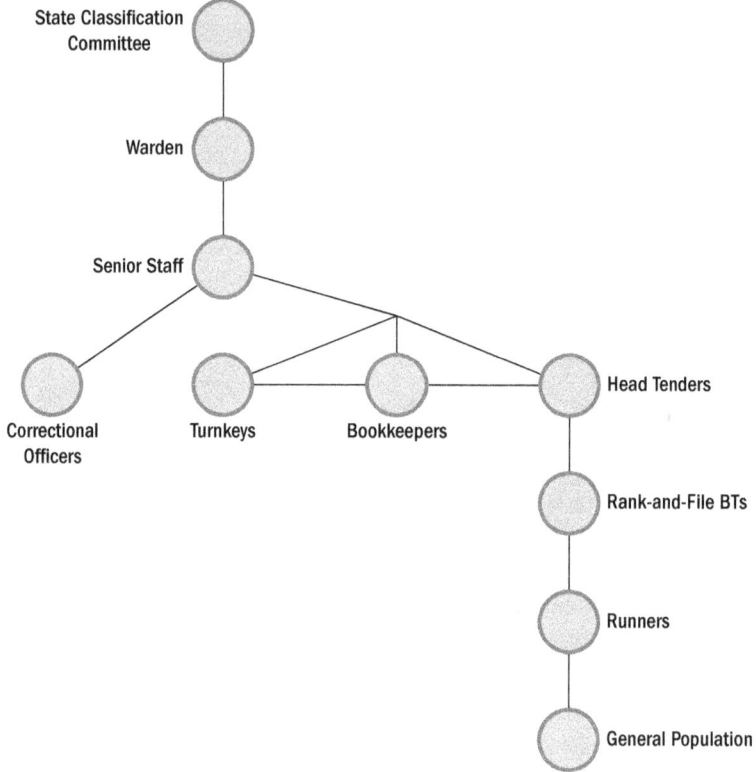

Figure 3.3. The Keepers Co-opt the Kept.

different skill set, needing to demonstrate good literacy, an aptitude for paperwork, and familiarity with office administration.

The bookkeepers ensured that the BTs were kept up to speed with any relevant developments within the institution and the BTs approached them if they needed a cell move. Sometimes this was to prevent a disagreement from becoming rancorous. Sometimes it was to facilitate the sexual exploitation of a weaker man who would be moved without his consent. Without this network of allies, the small guard force would have struggled to maintain order. (As noted below, in "Justice Does Justice," the staffing ratio in Texas was abysmal compared to other states.) The network of relationships is summarized in figure 3.3. It is less complex than Isir Bet's (figure 4.7) but more involved than the relatively flat and disconnected situation in the H Blocks (figure 2.4) and the spartan simplicity of ADX Florence (figure 5.7).

Seniority and power were related to skin color. Of the eighteen head BTs in the Eastham Unit, fourteen were white, three Black, and one Hispanic (Marquart and Crouch 1985: 567). If the allocation of these posts had properly reflected the racial makeup of the unit's population, it would have been nine Black, six white, and three Hispanic. All of the major's office bookkeepers were white (Crouch and Marquart 1989: 111). This institutional racism reflected a lack of diversity among the staff.

The Texas system was brutal but cheap, satisfying a public demand for secure custody the cost of which was largely offset through unrelenting prisoner labor. Figure 3.4 shows men at work on the Eastham farm in 1972, the year Ruiz submitted his petition. The system was not self-sufficient, but agricultural work (for which prisoners were not paid) defrayed a substantial portion of costs that were already kept low by a fiscally conservative state. The BT system, in other words, made sense economically. Another advantage was that BTs could communicate directly with the other prisoners in a way that was beyond the ability of the

Figure 3.4. Field Work on the Eastham Farm. Credit: Texas Department of Criminal Justice.

largely white, rural guard force. Sometimes this was because they spoke the same language (literally). More often it was because they understood the code of the urban streets from which so many were drawn.

Like prisoners everywhere, the men at the Eastham Unit hailed from the cities. They were closer to home than their counterparts at ADX Florence would be when the latter institution opened in the closing decade of the twentieth century, but they were further away than those in the H Blocks or Isir Bet. While they could receive supervised, non-contact visits at the weekends, the relative remoteness of the farm made this difficult for anyone without access to a car. For those who could read and write, keeping in touch by letter was another option.

The BT system survived on a combination of staff duplicity (in terms of ignoring the prohibition on inmates taking on a supervisory or disciplinary role at the same time as maintaining that they were abiding by it) and complicity (with inmate exploitation of their peers, which was necessary for the system to function).

"Institutionalized Snitches"

DiIulio (1987a: 207) described the BT system as "a calculated gamble aimed at turning the leaders of inmate society into the official allies of the administration." The rationale was that if the authorities did not pick the leaders, the prisoners would, and this would mean ceding a vital measure of control as the most antiauthoritarian and incorrigible among them jostled for position. However, the price of such a system was eternal vigilance and if the authorities relented in their oversight it could mutate into the very thing that it was designed to prevent—dominant inmates and corrupt relationships between inmates and staff. The fact that it required considerable effort to prevent the system from descending into savagery is evidence of its essential instability. The BTs capitalized on the entrepreneurial spirit that had led to their appointment by exploiting managerial weakness to consolidate their position. If the theory was that the BTs would be a cadre of dependable prisoners who would put the institution first, this certainly came to pass. But it was accompanied by a level of predation that critically undermined its stated rationale. The "calculated gamble" did not pay off.

The creation of a privileged class gave rise to a deep fissure in the prisoner society. When some of the most powerful among them aligned their interests with those of the authorities, the damage to solidarity was irreparable. This was a highly demarcated social life with clear winners and losers. Marquart and Crouch (1984: 498) described BTs as "institutionalized snitches." The inmate code was more honored in the breach in Texas, where the BTs fraternized with correctional staff and informed on their fellows. They created a barrier between prisoners and staff rather than siding with the former against the latter. To ease their own confinement, they were prepared to pass on information even if this was to the detriment of others. They were the embodiment of values that were supposedly abhorrent to prisoners. In other prison systems, snitches were likely to be on the receiving end of violence (or at least the opprobrium of their peers); in Texas it was the snitches who dispensed the violence.

The BT system was hierarchical, the rewards associated with power were considerable, and it was backed by staff. Prisoners who were not part of the elite were too exhausted (and too fractured) to organize themselves collectively. And, in any event, opposition was futile when it was likely to excite a coordinated and punitive response from an alliance of staff and BTs; this was an unwinnable conflict. Prisoners were systematically subjugated by their peers; violence and fear were the engine; the slave-like conditions on prison farms were replicated within the cell blocks and dormitories. From a prisoner's perspective, according to Delgado (2007: 176): "The law of survival was to be mechanical, obedient and brain-dead."

Prisoners viewed each other as sources of threat rather than potential allies. Their relationships were often antagonistic. They were vulnerable to the predations of the BTs and the casual violence of the guards. They existed in a world where they could be beaten and threatened with impunity but knew that if they responded in kind their punishment would be severe. This was a painful double bind. As we will see, it took the intervention of the courts to overturn the system, eventually.

Perkinson (2010: 242) noted that, after 1941, whipping was illegal in prisons in Texas, but the guards were not laggards when it came to administering informal punishments on a sliding scale from "tune ups" to "ass whippings" and, occasionally, severe beatings that required hospitalization or even led to death. Staff fought prisoners regularly, with Marquart and Crouch (1985: 568) reporting that, in the Eastham Unit in the early 1980s: "Inmates were roughed up daily as a matter of course." This ranged from slaps, kicks, and punches to coordinated thrashings with weapons. Nonetheless the bulk of the chastisement was administered by other prisoners.

Marquart and Crouch (1984: 497) described how an inexperienced guard was reported to his superior by a BT when he attempted to intervene directly in "tank business." He was told that he had been operating outside of his jurisdiction and was never reassigned to the area in question. Delgado (2007: 176) never saw a guard enter a cell block "unless invited." Guards who repeatedly intruded on the work of senior BTs faced reallocation to (the sweltering heat of) outside duty or (the rarely broken tedium of) a gun tower. Guards could confer status on prisoners, but this also worked in the opposite direction in that the guards with the most reliable flow of information could move up the ranks.

The relationship was more than simply transactional. BTs became invested in the role and went beyond what was required or expected in terms of supporting the authorities. Unlike paid employees, they were never absent from the facility, did not show up to work late or leave early; loyalty was assured and turnover was low. They were on call around the clock. Vicious officers completed their shifts and went home, they enjoyed rest days and vacations; the BTs were always there. According to Crouch and Marquart (1984: 498): "Some BTs were so loyal to the staff that they said they would kill another inmate if so ordered." In addition to showing "loyalty," this indicated that they felt they would be protected from the consequences of their actions. There was a degree of insulation from formal proceedings if their actions were on behalf—and at the instigation—of those who might have initiated the proceedings. Why exercise restraint if they were not going to be taken to task for not so doing?

Perquisites

BTs wore starched and pressed prison whites. In addition to being neatly laundered, Chase (2020: 113) noted that they were easy to identify based on the way they sported the uniform: "BTs characteristically wore their shirts untucked, and they often wore knit skull caps." This gave them a freedom of expression denied to other prisoners, who were required to wear the regulation clothing in the specified manner or risk disciplinary action.

They had preferential access to accommodation. According to Marquart and Crouch (1984: 496), the head BT always occupied a cell on the first tier, just off the main hallway. As well as being easiest to access these were relatively cool during the summer. Other BTs, turnkeys, and bookkeepers were housed in the middle and last cells on the first tier and the first cell on the second tier. Runners, whose position was informal and whose status was low, had no particular living quarters and they were scattered throughout the cell blocks. The less favored had to climb up to the third tier in their crumpled uniforms, where the temperature was highest and the ventilation poorest. (Having toured the Eastham Unit in June 2019, I can vouch for how hot it gets.)

Some BTs had pets such as cats, owls, turtles, and fish. In the Eastham Unit their doors remained open between 3:30 a.m. and 11 p.m. (Crouch and Marquart 1989: 108) so they could move freely and receive visitors at will. Head BTs could roam the corridors and they spent a lot of time in the vicinity of the major's office. They had privileged access to the mess hall and craft shop (where goods such as boots, belts, and holsters could be made for sale). They maximized the possible freedom within a tightly constrained environment.

Operating the television and choosing which programs to watch were the sole preserve of the BTs. Delgado (2007: 176) recalled from his time at the Eastham Unit: "There was no democratic system, the BTs watched on television what they chose to watch. The front row benches [were] reserved for the BTs and their wives, everybody else took a back seat." On Saturday nights when the prisoners gathered in the gym to watch a movie, the same rule applied, with the BTs selecting the movie and occupying the best seats.

Other perks of being a BT included the promise of early release, allocation to a single cell (a huge bonus in an overcrowded prison system, with the collateral advantage of providing an opportunity to run a store), separate shower times (to minimize the risk of attack from dissatisfied underlings), and access to the sexual services of weaker prisoners (on a scale of coercion ranging from implied threats to savage beatings). They could thrash potential competitors with impunity under the guise of enforcing the prohibition on sexual activity.

Perkinson (2010: 245) described how sex was integral to the BT privilege system, and that "one of the most coveted benefits was first choice of 'punks,' young, slender, often broken-spirited inmates who would do a BT's laundry, keep his cell clean, cook special meals on his hot plate, and provide other services on demand." The staff turned a blind eye to this exploitation on the basis that they could depend on the loyalty of the BTs in a crisis. As another commentator put it: "In the highly gendered domain of Texas men's prisons, sexual violence became the foundational form of control. . . . When the rapist was a state agent, rape became a tool of statecraft" (Blue 2012: 104).

BTs in the Eastham Unit made no attempt to conceal the clubs, chains, and blades in their cells and lockers. That they did not fear confiscation of their armory is unsurprising given that the staff viewed them as an auxiliary security force. By disarming their allies, they would be heightening their own vulnerability in an environment where they were already greatly outnumbered. The system engendered malign mutual obligations between prisoners and staff.

While there was a high level of anxiety and resentment among prisoners who were not part of the elite, and verbal abuse and beatings were routine, there is no doubt that the BT system created an orderly environment. Crouch and Marquart (1989: 112) noted that in the Eastham Unit, despite its population of mature, violent recidivists, there were only two inmate murders, two work stoppages, and a single disturbance in the decade following Ruiz's petition and preceding the system's abolition.

Crouch and Marquart (1989: 61) quoted a sign in the main hallway of the Eastham Unit that declared, in English and Spanish: "No smoking; No talking; No loitering; Single file." As they moved along the hallway, members of the general population were expected to remain between the wall and a green line painted about four feet from it. BTs could saunter along the center of the corridor with staff and turnkeys (Martin and Ekland-Olson 1987: 120). The fact they were not curbed in the same way as the other prisoners was a clear marker of status in an environment where meticulous temporal and spatial ordering was an integral—even defining—feature of daily life. Anyone else who crossed the line (literally) was vulnerable to disciplinary action.

Given how austere prison conditions were in Texas these were enviable privileges. In return, BTs acted as the eyes and ears (and fists) of the staff.

Order and docility were maintained through fear. Prisoners were compliant because they were cowed into submission. Perkinson (2010: 237) put it well when he observed: "Texas's prisons were quiet, disciplined, and economical, administrators proclaimed at every turn. What they seldom, if ever, acknowledged was that Texas's prison peace was purchased, just as it always had been, with force and fear." Blue (2012: 245–46) echoed this sentiment when he wrote of the low level of collective and lethal violence in Texas prisons in the following terms: "Their quiescence was the fruit of domination rather than consent, the application of violence rather than its diminution." Underpinning the BT culture was a staff culture of pervasive violence, threats, and verbal abuse; these cultures were mutually reinforcing.

The BTs' priorities were those of the institution rather than those of their fellows. Their presence was antithetical to integration and solidarity. They were inherently divisive and operated against a background of low regulation. It was a disintegrative and manipulative system, undermining the possibility of cooperation or altruism. It sundered relationships and kept people on edge. The threat of violence was so successful that it seldom had to be deployed with lethal effect. The BTs were co-opted and their collaboration was not covert but formalized and highly public. Despite the TDC's denials there is no doubt that the BTs derived their authority, and sense of immunity, from the explicit support of the administration.

A BT lived on his wits. If he did not satisfy his prison bosses, he risked losing his position, but if he was seen as being too close to them, he was vulnerable to attack. The dilemma of a reluctant BT is captured in the following observation made by one of their number in 1973: "If I do what the Man says to do, I'm messin' on the inmates, and if I don't do like the Man wants me to do I'm going to the field" (cited in Martin and Ekland-Olson 1987: 72). This was a difficult balance to maintain; the role was both welcomed and despised by those who occupied it, some of whom seemed able to beat up (other) snitches and (other) sexual predators without being struck by the savage inconsistency. BTs needed to be able to look after themselves in a combat situation and were selected accordingly. The extra freedoms made the risks worth taking. They were men who were accustomed to violence and would not hesitate to dispense it. Besides, they had the backing of the staff, which deterred potential assailants. This was a world where force prevailed. If physical prowess was not enough, a shiv was used to reinforce the message.

An extreme example of BT brutality is seen in the beating to death of Harvey Mayberry at the Eastham Unit on May 13, 1971. Doused in boiling water by BTs for making noise, his repeated calls for medical attention were ignored. When his cell door was eventually opened it was not to allow access to a doctor but rather to enable at least two BTs to reprise their attack. The perpetrators were not identified and the cause of death was attributed to "blunt trauma to the abdomen" (Martin and Ekland-Olson 1987: 49).

Seeking Relief in the Courts

On June 29, 1972, David Ruiz (see pen portrait) filed a handwritten petition alleging that the conditions under which he was held at the Eastham Unit were unconstitutional, that he was being harassed on account of his legal activities, placed unlawfully in solitary confinement, denied adequate medical treatment, and that he had repeatedly self-mutilated as a consequence. His treatment was exacting a psychological as well as a physical toll. Reavis (1985: 152) described this petition, which opened with a pauper's oath, as "a sheet of paper that has eclipsed the Texas constitution, the laws of our Legislature, and traditions that have guided us since the days of the Republic." Ruiz may have been cut off from family and friends, but he had access to the courts. On April 12, 1974, Judge William Wayne Justice consolidated his petition along with seven others into *Ruiz v. Estelle*. Ruiz's petition had become a civil rights claim on behalf of every prisoner in Texas, looking at the totality of conditions right across the TDC.

According to Chase (2020: 311), "the chief subject of the trial was the building tender system." Similarly, for Gulick (1984: 12) this was "the single most bitterly fought issue." Ruiz was particularly exercised by the BT system and when asked by an Eastham guard to explain his antagonism toward it, made no effort to veil his hostility, replying bluntly: "I will take orders from officers and not building tenders; and if I am ever assaulted by a building tender, book keeper or turnkey, they better kill me because I ain't taking no more beating and I been ready to die since the first day I entered this shithole prison" (cited in Chase 2015: 848).

David Ruiz (1942–2005), Writ Writer

David Ruiz was the third-youngest of thirteen children born to migrant farmworkers. He grew up in the Chicano neighborhood of East Austin and spent most of his life behind bars, starting with a stint in reformatory school aged twelve.

He was a serial self-mutilator, slashing his arms and body many times. He also directed his violence against others, telling Perkinson (2010: 254) that he attacked a BT with a file that he had taken from the tool shed, plunging it into his chest and neck. His payback was a beating so severe that both knees were broken, along with several ribs and one of his hands. On another occasion he almost beheaded a prisoner with an ax.

He escaped from the Eastham Unit in 1968 but was picked up the next day by the warden, accompanied by none other than George Beto, director of the TDC. Little did Beto know that this cold, tired, and hungry inmate would do so much to destroy the system of harsh discipline, subordination, and grinding labor that he had worked so hard to maintain. He spent a week at the Eastham Unit hospital recovering from the ordeal of the escape and was then sent to a pitch-dark solitary cell for forty-five days on a bread and water diet.

During this time alone Ruiz thought deeply about his life and concluded that the pen was mightier than the shiv. Inspired by the civil rights and antiwar movements he decided that his fight should henceforth be for principles rather than personal advancement. When he emerged from solitary, he announced that he would no longer work in the fields like a slave. When BTs threatened him with violence unless he complied, he returned to his cell, removed the blade from his razor, and severed his Achilles tendon.

Unfit for work, he determined to devote his life to using the courts to turn the state against itself. His twelve-page petition, handwritten on toilet tissue according to prison lore, eventually led to the ruling by Judge William Wayne Justice that incarceration by the TDC constituted cruel and unusual punishment.

A former TDC chaplain felt that Ruiz's actions had led to the ruination of all that was good about Texas prisons. In a book published three years before Ruiz died, he described him (with a distinct lack of Christian charity) as "a small, sour-faced man who had spent his life robbing, stealing, and living behind bars" (Pickett 2002: 134). He painted an unflattering portrait of a vainglorious, violent, and manipulative person with a penchant for self-aggrandizement.

It is a cruel irony that Ruiz spent the last twenty-one years of his life in administrative segregation, the housing "solution" that had been expanded dramatically to counter the violence that shook the system after the BT system was dismantled on foot of his petition. That he could not live among his peers in an inmate society that his actions had transformed tells its own story. When asked how he viewed his legacy, he opined: "The facilities are better. The guards aren't beating on people like they used to, not as much. There's more respect for the law" (cited in Perkinson 2010: 357). He died in custody and Judge Justice, then aged eighty-five, attended his funeral.

In "Steel on Steel," a poem published posthumously in the *Texas Observer* magazine, Ruiz (2005) described himself as "the huevon Mexican, cell-taught, self-taught, the original writ-writer, chained up and locked down for a lifetime." He titled his (unpublished) memoir *Tough with a Knife, Hell with a Writ* (Chase 2020: 277).

A letter writer to the *Austin Chronicle* on November 29, 2005, responded to the newspaper's obituary of Ruiz with the comment that, had he not achieved fame as a writ writer, "he might have been better known as a habitual felon whose hobbies included using deadly weapons to separate noncriminals from their money and property." He continued: "While his influence on making the Texas prison system less inhumane cannot be doubted, it's only fair to his victims that his entire legacy be remembered. No lawsuit is going to improve his current living conditions." The letter bore the title, "Ruiz Gone to Hell."

Sample (1984), a long-term prisoner with experience of several Texas prisons including the Eastham Unit, was released in 1972, the year Ruiz submitted his petition. He pithily summarized the power of the BT as "to whup you . . . kill you . . . or snitch on you" (p. 158). Justice concurred that "aggressive and predatory inmates are free to do as they wish in the living areas, and their victims can be threatened, extorted, beaten, or

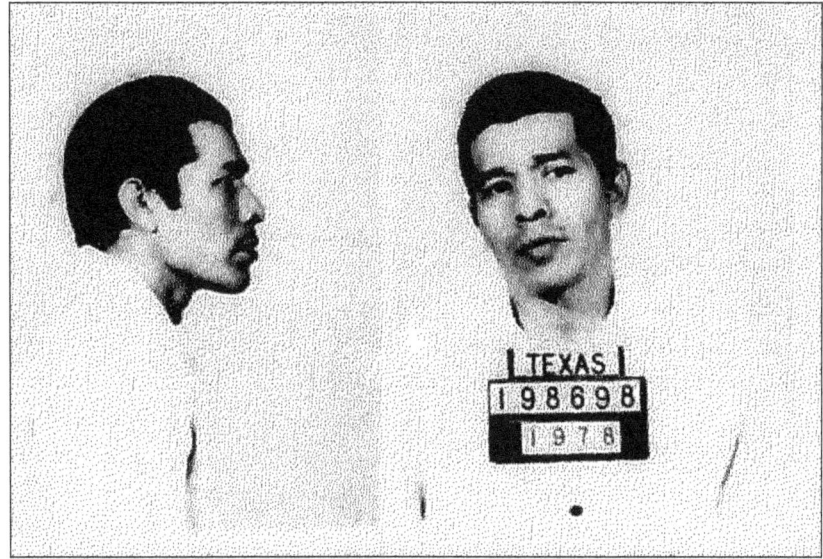

Figure 3.5. David Ruiz in 1978. Credit: Texas Department of Criminal Justice.

raped" (*Ruiz v. Estelle* 1292). This marked imbalance is glaringly different from the routine victimization, violence, and conflict that define prison life, which are often reciprocal, with individuals shifting between the roles of "victim" and "perpetrator" depending on a variety of contextual and interpretive cues (Edgar and O'Donnell 1998). The roles in the Eastham Unit were much more static.

Someone else could as easily have been selected by Judge Justice as the figurehead for this action. Ruiz was by no means the most accomplished jailhouse lawyer and his long history of violence compromised his perceived integrity and reliability. He comes across as an unlikable man, not reluctant to inflict violence on himself or others, whose biggest stroke of luck was that Judge Justice put his case on his docket. Another writ writer described him as "no great brain," whose main concerns during the trial were "(1) his clothes, (2) sex, (3) publicity, good or bad" (cited in Chase 2020: 326).

The trial began on October 2, 1978 (figure 3.5 is a mugshot taken of David Ruiz the same year). It concluded on September 20, 1979, having heard the testimony of 349 witnesses (Ruiz testified first and was on the stand on October 3 and 4) and received approximately 1,565 exhibits into evidence. The TDC dug in and defended tenaciously. Its plodding and ham-fisted approach was summarized by Perkinson (2010: 274) as being built on three pillars: "Delay, admit nothing, fight everything." Perkinson noted the delicious irony here, in that "the Texas Department of Corrections was suddenly reliving the experience of many of its inmates: reluctant to go to trial, probably guilty as charged, and ineffectively represented by counsel" (p. 275).

The TDC defense was to argue that the BT system did not exist. The authorities held that, in line with the penal code, the only duties carried out by prisoners were janitorial, not supervisory or disciplinary. The director of the TDC, W. J. Estelle, supported House Bill 1056 (see chapter epigraph), legislation that, he asserted, simply restated existing policy (Martin and Ekland-Olson 1987: 63). The denial concealed a series of pragmatic adjustments. So long as things were never formally acknowledged a state of (barely) plausible deniability existed.

Given the mountain of evidence to the contrary this was a stance that caused widespread incredulity. To give just one example, in an article in *Corrections Magazine*, published before the trial ended, Gettinger and Krajick (1978) described how they had collected affidavits from several prisoners claiming to have witnessed beatings by BTs, one of which was disguised as a suicide attempt. They quoted from an internal memorandum that made it quite clear BTs were more than janitors, defining their role as to "advise Staff Officers of any problems or conflicts which an inmate may have. . . . He shall NOT allow sex malpractice, brewing of alcoholic beverages, gambling, possession of contraband items, or fights in his wing" (p. 24). This document was prepared *after* the law prohibiting prisoner involvement in supervision or administration came into force in 1973. The article was accompanied by a photograph of a turnkey on gate duty. Repeated assertions that the BTs were little more than cleaners and message boys collapsed in the face of even the most cursory examination.

Examples of horrific and endemic violence were given during the *Ruiz* proceedings. For example:

> At the Eastham Unit, when an inmate resisted sexual overtures from building tenders Butch Ainsworth and Charlie Robertson, they decided

to apply force. A former building tender, a witness to the incident, credibly testified as follows:

They wrapped a wet blanket around him first; plugged an extension cord into a socket. The ends of the extension cord were insulated, and they stuck this energized electric cord to the wet blanket.

This wasn't getting the results that they wanted, so they unwrapped [the] inmate ... made him stand up on the commode in Ainsworth's cell and then placed the electric wires to his body and into the water.

This caused [the] inmate ... to scream from extreme pain, to begin to tremble, even to cry, and to submit to the homosexual act.

Besides sexually abusing the inmate, Ainsworth and Robertson confiscated his "commissary," as was routine with them. (*Ruiz v. Estelle* 1297, note 64)

This was not an isolated incident. Another witness told the trial that he had been raped at knife point in July 1978 by Robertson who, he alleged, had committed murder four years previously (Martin and Ekland-Olson 1987: 122). The victim in this case reported the sexual assault, but no disciplinary action was taken. Robertson was a BT whose propensity to cause serious harm seems beyond doubt. Ainsworth was no better, with the court hearing how he "was characterized by the former warden of the Eastham Unit as the most violent inmate he has ever known. Several blood chilling incidents involving inmate Ainsworth were described by TDC officers and inmates. On one occasion, Ainsworth ... cut off several of his own fingers and delivered them to a guard" (*Ruiz v. Estelle* 1295, note 57). With grim understatement, a man who served time in the Eastham Unit with Ainsworth described this self-mutilation as "an unusual way of protesting the transfer of his lover" (Delgado 2007: 172).

One prisoner described to the court the weapons held by BTs as including "a free world hunting knife approximately a foot long with a stainless steel blade about three inches wide and a bone handle" (Martin and Ekland-Olson 1987: 124). Ease of concealment was clearly not a concern for the owner of this terrifying implement. Justice concurred about the range of weaponry openly available to BTs in the Eastham Unit. In addition to knives he listed "two mop handles taped together, pieces of trace chain, pipes, and 'baseball' (small wooden) bats" (*Ruiz v. Estelle* 1296, note 62).

The TDC denying the existence of BTs is akin to the Northern Ireland Prison Service denying that prisoners engaged with staff via their own command structure rather than as individuals, or the BOP denying the existence of solitary confinement. Just because something is repeated ad nauseam does not make it true.

Justice Does Justice

Justice's lengthy memorandum opinion appeared on December 12, 1980, fifteen months after the trial ended. He described the proceedings as having "lasted longer than any prison case—and perhaps any civil rights case—in the history of American jurisprudence" (*Ruiz v. Estelle* 1391). In addition to its length it was notable for its breadth, described after its conclusion as "the most sweeping prison conditions case in American history" (Alpert et al. 1984: 291).

Justice found that the conditions in Texas prisons were unconstitutionally cruel. His conclusion: "In short, TDC officials have not adequately controlled the unlawfully maintained building tender system, and they have directly and indirectly permitted its abuses to be visited on the inmates of Texas prisons" (*Ruiz v. Estelle* 1298). There are two important points in this pithy summation that go to the heart of the TDC's "moral performance" (Liebling 2004). The first is that the system was "unlawfully maintained." The second is that the abuses were "permitted." As he elaborated:

> Building tenders have unofficially been given such specific powers as issuing orders to other inmates, assisting in taking daily counts of the population, keeping track of inmate movements, escorting inmates to different destinations within the prison, and distributing correspondence and commissary scrip. Some are authorized to be in possession of keys outside the presence of civilian personnel, and others operate the automated opening devices which control access to cell blocks, day rooms, and other parts of the institutions. In the day rooms, building tenders are in complete control; *e.g.*, they enforce order and silence, operate the controls of television sets, and regulate the games that can be played. . . . Some have access to records concerning inmates' financial resources, and others are authorized to assist in preparing and editing disciplinary reports. Certain building tenders are able to view general inmates' files

and use the information to operate extortion, prostitution, and usury schemes.... Of overriding significance is the fact that building tenders are often permitted to carry weapons. (*Ruiz v. Estelle* 1296)

Justice established the office of the special master to oversee implementation of, and compliance with, his orders. The system of prisoners in positions of authority over their peers—outlawed by the Texas legislature in 1973, condemned by Justice in his opinion, and denied by the TDC—was the subject of the first report from the special master's team of monitors, one of whom had been assigned the task of gathering data about whether it had been dismantled. This report, based on numerous interviews and site visits, was filed on October 16, 1981, and it ran to 548 pages, including appendices (Martin and Ekland-Olson 1987: 190). The report detailed a climate of fear within the prisons and a litany of ongoing abuses by BTs, who remained armed, controlled access to many areas, possessed keys, and perpetrated beatings and rapes with impunity.

Bobby Delgado arrived in the Eastham Unit in October 1979, just after the *Ruiz* trial had concluded but before the judgment had been delivered. He recalled an experience that was even worse than he had feared, with BTs who were fiercer than their counterparts in other prisons he had served time in. They "stood in a class of their own... different in character, attitude and temperament. The warden was recruiting monsters; most of them killers" (Delgado 2007: 171). Bashings were routine and sexual violence was rampant. Delgado captured the Eastham Unit's fearsome reputation with his summary appraisal (and emphatic capitalization) that "two alphabet letters and one prison unit became a synonym for injury and death; THE BTs AND THE EASTHAM UNIT" (p. 88).

The report was released to the press as soon as it had been submitted to the special master. A hearing on alleged abuses by BTs began on March 15, 1982. On the first day, two of the men who took the stand were former BTs who told the court they were allowed to keep weapons such as knives and nunchucks. Others followed suit, testifying to a litany of BT abuses. Against the background of a riot at the Eastham Unit (Press 1986) and the prospect of further damning testimony, the TDC recognized its vulnerability and, after a week, decided to negotiate a settlement. The following month agreement was reached. It was only at this point that Butch Ainsworth, who was still working as a BT at the

Eastham Unit, was finally stripped of his role and moved to another prison (Martin and Ekland-Olson 1987: 212). The fact that this man, who had been the subject of such adverse comment during the *Ruiz* trial, had carried on regardless speaks volumes about how seriously the judgment was taken, at least initially.

To allow for the dismantling of the BT system, staff recruitment had to be boosted. At the same time prisoner numbers were steadily increasing and new institutions were being built. This did not come cheap. Martin and Ekland-Olson (1987: 238) estimated that the budget allocated for Texas prisons ballooned from under $100 million in the two-year period 1974–75 (when Ruiz's petition was consolidated with a selection of others that had arrived at Judge Justice's chambers) to almost $1 billion in 1985. Judicial action led to the ending of the BT system because the state was forced to accept that prisons cost more to run than it had hitherto been willing to spend and that their occupants were more than penal subjects who had forfeited any right to decent treatment as a result of their criminal conduct. Ruiz cost the state billions. He may have been the dearest (in just one sense of the word) prisoner in US history.

Not everyone felt that Justice was a force for good. According to the judge's biographer, "It was said that he was the most hated man in Texas" (Kemerer 1991: x). In a long essay in *Texas Monthly*, Reavis (1985) captured a wide sense of disappointment at the disappearance of a time when convicts were fearful, homicidal violence was kept in check, and prisons were cheap to run. It is probably fair to say that those who lamented the system's demise had never been required to survive within it.

Pickett (2002: 140) took a benign view of the BTs, seeing them as tough men, akin to "a squad leader in an army barrack . . . who saw to it that the convicts under their watch lived as close to a democratic lifestyle as prison would allow." In his capacity as a prison chaplain he described being called to the hospital when badly beaten men were sent there for treatment. (A chaplaincy team, supported by community volunteers, catered to the needs of Catholics, Protestants, and Jews. Muslims in Texas prisons had few opportunities to worship together.)

Broken jaws, missing teeth, and cracked ribs were the currency of BT discipline, but Pickett seems to have been untroubled by the human suffering, "explaining" how he usually learned afterward that the victim had been stealing from or assaulting others. He accepted this rough justice, to which correctional staff turned a blind eye, as an effective way of maintaining safe and orderly prisons. Accompanying Pickett's dismay that the system was dismantled was a sense of regret that "the good done by these men was never recognized" (p. 142). He saw them, in the main, as church goers, "more respected than feared" (p. 142), whose primary concern was the well-being of their fellow men. He was convinced that many suicides "were averted by alert and caring building tenders. . . . I found their input invaluable and their presence a benefit to my role as chaplain. I came to depend on their knowledge and insight" (pp. 142–43).

Pickett felt that when the system was dismantled, the resulting interference with the flow of information upon which he had depended greatly affected his ministry. Given that the chaplain worked closely with the prison administration it is not entirely surprising that he shared its view, but it does seem strange that he would so unhesitatingly—even naively—accentuate the positive features of a system that caused such fear and loathing among his flock. Clearly the BTs handled communications with spiritual leaders just as effectively as with other senior prison staff.

Across the state of Texas, the reliance on BTs increased over the course of the *Ruiz* litigation as a result of a rising prison population and no commensurate increase in staffing. Chase (2020: 297) gave figures of around eight hundred BTs in 1974 (constituting one in twenty prisoners) rising to almost twenty-three hundred by the end of the decade (one in eleven prisoners). At the same time as their power was increasing, they were being subjected to less supervision and scrutiny. The ratio of staff to prisoners was 1:12 at the time of the *Ruiz* trial, possibly the worst in the nation, compared to a national average of 1:5 (*Ruiz v. Estelle* 1290). Even W. J. Estelle acknowledged that such a ratio was "extremely dangerous" (para. 1291). It improved to 1:6 by 1986 (Crouch and Marquart 1990: 117).

The trial tested the formal legal position—as expressed in the epigraph to this chapter—against the reality of the prisoner experience, with Justice concluding: "As the evidence makes apparent, both this Texas statute and the federal Constitution have been violated by the building tender system as operated at TDC" (*Ruiz v. Estelle* 1304). But prisoners were not only at risk from their peers. Justice declared: "The widespread staff brutality at TDC is also in contravention of the Constitution" (para. 1304.). This was some distance from the scenario described by DiIulio (1987a: 210), who saw the system as "marginal, if ultimately corrosive," serving as little more than "a rotten crutch, a species of inmate self-rule that contributed nothing essential to TDC's control efforts." The case exposed what had long been in plain view for anyone who cared to look—that Texas prisons operated in defiance of the law and prisoners were helpless (and hopeless) in the face of threats and beatings administered by guards and BTs.

End of an Era

The BTs were stripped of their duties and reassigned to regular jobs in the Eastham Unit in September 1982, having surrendered their weapons, pets, and other perks. The bookkeepers had already been made redundant, having spent several months training the officers who succeeded them in the intricacies of the unit's filing system and clerical arrangements. During November and December 1982, a total of 141 new recruits arrived at the Eastham Unit, almost doubling the guard force (Marquart and Crouch 1985: 571). The turnkeys showed the new guards how to operate the doors and the BTs showed them how to carry out the counts, something that staff had never done before.

To ensure there were no repercussions against former BTs, many of them were grouped together in cell blocks and dormitories for the purposes of mutual protection. They did not appear to fear retaliation and those they had previously subjugated did not appear to seek it out. Their reputations for violence continued to serve them well in this regard. The turnkeys were similarly reassigned in December 1982, having taught their salaried successors how to operate the barricade doors in the corridors, and neither did they experience retribution at the hands of the prisoners they had long oppressed.

From January 1, 1983, the system no longer existed in the Eastham Unit and two other prisons that had particularly bad reputations for BT abuses. Remaining units had until January 1985 to fall in line. Henceforth, what were known as support service inmates were limited to janitorial or clerical duties, under direct staff supervision, for which they received no special privileges. These typically became jobs for nonviolent men who could exercise no dominion over their peers (Crouch and Marquart 1989: 131). Court-appointed monitors ensured that there was no reversion to prior practice.

There was another first in the Eastham Unit's long and turbulent history in that guards were assigned to the living areas. They were told that they could no longer use physical force as an unofficial way of maintaining order and anyone who did so faced investigation and the possibility of dismissal. In the space of a few months a decades-old system was abolished. Alpert et al. (1984: 303) suggested that the way *Ruiz* was fought added to the febrility of the situation, contributing to the disruption that accompanied its conclusion, in that "an almost purely adversarial climate evolved around the case, with the judge, the TDC, and the special master involved in open conflict just as much as the inmates and the guards. Under such circumstances, it is little wonder that the fragile social system of the prison erupted in violent conflict."

A balanced assessment is probably that the *Ruiz* decision tilted the system into turmoil not only because the abolition of the BTs created fear and uncertainty among prisoners that caused them to band together (along racial lines) and to provoke intergang conflict, but because it resulted in demoralized and disengaged staff whose desire to maintain order had been softened to the point that potential exploiters saw an opportunity worth seizing. When the enforcement of rules is lax, and infractions are downplayed, a culture of impunity is cultivated; this had murderous consequences for a time, as shown by the second peak in figure 3.6.

Before *Ruiz*, Texas prisons were relatively free of homicide, economically productive, and cheap to run. Chase (2020: 121–22) observed: "Under the building tender system, Texas had the nation's lowest prisoner murder rate with only four homicides between 1973 and 1976." This compared with 66 in California, 30 in Florida, and 23 in Missouri over the same period. The raw numbers understate the disproportionality. While there were more prisoners in California than in Texas, there were half as many in Florida and one-fifth the number in Missouri. The annual average homicide rates per 100,000 prisoners, in descending order, were Missouri's 176, Florida's 89, California's 74, and Texas's 6 (recalculated from Chase 2020: 121, table 7). In the wake of *Ruiz*, Texas prisons became more deadly places as newly emergent gangs fought

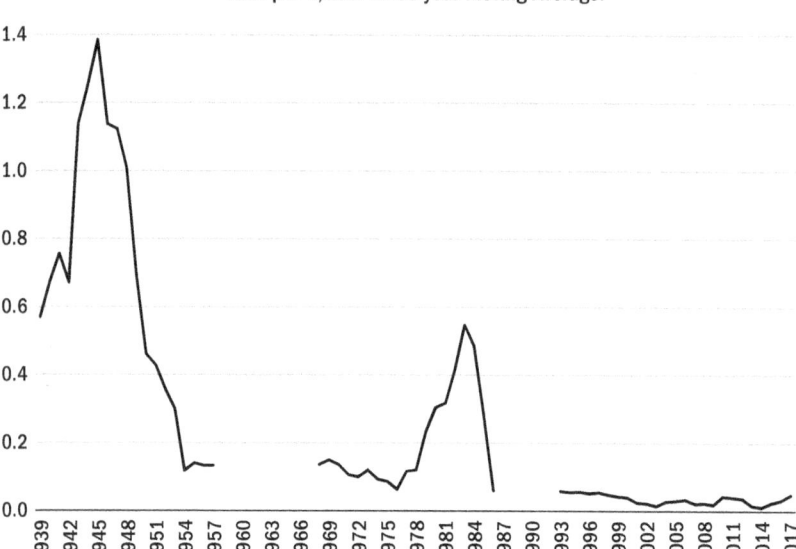

Figure 3.6. Prisoners Killed by Other Prisoners in Texas, 1939–2019. Sources: Bureau of Justice Statistics (personal communication), Chase (2020: 67), Ekland-Olson (1986: 398), Texas Department of Criminal Justice (personal communication), Texas Justice Initiative (personal communication).

each other for supremacy. But prisoners in general were relieved that an abusive system had been removed and, as matters transpired, the spike in violence was transitory.

Justice reflected in his opinion on the difference between what might be described as superficial and deep safety: "While inmates may not be subject to murder at excessive rates, that does not relieve their well-founded apprehension of extortion, assault, and rape. Therefore, TDC's low homicide rates do not preclude or modify the finding that TDC institutions are unsafe and charged with a climate of fear" (*Ruiz v. Estelle* 1294). The persistent overcrowding exacerbated the generally hostile relations between staff and the general prison population and the rancor that existed between the latter and the BTs.

Justice's summary of the pre-reform period was stark and unequivocal. Notwithstanding the low level of homicide, he opined, prisoners did not feel safe and sometimes went to extreme lengths to evade the tension, threat, and anxiety that defined everyday life. "Indeed," as he expressed it, "to escape threatened physical attacks, several inmates have deliberately violated rules in order to be consigned to some form of punitive segregation. Self-mutilation being a disciplinary offense, some have gone to the extent of cutting their arms, legs, or heel tendons to achieve temporary transfers to administrative segregation, solitary confinement, or the hospital" (*Ruiz v. Estelle* 1293). That prisoners would engage in something as cripplingly painful as heel stringing, and face the prospect of a punitive response afterward, is a lacerating comment on how they apprehended prison life. It is excruciating to exist in a place where the threat of violence is omnipresent and there is a complete absence of horizontal legitimacy.

Pressure came from several directions. The prisoners were emboldened by the reforms ushered in by *Ruiz*. The guard force was suddenly swollen with new recruits who had been taken on to improve the staffing ratio and to make the BTs redundant; veterans were demoralized, rookies were anxious and confused. New administrative systems and wide-scale management changes meant that officers could no longer depend on their superiors for support when clashes with prisoners occurred. There was a great deal of uncertainty about how the parameters of acceptable conduct were being redrawn. (Indeed, some staff may have been clear about what constituted impermissible conduct but decided not to act in order to accentuate the deleterious effects of the judgment. Some were hesitant, others cynical.) During this turbulent period the security staff was transformed from being small, racially homogeneous, and cohesive to large, diverse, and fractured.

Good Ol' Boys

While the staff—supported by the BTs—were in control they may have been few in number, but they were a tight knit group of white, rural men with low levels of formal education. It was not an occupation that suited everyone, but among those who decided to make a career of it there was a strong esprit de corps. There were close personal and familial ties among the guard force and a clear sense of institutional loyalty. A high value was placed on toughness, self-reliance, paternalism, the importance of hierarchy and subordination, and the ability to work as long and as hard as the situation demanded. The pay was not great, but there were reputational rewards associated with being able to command a reluctant workforce to hoe and to harvest at breakneck pace or to face down and overpower a dangerous felon. The sense of interdependence was reinforced by the isolated location of the Eastham farm, which meant that the staff lived together on site. Work life and family life were enmeshed.

Under the ancien régime, the staff knew their prisoners, especially those who acted as BTs, with whom there were strong bonds of mutual reliance. But they knew indirectly about the others, particularly which ones might be potential threats to order, due to the information being channeled to them by the BTs. When the system was dismantled, the distance that quickly grew between staff and prisoners potentiated disorder, not only because staff could no longer call upon their prisoner allies to break things up, or because the presence of the BTs had acted as a deterrent, but because the staff did not know from whence a control problem was likely to emerge on account of the stream of information ceasing.

Even the most enthusiastic guard force would have found it difficult to run the prison in the absence of reliable intelligence. Cultivating snitches takes time, skill, and mutual trust; the latter two ingredients are not possessed in sufficient quantities by neophyte officers. A small cohort of well-informed and experienced correctional staff could hold the line at a time when mutual expectations were understood, if not welcomed, better than a larger and more diverse body that was deprived of a reliable flow of data, unsure about acceptable occupational norms, anxious about the extent and malleability of their authority, and faced by a prison population that was growing in terms of numbers and confidence.

Many of the new and inexperienced staff were afraid of the imprisoned men with whom they were in direct contact. Rather than being white and rural, they tended to be minorities from urban areas. They were young and often lacked deep vocational commitment. Without the buffer of the BTs they were exposed to hostility and abuse that compounded their hesitancy to impose order. The more hands-off approach that resulted was exploited by the prisoners. The rush to recruit had adverse implications for selectivity and training as well as informal socialization. The drive to get more staff into the prisons overrode the need to ensure competence, suitability, and job readiness and, in less busy times, some of those taken on might have been deemed not to make the grade. Martin and Ekland-Olson (1987: 239) reported that the number of correctional officers employed by the TDC almost quadrupled between 1979 and 1985 (from a base of around two thousand). The pool of potentially suitable recruits was reduced by a booming economy in the early 1980s and the availability of better-paid jobs in the oil industry. Some of those given an officer's gray uniform had more in common with the prisoners than the senior staff.

The guards in the BT era had more autonomy, more discretion, less accountability. They lamented the loss of their ability to deploy violence in response to perceived infractions post *Ruiz*. As one Eastham Unit sergeant put it in 1984: "Every time you put your hands on one you got to do a lot of paperwork and stuff. . . . You got to cuff 'em, kiss 'em, and read 'em their rights." One of his more junior colleagues elaborated: "The greatest change is when we had to quit giving ass whippings. . . . You slap him two or three times. The next time you talk to him, he is liable to do anything you ask him to do" (cited in Crouch and Marquart 1989: 151). For tough men, used to subordination and summary justice and skeptical about form filling, due process was an impediment to good order and discipline.

The Center Cannot Hold

DiIulio (1987b) argued that the descent into insubordination, assaults, and lethal violence, which characterized the Eastham Unit and other prisons across the state, was due not solely to the abolition of the BT system but also to a breakdown in morale among correctional staff. The chain of command was weakened by the barrage of adverse publicity that accompanied the *Ruiz* case and its aftermath, and security became lax. In his words: "Out of a mix of spite, wounded pride, and simple confusion about the state of their authority, officers in some prisons started letting inmates congregate freely out in the yards and inside the cell blocks . . . standard operating procedures governing cell searches, contraband interception, and the like were weakened and, in some places, abandoned" (p. 83).

The social life of the Eastham Unit was not only affected by a change in the organization of prisoners. The wider context had been fundamentally destabilized, staff morale had plummeted, and an air of laissez-faire had crept in. This contributed to high turnover, further weakening the guard force's capacity (and inclination) to restore order. Many senior staff resigned or were fired. Long-established informal practices, and a parsimonious approach to paperwork, were replaced by rules and bureaucratic demands. The warden's autonomy was curtailed. The staff subculture came under pressure from a sudden influx of new recruits, including women and minorities, many without the familial ties that had defined the staff in the past and that had secured their loyalty despite poor pay and arduous hours. The old certainties were gone; a state of anomie ensued.

Post-*Ruiz*, the men incarcerated in the Eastham Unit became much less inclined to obey the staff unquestioningly for fear of violent repercussions if they dared to do otherwise. Marquart and Crouch (1985: 573) found that assaults on staff, threats against staff, refusal to obey orders, and swearing at officers were five times higher in 1983 and 1984 compared with 1981 and 1982. Some of the increase in recorded insouciance, insolence, and aggression was no doubt attributable to improved reporting; tune-ups were replaced with write-ups. Also, there were many more staff to abuse and they were now interacting more closely and regularly with prisoners. But, more importantly, the prisoners knew that the BTs would no longer rush to the defense of the staff and without this buffer the officers were more vulnerable.

One of the steps taken in light of the abolition of the BT system was the replacement of metal cutlery with disposable plastic utensils (Pickett 2002: 144). This was because so many knives, forks, and spoons were being stolen from "chow halls" (prison cafeterias) and refashioned as weapons, indicating a high level of readiness to attack or to not be found wanting if called upon to defend oneself.

The increase in regulation (i.e., more rules and more staff) was not yet having a consistent effect and the prisoner body remained fragmented, albeit differently in the absence of the BTs. The surge in noncompliance suggests a dramatic change in the social life of the cell blocks, workplaces, and corridors. It was often accompanied by verbal abuse and staff now found themselves on the receiving end of vulgar and profane name-calling. When not being ignored they were being cursed and they could no longer resort in their defense to the tried and tested methods of informal corporal punishment. This was quite a change, in a very short space of time, from the deference they had been used to. The respect they had won was based on fear, tradition, violence, and a vicious surrogate guard force of BTs. When these props were removed it soon evaporated and their vulnerability was starkly revealed. The anxiety that accompanied the erosion of role certainty was compounded by a threat of attack that was all too often realized. To make matters worse, the steady stream of tip-offs that would previously have been conveyed to them by the BTs had dried up—the risks of informing now outweighed any possible rewards—so they were unsure where the most potent threats lay and what the prisoners were planning.

Prisoner-on-prisoner violence increased. Three homicides took place on the Eastham Unit in 1984, with another three the following year (Press 1986: 53). This compared with a single fatality during the previous three years. The secular trend is shown systemwide in figure 3.6. Many more prisoners were found carrying weapons and striking out with them. This marked a major departure from previous arrangements, when BTs would have dealt severely with any prisoner (other than one of their number) who armed himself. Moreover, the BTs tended to deal with conflicts that emerged in their living areas and other residents were seldom permitted to take matters into their own hands. If they did, they risked reprisals from the BTs for usurping their authority. While the BTs were no slouches when it came to exploiting their fellow prisoners, they prevented anyone else from behaving similarly. When they were dismissed, predation spread out more widely across the prisoner society and the weak were more exposed. It is also true that the uptick in violence must have reflected, to some extent at least, more reliable recording. Assaults perpetrated in the past by BTs, and staff, were unlikely to have been faithfully logged as such.

Justice was worried that an unintended consequence of his decision would be the emergence of powerful gangs, of which there was no tradition in Texas prisons, to fill the control vacuum that had been created by dismantling the BTs. In what Ekland-Olson (1986: 415) described as a "prophetic warning," he cautioned: "Aggressive and predatory prisoners, disorganized or otherwise, will seize the opportunity to achieve control. As the experiences of other states have demonstrated such illegal power structures, once they arise, take root quickly and defy the most vigorous efforts aimed at their elimination." To forestall this, he urged the recruitment of more staff. The gangs emerged, as predicted, and staff numbers were increased, but it took some time for the latter to impact on the former.

According to Fong (1990: 36–37), TDC statistics show that there was only one prison gang in existence in March 1983, namely the Texas Syndicate (formed in 1975; Camp and Camp 1985: 20) with fifty-six members. Fong (1990: 41) stated: "The Texas Syndicate was originally formed for the purpose of self-protection against the 'building tenders.'" This view was confirmed by one of its members who described the debate within the gang around a move away from opposing BTs and toward criminal activities such as gambling and the distribution of drugs and alcohol, which were at the time tightly controlled by the BTs (Delgado 2007: 193).

By September 1985, things were much more balkanized. There were eight recognized gangs across the state, along with several small groupings, and a combined membership of fourteen hundred. Now the prisoners were organizing their own protection and enforcement mechanisms rather than this being the exclusive preserve of the administration, whose own gang—the BTs—had always been strong enough to deter the emergence of any rivals. As Chase (2020: 189) expressed it: "The comprehensive power of the building tender system rendered any attempt at gang organization nearly impossible."

Contrary to the predictions of governance theory (see chapter 1), it was not a rising custodial population in Texas that caused prisoners to turn to centralized mechanisms of extralegal governance (i.e., gangs). Rather, it was the abolition of another centralized mechanism of extralegal governance (i.e., BTs) that had been a feature of the Texas prison system since its inception. One form of extralegal governance, in other words, was exchanged for another. BTs were a brutal presence even when prisoner numbers were very small. They were extralegal (in that it was prohibited for prisoners to exercise a disciplinary function) but so deeply embedded that they operated in plain sight until the *Ruiz* judgment. It was a hybrid arrangement in that BTs did not draw up the rules, but they were selected according to clear criteria. Also, their reputations often preceded them. There is nothing inevitable about the emergence of gangs, even when the conditions specified by governance theory are met.

There is some continuity here in that the BTs and the gangs attempted to dominate through fear of violence. But the gangs were organized statewide (as opposed to on an institution-by-institution basis), they did not join forces with staff, they were racially divided, they had rules and constitutions, they were organized to obtain criminal ends, and they were much more lethal during a brief period. The BT system, by contrast, was based on local divisions and, while inherently violent, its effects were seldom fatal. BTs were chosen by the wardens and could be dismissed by them. No such leverage existed with gang leaders.

A Bloodier Life (for a Time)

There is no simple causal relationship between the demise of the BTs, the rise of the gangs, and a (brief) descent into chaos in the mid-1980s. As noted above, the collapse of staff morale also contributed. So too did the completion of racial desegregation. Prisons in Texas were segregated until 1965. The lack of mixing meant that racial tension was not a major problem. Cell blocks and job assignments remained segregated until the late 1970s, when this practice was eventually abolished as a result of *Lamar v. Coffield* (1972), a long-running lawsuit (in which the indefatigable David Ruiz became involved as a plaintiff). The process was not completed until the integration of individual cells began in earnest in the early 1990s.

The Eastham Unit had long been viewed as the "white boys' farm," where the dominant white prisoners were supported by the white staff (Crouch and Marquart 1989: 193). When the BTs were abolished and the staff became more racially mixed, Black prisoners grew in assertiveness. As a result, whites banded together for protection and so did Mexicans. Despite being formally integrated the prisons became very racially polarized. Based on testimony from one of the gang's founders, Pelz et al. (1991) drew a clear line from the ending of the BT system to the creation of the Aryan Brotherhood of Texas. The requirement in *Lamar* that every cell block reflected the racial mix of the institution meant that Black prisoners were in a plurality everywhere. When whites found themselves in a numerical minority in the cell block and stripped of the status that had come with their occupancy of senior positions within the BT hierarchy, they joined forces for mutual protection and enhanced power. This happened during 1981 and 1982 (Pelz et al. 1991: 28).

Another factor that contributed to destabilization was that expectations rose steeply when copies of the court's order in *Ruiz* were distributed via the *Echo* prison newspaper in 1981, but they were not matched by meaningful change on the ground; dashed hopes led to dissatisfaction that—in the context of emboldened prisoners and uncertain staff—created a context for widespread disturbances (Alpert et al. 1984: 299). The staff were not sure how to deal with assertive prisoners whose claims for improved treatment had the backing of the courts.

Also feeding into the crisis of control in the prisons, according to Gulick (1984: 179–82), was the sweeping political and economic change that took place across Texas society throughout the 1970s. This included financial scandals, electoral reform, changing political structures, a booming economy, and rapid modernization in terms of infrastructure as well as mores. Penal change cannot be divorced from wider developments, especially when considering a legal process that extended for as long as the *Ruiz* case and coincided with a period of unusual social, political, and economic upheaval. Gulick's argument is that the crisis of control in Texas prisons cannot be understood in isolation and that, to some extent at least, it mirrored a crisis of control that was unfolding in parallel in the state. By this account, even without *Ruiz*, these would have been challenging times for the penal system. Possibly, but given the hostility of the state to what was perceived as judicial interference, it is not clear what shape this change would have taken, or what weight would have been accorded to prisoner concerns.

In other words, the violence emerged from profound social disorganization in the Eastham Unit and other Texas prisons. The abolition of the BT system was part of this to be sure, but there were other factors at play. Returning to the discussion of compliance in chapter 1, the removal of the BTs meant that the degree of coercive power that could be brought to bear on prisoners was suddenly, and massively, reduced. The regime had been found illegitimate by the courts. It was no longer in prisoners' interests to remain in thrall to the more powerful among them, who had lost the backing of the staff. This was an instance of delegitimation. It took some time for new norms and behaviors to emerge and become embedded. In other words, there was a legitimacy deficit (see box 1.1). Additionally, routines were upended along with the unreflective, ritualistic aspects of life that allowed prisoners to progress through the day almost automatically ("dull compulsion").

As all the bases of order—coercion, calculation, consensus, and dull compulsion—were demolished simultaneously, it is not surprising that upheaval resulted. This was a predictable outcome of the court's determination that the regime was not legally valid. When this "rotten crutch," based on tradition—and a sense of fatalism—rather than law, was taken away, collapse followed. (The periods of volatility experienced in the other case study prisons, such as occurred after the creation of the League of Communist Republicans in the H Blocks, and the dashing of expectations around a possible amnesty in Isir Bet, resulted in much less death and suffering. At least in part, this was on account of them happening against the background of a variety of life that was more robustly legitimate.)

There were some skirmishes in advance of the gang-related lethal violence that peaked in what became known as the "war years" of 1984 and 1985 (Ralph and Marquart 1991: 43). Ekland-Olson (1986: 404) charted the trajectory, post-*Ruiz*. An increase in group disturbances (e.g., work stoppages, riots) was followed by a rise in direct confrontations between prisoners and staff (e.g., disobedience and assaults), and then—when the latter group had been tested and found wanting—a series of homicidal encounters between prisoners to establish a new locus of control.

According to Fong (1990: 37), 20 of the 25 homicides recorded in prisons across the state of Texas during 1984 were gang-related (and often intraracial). The same was true for 23 of 27 that occurred the following year, of which 13 were committed by members of the Texas Syndicate against members of the Mexican Mafia, another Hispanic gang. (The Texas Syndicate had killed six Mexican Mafia members in 1984.) Fong estimated that the Mexican Mafia had 351 members around this time, which yields a shockingly high mortality rate of 5.4 percent during a two-year period. The overall mortality rate for gang members was 3.1 percent (43 out of 1,400). This was an unsustainable level of casualties.

Eight homicides were perpetrated by members of the Aryan Brotherhood of Texas in 1984 and another five the following year (Pelz et al. 1991: 29–30). This gang committed one in four of all killings during the war years—a lower tally than the Texas Syndicate but still a staggering contribution to the wave of violence that threatened to submerge the TDC. They lashed out at the Blacks, whom they blamed for the diminution in their status.

Homicides were the tip of the iceberg, with widespread racial violence instigated by whites, angry at what they saw as a disruption to the natural order of things where they were at the top of the racial hierarchy. As Pelz et al. (1991: 30) described: "Analysis of written correspondence during this period reveals AB [Aryan Brotherhood] members chasing blacks around recreation yards with knives, harpooning others through open food slots, fire bombing and assaulting blacks on the way to/from showers, recreation, and legal visits, as well as stabbing, beating, and murdering inmates thought to be enemies of the Brotherhood."

There must have been an impetus from the gangs themselves to reduce the level of violence, which for some of them was devastating, and others must have feared the consequences of retaliatory strikes as well as the depletion of their numbers through the widespread use of administrative segregation. A gang will not succeed if its members' lives are in jeopardy. While it might be an overstatement to suggest that the bloodbath led to a truce, it would be fair to say that gang members who had not been segregated knew that organizational survival required less homicidal violence. Crouch and Marquart (1990: 120) reported that most of the gang-related killings perpetrated in 1984 and 1985 occurred in the administrative segregation cell blocks. In other words, the violence was ferociously concentrated and highly localized.

It was not the case that the turbulence in prisons reflected a tidal wave of lethal violence in Texas more generally. Figure 3.7 presents data from across the state and within the prisons for the period including the war years and two decades later. The state's homicide rate (murder and non-negligent manslaughter per 100,000) doubled from 8.6 to 16.9 between 1960 and 1980 before tumbling to 5.9 by 2000, and even further afterward (e.g., 4.9 in 2010). This suggests that to explain what was going on we must look at factors internal to the TDC.

The immediate aftermath of the abolition of the BT system saw a spike in violence and a precarious state of affairs for prisoners, especially the minority among them who became involved with the emerging gangs. However, we should not lose sight of the fact that the social order that was dissolved was far from harmonious. Indeed, the reason

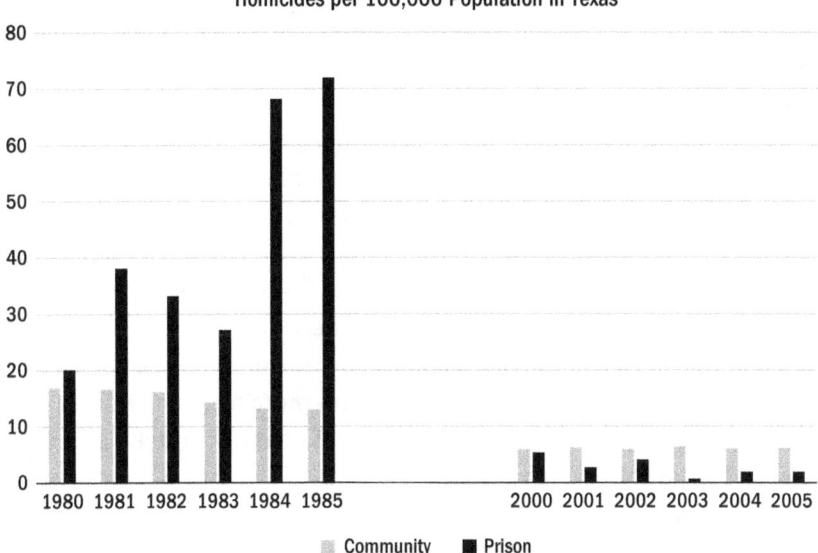

Figure 3.7. Lethal Locations. Sources: Ekland-Olson (1986: 398), Federal Bureau of Investigation (2020), Texas Department of Criminal Justice (personal communication).

for the *Ruiz* reforms was that the status quo was a threat to prisoners' bodily integrity. The courts intervened, order was restored, and prisons became safer. Some of the difficulties that emerged related to the administration's resistance to the proposed reforms rather than the reforms themselves; enthusiastic and sincere compliance would have had less pernicious consequences. By the late 1980s, the widespread use of administrative segregation and the fact that prisoners had become used to racial integration meant that the support for white supremacist groups declined and the lethal threat they presented diminished.

It seems clear based on the available evidence that Texas prisons were not safe before the *Ruiz* judgment. Limited lethal violence and the associated impression of stability had shallow foundations. While the reforms may have created the context for a surge in gang-related killings, this did not endure and even at its height did not have adverse implications for prisoners' perceptions of safety. From the official perspective, the prisons may seem to have operated smoothly, but prisoners did not feel safe. Closer examination reveals an environment that appeared orderly on the surface was underpinned by inequality and fear. What was envied by managers and some observers was grudgingly endured by those who labored under it, whose compliance was manipulated rather than freely given.

Crouch and Marquart (1990) surveyed prisoners' perceptions of safety across nine prison units in Texas, one of which was the Eastham Unit. Their research revealed that most did not consider the prisons safe in the 1970s. While they were unlikely to be killed, they did not feel out of harm's way from BTs or staff. There were few changes in perceptions during the war years, probably because the violence was gang-related so prisoners without gang associations—the majority—were not unduly perturbed. Or, more precisely, they were no more fearful than they had previously been of attack from a BT or staff member. In 1986 and 1987, the final years studied, prisoners felt safer than ever; the BTs were gone, the staff could no longer behave with impunity, and many gang members had been taken out of circulation and placed in administrative segregation. Unlike some prison officials, the prisoners did not rue the passing of the BTs. The dismantling of this control system was not lamented by those who had been subjected to its rigors. The removal of a source of constant tension and division was not a matter for regret or nostalgia. (There were some interesting racial differences in that whites, who were most likely to be represented among the BTs and staff, felt safer than Blacks during the 1970s. Hispanics felt safest of all, with a strong sense of solidarity that was bolstered by a shared language and heritage.)

The prisoners did not miss being spoken to in a derogatory fashion by BTs and staff and being beaten at will by the same groups without the possibility of lodging a complaint that would be taken seriously. To live with people who can thrash you without facing consequences is not conducive to harmonious coexistence. The only thing in favor of this heavy-handed approach to discipline was that it was predictable. It was a cause of general relief that a measure of horizontal and vertical legitimacy was introduced post-*Ruiz*. This led to an improvement in the quality of life for the majority.

Extending Temporal Parameters

A longer time frame is required to make sense of the waxing and waning of violence in Texas prisons and to put the war years into context.

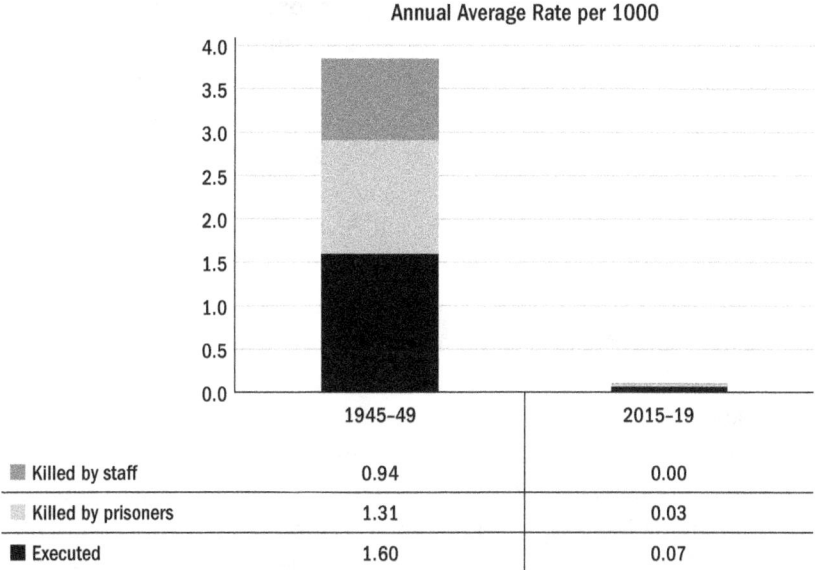

Figure 3.8. Texas Prison Homicide: Then and Now. Sources: Chase (2020: 67), Death Penalty Information Center (2020), Texas Department of Criminal Justice (personal communication), Texas Justice Initiative (personal communication).

(Unfortunately, the available data do not allow such an analysis specifically for the Eastham Unit.) As figure 3.6 shows, prisoners in Texas were more likely to be killed by their peers in the 1940s than the 1980s. Interestingly, while homicides were rare in the 1970s, it was noted during the *Ruiz* proceedings that the victims were disproportionately drawn from among the ranks of the BTs: "It is not without significance that, of the relatively few homicides which TDC reported for the years 1974 to 1979, a substantial percentage named building tenders as the victims" (*Ruiz v. Estelle* 1298, note 68).

If homicides caused by correctional officers (i.e., beatings and shootings) and the state (i.e., executions) are included, the contrast is even more striking. Figure 3.8 presents average annual homicide rates in Texas prisons during two quinquennia, separated by seventy years. The rates were 3.85 and 0.10 respectively, an almost fortyfold difference. The actual numbers were ninety-two (between 1945 and 1949) and seventy-seven (between 2015 and 2019). Consider that there were almost fifty times as many prisoners in 2015 as in 1945, but that a greater number were killed by other prisoners (seven vs. two) and by staff (two vs. zero), in the earlier year. In other words, there was proportionately more lethal violence in earlier decades, albeit the direction of the violence was not only from other inmates but also from staff and the state. In 1985, the peak of the war years, the rate of prisoners killing other prisoners was one-third of the rate in 1945. If killings by staff are included, it falls to one-quarter. If executions are added, it drops to almost one-fifth. This analysis challenges the received wisdom that the violence that followed the dismantling of the BT system was unparalleled.

In the past, prisoners were fewer in number but at higher risk of death at the hands of staff (either through use of force or in the execution chamber) and their fellows. The 1940s, when the legacy of the plantation had not been fully shaken off, were very violent times. In addition to prisoners deliberately slain by other prisoners, guards, and the state, others died from heat exposure, accidents, escape attempts, suicide, general maltreatment, and medical neglect. In other words, figure 3.8 underestimates the human toll exacted by the system. Worked to death and beaten in the fields, prisoners were further subdued when they returned to the prison in the evening. Violence permeated everything. The labor was violent, the supervision was violent, the relationships with staff and other prisoners were violent, the language was violent and casually racist. There was a level of self-directed violence and mutilation. These were desperate people attempting to survive in desperate times. (It should be noted that some cuts recorded as "self-mutilation" were likely to have been inflicted by third parties, such as BTs, whom the authorities were keen to protect from the consequences of their aggression.)

Given that the staff were so scarce they must have been enthusiastic punishers. The evidence shows that the Texas system was violent at all levels in the 1940s (ranging from lethal violence, assaults, and beatings to cruel work practices and self-mutilation). Then it became the jewel in the corrections crown, lauded as cheap, disciplined, and orderly. Then it descended into violence again in the 1980s (but not as far). Then control was regained and there has not been another downward spiral since. The long-term story in other words is about the pacification of Texas prisons, with a short-term, but bloody, reversal of the trend in the mid-1980s.

Restoring Order

Crouch and Marquart (1990: 110) referred to evidence given by TDC officials during the *Ruiz* trial that only sixteen prisoners were murdered between 1970 and 1978, an average of two each year. Comparing this with 1984 and 1985 shows how rapidly things deteriorated—with an average of twenty-six murders in each of these two years. But comparing this with 1986, when there were two killings, shows how swiftly things were brought back under control. Crouch and Marquart (1990) set out the chronology. In late 1984 special administrative segregation cell blocks were built in several units, but they were not used extensively at first. In the fall of 1985, in response to political pressure to bring the prisons back under control, and no end in sight to the escalation in violence, the TDC ordered a "massive lockdown" (p. 119) of men who were known to be violent or gang affiliated. A lot of people were caught up quickly in the dragnet, and by Christmas nearly 3,200 men had been confined to single cells under a high degree of security. According to Chase (2020: 380), the administrative segregation population in 1983 (on the cusp of the war years) was 345 and by 1987 it had grown to 3,055. As a proportion of the prison population this is a ninefold jump from (just under) 1 percent to (just over) 8 percent. There was a strong inverse relationship between the numbers in administrative segregation and the annual death toll.

The lockdown worked because it took predatory prisoners out of circulation and reminded staff that they had not lost control completely. By the late 1980s staff numbers had risen substantially, there was greater familiarity with what the courts required, and those whose allegiance was to traditional control strategies were a dwindling number. Fewer staff remained whose nostalgia for a racist and repressive past would be tolerated, if they dared to articulate it. A more diverse guard force was settling into place. A more regulated environment was beginning to stabilize. All these factors served to boost morale.

Crouch and Marquart (1989: 201) presented data on serious assaults across the TDC units that housed violent recidivists (including the Eastham Unit). The rate per thousand inmates for fighting with a weapon fell from twenty-four in 1985 to eleven in 1987, with even greater proportionate declines for fighting without a weapon (sixty to twelve over the same period) and possession of a weapon (fifty-five to nine). Administrative segregation clearly had an impact. It took dangerous armed men out of circulation and it reduced the perception on the part of potentially vulnerable prisoners that they needed to be prepared to defend themselves with force should the need arise.

After the war years things settled down and, despite a steeply rising prison population, the number of homicides was never as high again. The fact that the system was brought back under control in 1986 and has remained stable since (figure 3.6) shows that there was nothing inevitable about prisoners holding sway with murderous effect. Prison violence can be controlled if the will and the wherewithal exist.

The removal of BTs demonstrated to prisoners that the administration could not co-opt its favorites and reward them for their service. Life may have remained grim, but the pain was more evenly shared. The informality of the past had benefited the few, the strong, and the white. While staff complained about the erosion of discretion and endless bureaucratic demands, those in their custody were reassured that they lived in an environment where rules mattered and where the courts could—and would—intervene to enforce them. This enhanced perceptions of procedural justice. Similarly, the prisoners were no longer vulnerable to the arbitrary use of force by staff, which had so often been a cause of fear, aggravation, and distress. All of the foregoing must have contributed to the stability that emerged from the late 1980s and that continued despite surging numbers behind bars.

Life post-*Ruiz* was more rule-governed and safer. The unquestioning repression of the past—reinforced with blows and racial epithets, and the availability of a surrogate guard force in the guise of the BTs—was no longer integral to prison order. Traditional ways of doing business were supplanted by centralization and increased bureaucratic demands; it might have been staid, but as far as most prisoners were concerned it was more legitimate and their autonomy and bodily integrity were more secure. Compliance may not have been normative, but at least there was clarity around expectations. In the past it was coercive and capricious, the worst of both worlds. Dull compulsion was a marked improvement on constant fear.

The new arrangements may have been seen as unduly restrictive, but at least they were not personal and there was some hope of making power holders accountable. Once the staff became accustomed to it, they appreciated the value of a system where procedures were clearly stated, if not the associated paperwork. They learned to use the new disciplinary protocols to their advantage and to see how writing someone up for a violation could impact his behavior as effectively as "whipping his ass." For persistent rule violators, administrative segregation beckoned. Staff realized that they had power. A different kind of life emerged—still tight, but safer. There was more and better regulation (moving along the horizontal axis of figure 1.1) and possibly more integration as the bloc that had divided the prisoner body was gone and prisoners were no longer stratified according to the administration's priorities. If the Eastham Unit's coordinates were to be replotted along the axes of integration and regulation, the result would show diagonally upward movement. In addition, it was more legitimate (horizontally and vertically).

When Ruiz returned to prison in 1984 he was sent to administrative segregation. While no doubt bolstered by the major public profile that accompanied his writ writing, his infamy in the TDC, and the support of his wife and family, he saw out his prison career in the very kind of solitary confinement that had led him to self-mutilate frequently when he was a young man.

The Eastham Unit is what a prisoner society can look like when both integration and regulation are low, and when whatever legitimacy exists is tenuous and falls foul of a legal challenge. When the state abdicates its role and takes a minimalist approach to regulation, instead enjoining selected prisoners as its agents, this creates a divided society where each is pitted against the other. The weak regulatory environment is exploited by the strong prisoner with official backing. The resulting splits are deep and exacerbated by racial, linguistic, and regional differences. The BT system was corrupt, racist, and hypocritical. It created a divisive carceral environment. But it was less murderously violent than what preceded—or immediately succeeded—it. Once the turbulence passed, the men held in the Eastham Unit were safer and less fearful. Their life in the late 1980s was a world apart from what had prevailed beforehand.

Coda

Texas was not the only state to exploit prisoner labor both in the fields (to make money) and in a supervisory capacity (to save money). In

Mississippi the inmate guards were armed, assigned to separate quarters with superior facilities, and neatly attired in bespoke clothing and well-shone cowboy boots. While they were expected to work long shifts with little time off, when not on duty they could hunt, fish, or go horse riding. They received generous remission on their sentences, were much more likely to receive parole, and were granted an annual ten-day furlough. They pursued escapees and some even worked on special assignments for community-based law enforcement agencies (McWhorter 1981). Jackson (2009: 15) described driving to Cummins Prison Farm in Arkansas in 1971. He was stopped on his approach by an armed man wearing a khaki uniform who was guarding a barrier on the road. Asked if he had any weapons in the car, he replied that he had a .22-caliber rifle and was told to make sure it was locked up while he was on the farm. The barrier was raised, and he was waved through. The armed man was a life sentence prisoner. The men working in the fields were supervised by other prisoners, some on foot and others on horseback, some with pistols and others with rifles. The inmate trusty systems in Mississippi (*Gates v. Collier* 1972) and Arkansas (*Holt v. Sarver* 1970) were reformed before the *Ruiz* action got underway as a result of successful challenges brought by prisoners whose Eighth Amendment rights (not to be subjected to cruel and unusual punishment) were found to have been violated. In other words, *Ruiz* caught a wave rather than starting something. What set Texas apart was that it clung to the system after other states relinquished it. Crouch and Marquart (1989: 86) found references to BTs, turnkeys, and inmate bookkeepers in Texas prisons as far back as the 1880s; they were classified under "Indispensables" and, as things transpired, they were to remain so for a hundred years.

4

Isir Bet, Ethiopia

The purpose of these regulations is to . . . enable prisoners to learn from their crimes in order to make them peaceful and productive citizens when they depart the institution . . . and to create a tranquil community, where work is plentiful, time passes quickly, and life is well ordered.
—Preamble to prisoners' code, promulgated in October 2015

With 115 million people in 2020, Ethiopia was the second most populous African country (after Nigeria) and significantly larger than any country in the European Union (Germany was top with 83 million) or any US state (California was top with 39 million). Ethiopia's economic performance is improving, but it remains desperately poor, with figures from the World Bank (2021) showing per capita gross national income of US$850 in 2019, and life expectancy at birth of sixty-seven years, compared with US$65,910 and seventy-nine years, respectively, in the US.

Ethiopia is one of the world's most ancient civilizations, currently comprising ten regions and two chartered cities. The working language of the government, and lingua franca for most of the country, is Amharic, but around one hundred languages are spoken nationwide. Little has been written about Ethiopian prisons and what does exist tends to be narrowly focused on health matters (e.g., Abera and Adane 2017) or relates to political imprisonment (e.g., Guutama 2003). There are some first-hand journalistic accounts (e.g., Schibbye and Persson 2015).

The Ethiopian prison that is the subject of this chapter resembled a tightly spatially constrained and bustling village, which I visited for a week in 2016, with shorter follow-up trips in each of the two subsequent years. My visits were at the invitation of Paddy Moran, a missionary priest, rather than in the context of a formal research project (see O'Donnell 2019a, 2021a). This is why I refer to it as Isir Bet (the transliteration of እስር ቤት, the Amharic word for prison) rather than identifying it by name. It is one of twenty-three prisons located in the Southern Nations, Nationalities, and Peoples' Region (SNNPR), the country's most rural and third most populous region, which embraces more than forty-five ethnic groups and borders Kenya and South Sudan. The prison was established in 1957, during the reign of Emperor Haile Selassie and opened with 10 inhabitants. It was rebuilt during the 1990s as a regional prison with capacity for 1,200. By the time of my first visit, the population had grown to 1,995 men and 119 women (accompanied by 30 of their children) who were distributed across eighteen dormitories (fourteen for men and four for women). There were no white prisoners. There were plans to move to an alternative site that would better accommodate the press of numbers.

The reference decade for this case study is from 2010 to 2020. This incorporates the period before Chalew Gebino was elected chairman, an office he held from 2012 to 2017, to a riotous interval in 2018, and beyond. Isir Bet is an example of what prison life is like when integration is high and regulation is low (see figure 1.1). Each chapter epigraph sets out an official statement of purpose that is then contrasted with the reality. The gap between official rhetoric and penal practice was narrow in Isir Bet, and wide in ADX Florence, the H Blocks, and the Eastham Unit.

A Gated Village

Isir Bet is located in a large town, close to a football stadium and surrounded by residential areas, as illustrated by figure 4.1. Normal life continued right up to the entrance gate, with children playing, traders touting for business, three-wheeled *bajaj* taxis dropping off and collecting passengers, and locals going about their daily activities. Just inside the gate stood a metal sign upon which one of the prisoners had painted an almost life-size representation of a member of staff in camouflage-style uniform bearing the injunction, in Amharic, to stop and cooperate with any security checks (figure 4.2). The figure in the painting offered a respectful salute to visitors, suggesting an ethos of cooperation rather than coercion. The prison provided the basics of food and water, bedding and shelter, education and healthcare. Its occupants were left to their own devices to source clothing, toiletries, and any extras that they required to ease the burdens of confinement. If they had a family outside,

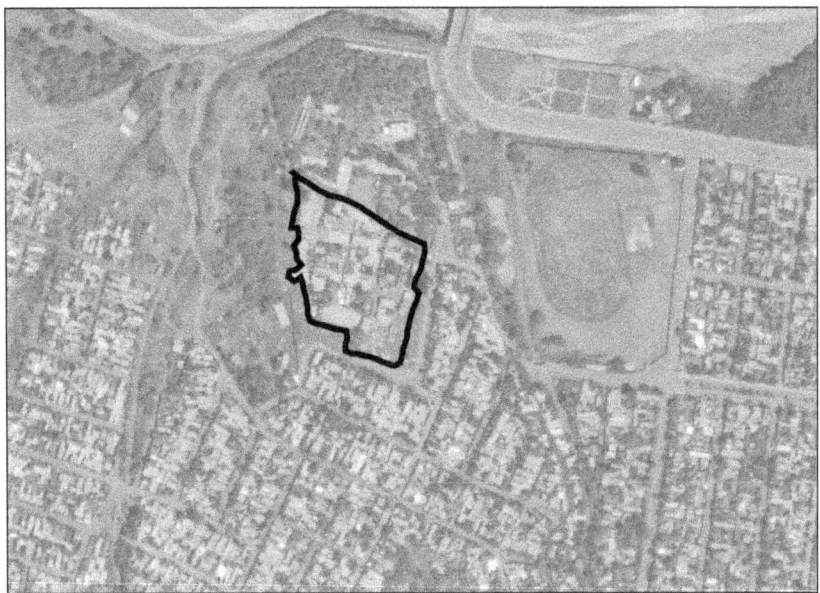

Figure 4.1. A Village within a Town. Credit: Esri World Imagery.

its support was an urgent concern. As a result, every available space within the compound was occupied by someone attempting to generate an income one way or another. Those who worked were rewarded in accordance with the market value of whatever they managed to produce. The prison operated as a cash economy, and the Commercial Bank of Ethiopia visited twice weekly to facilitate deposits and withdrawals.

Entering the prison for the first time I was struck by the vibrant colors and the sartorial range. Some wore threadbare, mismatched items, while others were impeccably groomed. Staff wore military fatigues. My guide and interpreter—who was the prisoners' chairman during my first two visits—wore a fresh outfit every day, neatly laundered and pressed. I was hot and bothered and somewhat disheveled. He was cool and collected. The other prisons that feature as case studies in this book were less polychromatic. When I visited the Eastham Unit in Texas, the prisoners were all attired in prison-issue whites and the staff wore gray. When I visited the H Blocks in Northern Ireland the staff wore the regulation uniform, but the prisoners dressed as they pleased. In ADX Florence, where visiting professors are not welcome, the only splash

Figure 4.2. Welcome to Our World. Credit: Ian O'Donnell.

of color is seen during visits when standard issue khaki trousers and khaki shirts are temporarily swapped for jumpsuits (white for the general population, yellow for the control unit, orange for anyone from the special housing unit).

The prison compound was an intensely sociable place, especially during visits when families brought messages and supplies and at mealtimes, when people came together to eat the *injera* (a sour, spongy flatbread made from teff, a national staple) provided by the prison. The daily dietary at Isir Bet consisted of *shai* (tea) and bread (a seven-ounce loaf made from wheat or maize) for breakfast, followed by a fourteen-ounce helping of *injera*, with vegetable stew, for lunch and dinner. Meat was provided about four times each year when a special holiday was being celebrated.

Sometimes men collected food for their companions, standing in line as the freshly prepared portions were doled out (figure 4.3), while the rest of the group found a suitable place to gather in the shelter of the dining hall. If they desired variety and could afford to do so they patronized

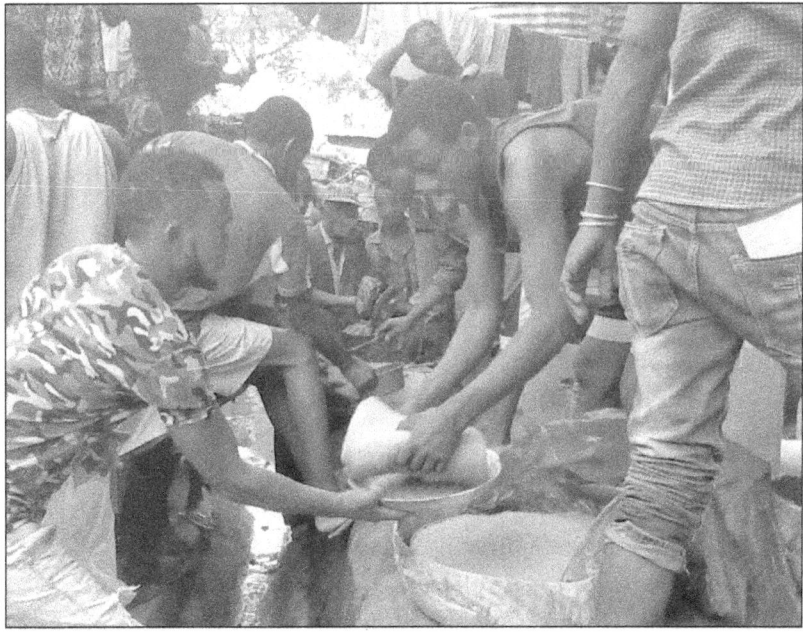

Figure 4.3. Dinner Is Served. Credit: Ian O'Donnell.

one of the prison's several privately operated cafés. (Having dined there, I can attest to the deliciousness of the sweet potatoes.)

Weldeyohannes (2017: 113) observed that food in Ethiopian prisons was generally in short supply and of poor quality, meaning that prisoners "are at increased risk of foodborne diseases, such as diarrhea, typhoid, and typhus . . . and there are no rules in state or federal laws or policies on nutritional standards of food." For those who could supplement (or disregard) the official offering either through the contents of parcels brought by their families or their ability to buy meals prepared by others, the dietary was adequate. For those who had to rely on what was provided to them, monotony was the order of the day. Regular supplies of water were a problem. On account of inadequate infrastructure, the prison struggled to provide sufficient water for drinking, food preparation, bathing, laundry, and cleaning.

There was a very high level of participation in organized religion. Orthodox and Protestant churches were packed during weekly services (around eight hundred congregants in the former and a thousand in the latter). There was a mosque for the small number of Muslims and prayer spaces for a handful of Jehovah's Witnesses and members of the Apostolic Church. Men of God were held in high esteem. Prisoners brought the rituals of everyday life into the prison and sometimes practiced them with enhanced fervor. The prison was an intensification of life outside. (Priests and preachers attended the Eastham Unit chapel on Sundays, and men in the H Blocks could attend Mass together. But believers at ADX Florence had to worship alone; as in so many other ways, theirs was a dilute version of community living.)

Accommodation

On admission, new arrivals were allowed to keep their money and any possessions with the exception of cell phones. They had a shower and haircut and a decision was made about where they would live. Single cells were unheard of and everyone was accommodated in dormitories. With the exception of one dormitory that was set aside for recidivists, and two for those awaiting trial or sentence, allocation was by gender and sentence length with no account taken of the nature of the offense, age, or ethnicity. While contrary to UN standards, which stipulate that dormitories should be "occupied by prisoners carefully selected as being suitable to associate with one another" (United Nations 2015: Rule 12), this integration policy did not seem to be a cause of dissatisfaction and tension or to heighten the risk of interpersonal violence. Indeed, it may have stifled the emergence of dominant groupings. One advantage of crowded dormitories is that the occupants are safer from staff predation than are their counterparts in single cells. Another is that social exclusion through physical distancing is not possible, so ostracization is more difficult. The method of dormitory allocation and the written code (see below, "A Living Code") seem to have reduced the opportunity for gangs to emerge.

The UN minimum standard space requirement per person in a dormitory is a little over 4 square yards (United Nations 2014: 7). Figure 4.4 shows the largest dormitory in Isir Bet. It measured 167 square yards and so, to satisfy this standard, should have had no more than 41 occupants. When I visited, 208 men, each of whom was serving eleven to fifteen years, were sleeping there every night. Ventilation consisted of a metal grill between the top of the wall and the roof, a simple method of allowing air to circulate without jeopardizing security. The smallest men's dormitory held 40 farm workers. Women, and some of their children, were held in a separate, but nearby, part of the compound. The biggest of their rooms, with a floor area of 69 square yards, accommodated 44 adults and 10 children; the smallest was home to 20 adults and 8 children. All dormitory doors were locked at around 5:30 each evening and their occupants remained enclosed until 6:30 the following morning. Once unlocked, they remained so all day.

At the time of my first visit, there was one (male) prisoner who had been sentenced to death, 94 were serving life sentences (90 male and 4 female), and 1,075 were serving at least ten years (1,036 male and 39 female). At the other end of the scale there were men and women serving no more than several months. As for the offenses committed, 652 had been incarcerated for lethal violence (617 men and 35 women) and another 249 for attempted murder (242 men and 7 women). Other common offenses included rape, theft, and robbery, with small numbers incarcerated for bigamy, deforestation, and trespass. The youngest person was sixteen years old. The oldest was estimated to be in his mid-eighties or early nineties, the lack of birth registration rendering a precise calculation impossible.

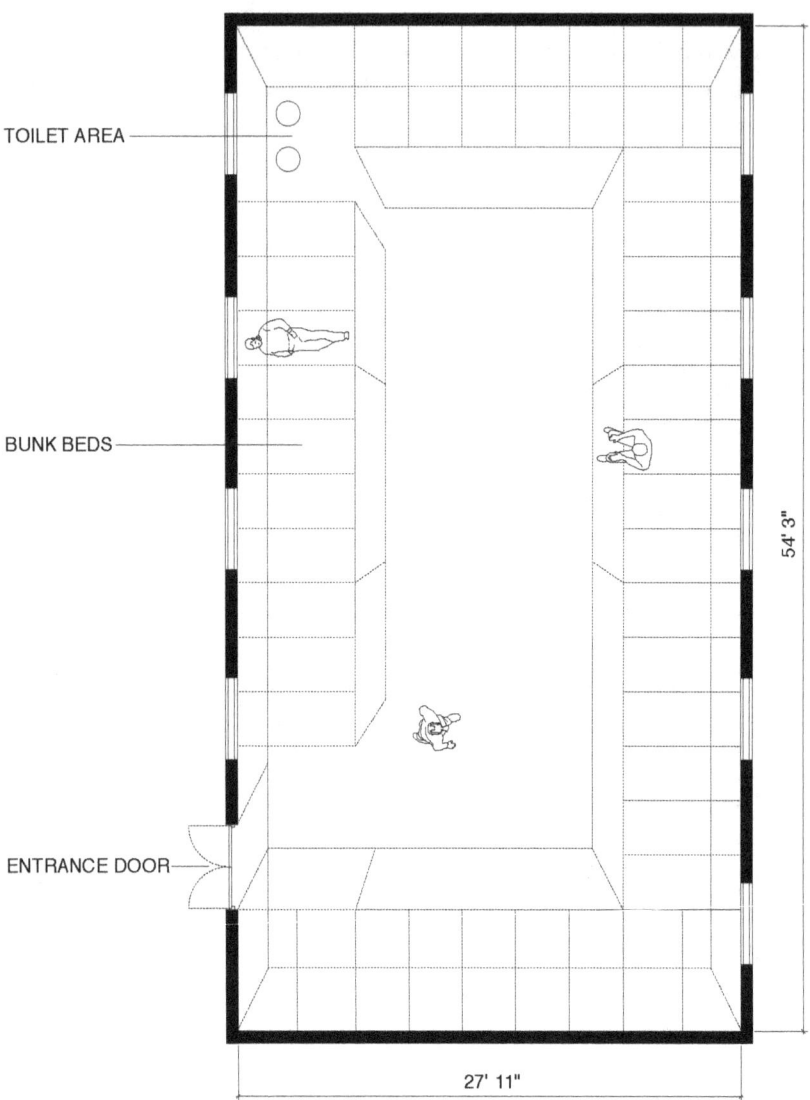

Figure 4.4. Cramped Confinement.

Double bunk beds were arranged around the dormitory's perimeter. Each person had a foam mattress (thirty inches wide and seventy-one inches long), and if the crowding increased these were squeezed more closely together. Anyone unfortunate enough not to occupy a bunk rolled out their mattress on the floor at night. Some spent several years on the floor until a combination of availability and seniority won them a bed. (One man serving a life sentence told me he had spent five years on the floor.) This was not as much of a problem for those in the short-term dormitories, where the turnover was high and beds became available quite often. Those with money could skip the queue by renting a bunk if they could find an occupant who preferred an additional income to nighttime comfort. Under such circumstances the two simply swapped places. To make the arrangement permanent cost up to one thousand birr (see table 4.2 for exchange rate).

Buckets were provided in a corner of the dormitory to meet the overnight demand for toilet facilities. They were carried away in the morning, sluiced out, and returned. This was a punishment duty or a poorly paid job toward the cost of which all residents contributed a nominal monthly amount. These precautions were vital to prevent the spread of disease in a place with too many people and too little plumbing. Prisoners also pooled their resources to cover the price of the satellite television subscription, making individual contributions of eight santim per month (there are one hundred santim in one birr).

Not all locations were equal. The chairman of the prisoners, a photograph of whom, taken during his final year acting in this capacity, appears as figure 4.5, had a top bunk, located in a corner (which meant he had only one immediate neighbor), near ventilation, and with his own electric light. This was a long way from the discomfort of an uneven patch of ground near the urine buckets. It was not so much an issue of bad odor, as hygiene standards were high, but a question of getting trampled upon by anyone who needed to use the facilities after lockup. Mattresses occupied by those who slept on the floor were rolled up and stored during the day so that dormitory residents could sit and talk, enjoy board games, take a break from work, or watch television if the weather was inclement. Bags of possessions were packed and stored, and the floors were thoroughly swept. Another disadvantage of not having a bunk was that one could not retire to the privacy of a bedspace for a

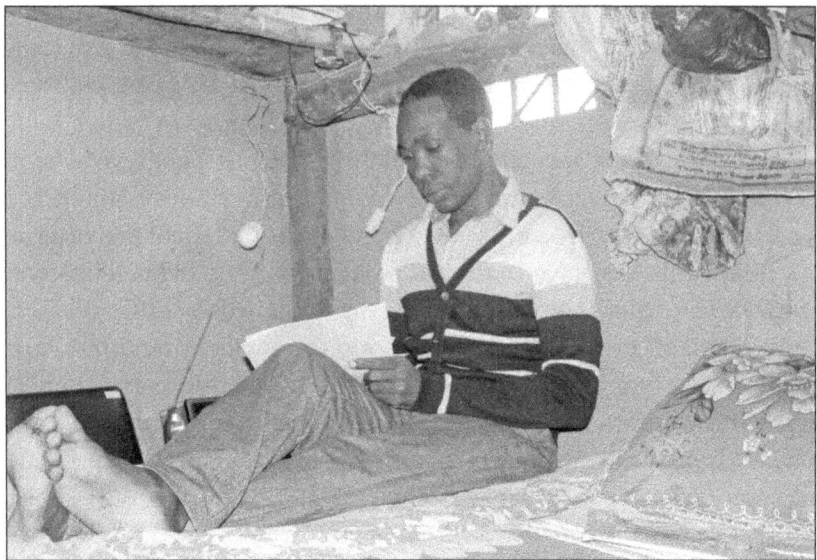

Figure 4.5. Chalew Gebino in 2017. Credit: Ian O'Donnell.

break during the day. Mattresses could not be rolled out on the floor before 8 p.m., while those with beds could occupy them at any time.

The compound was not paved. Rather the ground was beaten earth, so it became muddy after heavy rainfall. To keep the dormitories clean, anyone entering was required to leave their footwear at the door. From time to time small groups would gather inside to relax or play checkers (figure 4.6). There was a high degree of organization and the available space was used to its maximum potential.

Poverty and Purpose

The biggest source of employment was weaving cotton yarn to produce *netela* (scarves) and *gabi* (blankets). Next came fishing-net making, then crochet, embroidery, cooking, wood carving, and shopkeeping. The numbers engaged in these various occupations are shown in table 4.1. In addition, several prisoners wove *mesob* (decorative baskets). Others chopped firewood, shone shoes, fetched food, ran messages, cut hair, collected money at pool and billiards tables, or stood watch over empty dormitories. A few tended sheep and chickens in an enclosure within the compound. Others grew fruit and vegetables or kept bees on a nearby farm to which they walked each morning under armed escort. They labored on the land for six hours, planting, weeding, and harvesting, and were then free to spend what remained of the day weaving or resting. This was probably the best place to work in the sense that it was spacious, there was fresh fruit to eat, and time was set aside to generate an income at the loom once the necessary quota of agricultural work had been completed.

As in any market society, there were large disparities in income. Some of the more entrepreneurial among the prisoners managed to acquire significant wealth and had greater earning capacity than the guards (a cause, on occasion, of resentment and exploitation), while others remained impoverished and reliant on the charity of their peers. While they lived communally and received no differential treatment from the prison authorities as regards their accommodation and diet, there were obvious differences in terms of standards of dress and extent of wardrobe, how frequently an individual patronized one of the prison's cafés, how often he could buy water, tea, or coffee, whether he paid to have his shoes polished and his laundry done, and his sleeping arrangements.

Figure 4.6. Dormitory Living. Credit: Ian O'Donnell.

TABLE 4.1. Primary Methods of Income Generation (Numbers Employed)

Weaving	1,000
Making fishing nets	300
Crochet	150
Embroidery	100
Food preparation	50
Wood carving	30
Shopkeeping	12

The prison was a noisy place with handlooms clacking, radios and televisions playing, and announcements being made over the public address system. The sheer amount of activity was impressive and brought to mind the line in the Ethiopian national anthem that declares: "We are people who live through work." Weavers and carvers were busy in their sheds; fishing-net makers worked wherever they could make room (including in the dormitories until an agreed cutoff time of 10 p.m.); barbers trimmed and clipped in their shops; cooks boiled, baked, and fried at their fires; messengers ran hither and tither; idlers walked and talked; visitors queued to gain admission, always bringing news and sometimes laden with supplies; traders manned stalls in the visiting area hoping for the arrival of *ferengi* (foreigners) with more money than sense, whose intermittent visits yielded a cash bonanza.

Some were bored and lacked the money to entertain themselves, or were well supported by their families so felt no need to seek employment, or were serving sentences so short that they would not have time to be allocated a workspace, learn a trade, and turn a profit. For those who were waiting for a workspace, there were opportunities to make money by providing services of one kind or another. For example, some prisoners fetched meals for the weavers so that their work would not be interrupted. The charge for this service was twenty birr per month and the person providing it could collect meals for several people at a time, thereby multiplying his income.

The school was highly regarded and well attended. Isir Bet was the only prison in the state that offered education up to grade twelve, at which point the Ethiopian higher education entrance examination can be taken. Success at this examination opened up the possibility of university attendance via distance learning, if there was some time yet to be served, or in person post-release. The provision of education at the prison was a relatively recent innovation. The Special Rapporteur on Prisons and Conditions of Detention in Africa (2004) reported that it had no schools for formal or vocational training. Nor was it clean and well maintained at the time of its inspection.

There had been marked improvements in the years before my first visit. The local Catholic mission had funded a sixteen-bed ward where patients could be accommodated prior to, and after, hospital visits. It also provided the finances required for improvements to sanitation, access to potable water (although a reliable, and adequate, supply remained a huge challenge), and ventilation in the dormitories. An art studio was built along with new classrooms and a variety of educational and training initiatives were supported. The mission funded the construction of a shelter for the weavers so that they could work in all weathers and a dining hall so that the men could eat in company and with dignity. All of the building work was carried out by the prisoners. These changes certainly eased the burdens of confinement.

There are concerns about how speedily, fairly, and consistently the Ethiopian judicial process operates, the use of prisons to warehouse the government's political opponents, the standard of staff training, the adequacy of material conditions of confinement, and the lack of independent monitoring (e.g., Senbeta 2015). There have been scathingly critical reports of torture, rape (of female prisoners by guards or members of the local paramilitary police), and routine humiliation and degradation at particular institutions (Human Rights Watch 2018). Ill-treatment at unofficial places of detention has been a particular concern (African Commission on Human and Peoples' Rights 2012).

Detaining the regime's opponents is a default response to political agitation in Ethiopia (Toggia 2008), and Guutama (2003) described a decade spent as a political prisoner in Addis Ababa under the Provisional Military Government, or Derg, that overthrew and imprisoned Emperor Haile Selassie in 1974. The conditions were cramped, torture was common, the prisoners were uncertain how long their detention would continue, and they feared execution. During the first years of his incarceration he was responsible for supplying his own food, clothing, bedding, and any other essentials. Later the government provided bread and tea three times a day. Guutama was released in 1989.

Human rights problems beset the Ethiopian criminal justice system (e.g., United Nations Committee against Torture 2011) and conditions in police detention are especially poor. One leading international nongovernmental organization documented:

> torture and ill-treatment . . . in federal prisons, police stations, military camps, and known and secret detention facilities. The perpetrators range from rural militia acting at the behest of local administrators, to high level officials at the federal and state level. Methods of physical torture and ill-treatment vary and include beatings with sticks, electric cables, rifle butts, iron bars, or other hard instruments; immersing individuals' heads in water; beating and kicking people while they hang upside down; tying bottles of water to men's testicles; and forcing detainees to run or crawl over sharp gravel for several hours at a time. (Human Rights Watch 2013: 16)

This brutality was all too often a response to political dissent (see Human Rights Watch 2018 for an account of the horrific treatment meted out to members of the Ogaden National Liberation Front, a banned opposition group).

Isir Bet was not a place with a reputation for abusive treatment.

Women and Children

Isir Bet is the only one of the four case study prisons where women and young children were held as well as men. (There were teenagers in the H Blocks, but they were there as a result of their own actions rather than their mothers'.) The women's compound, which was separate and self-contained but located within the same secure perimeter, was marked by a lack of constructive activity, particularly for the children. There were few opportunities for employment or diversion and life was less rewarding, more monotonous, and more cramped. The available space was limited, especially the communal ground outside the dormitories, and the women seemed less content than their male counterparts. There were lots of small fires where food was prepared for the children; the overall impression was of a smoky and claustrophobic environment.

Women went to the same school as the men, but there was no formal contact. They could attend religious services with a staff escort; they sat apart from the men. They seemed bored and underemployed. The men could afford large televisions with satellite subscriptions. The women had inferior sets with poor reception. Just as in other countries where female prisoners are in a small minority, they occupied a peripheral place in a system designed for men. Dagne (2013: 7) argued that "human rights of women prisoners are violated within prisons." Because they are few in number, and submissive in line with cultural expectations, women tend to fare worse than men if they are incarcerated in Ethiopia.

The children had access to a kindergarten in the mornings but otherwise lacked the kind of intellectual nourishment required for adequate cognitive development. At least they were not denied the opportunity for maternal care and affection and this, no doubt, went some way toward compensating them for the tight parameters within which they spent their formative years. The potential failure to thrive must be weighed against the bleak prospects of growing up outside prison in the absence of a mother, a challenge faced by any siblings who remained at liberty.

The level of noise was high in the women's quarters, where the children—like children everywhere—were insistent in their demands for attention. During one of my visits (accompanied, as always, by a female member of staff), a sick child wailed incessantly from his bunk. He could not be soothed and his anguish could not be ignored. A hospital visit was planned but, until it took place, the only respite for the other residents was when he slept, fitfully. This added to the overall level of discomfort, especially at night when the dormitories were locked and relief could not be sought by moving outside and attempting to remain out of earshot or to dilute the intensity of the child's cries with the cacophony of everyday life. Many of the women were mothers themselves and their collective inability to relieve a child's suffering must have weighed heavily; a parental imperative was fatally compromised, providing a powerful reminder of how incarceration exacerbates distress.

Mekonnen (2012) examined the situation of children imprisoned with their mothers in the SNNPR. State law allowed for infants who were less than eighteen months of age to remain with their mothers until they were four years old, at which time—in order to mitigate the adverse physical and psychological consequences of growing up in custody—the prison should endeavor to find a guardian to whom the child would be surrendered. Such arrangements were difficult to put in place due to mothers' unwillingness to give up their children and problems contacting families if they lived far away, and the practice was that they could remain until they were thirteen years of age. The prolonged detention of innocent children is not unique to this region, and the African Child Policy Forum (2007: 57) reported that children imprisoned with their mothers remained until the mother was released, sometimes more than ten years later, with obvious and adverse implications for their subsequent resocialization. It is difficult for a child who has known only captivity to cope with freedom.

Mothers received an additional allowance to feed and otherwise care for their children. In Isir Bet the prison commander was allocated thirteen birr per day to cover the costs of each prisoner and this was given directly to the women by way of a monthly payment of 390 birr. While welcome, this sum was insufficient to buy nutritious food let alone clothes or bedding for the child. There was another hurdle to be overcome by pregnant women for whom the law required "a recommendation from medical directors to get additional food" (Weldeyohannes 2017: 121).

A Living Code

The creation of a written code in 2015 was an attempt to displace the personal with a set of rules that promoted predictability and fairness. It marked a shift away from capriciousness to principled and consistent decision-making. The introduction to the code expressed the hope that if the disciplinary process was made transparent this would "eliminate the sense of revenge" (para. 3) that can sometimes be kindled by rule enforcement. It was drafted because of the perceived ineffectiveness of the state's rules for the administration of prisons, which were couched at a high level of generality and could not be directly applied to the situation on the ground at Isir Bet. It was not intended to replace state law, but rather to complement and amplify it. The code stated that it was not in opposition to the institution's rules but rather was subordinate to them, and any action taken under the code did not preclude prosecution in a court of law.

Chalew Gebino (see pen portrait) introduced the code after three years in office as the prisoners' chairman. This was his initiative and his outstanding achievement. It was an attempt to eliminate the kinds of disparities that arose when treatment was based on ties of friendship, ethnicity, and graft. He felt it was unfair that a person in one dormitory might be dealt with very differently than a person in another dormitory even if their behavior was identical. The code made it easier for leaders to be consistent and to place some distance between themselves and their decisions on the basis that it was nothing personal, that their hands were tied, and that just like everyone else they were required to abide by the rules. The code was designed to copper-fasten legitimacy. It created a context where the prisoners' leaders no longer stood to gain financially from their position and role expectations were transparent. It required—and boosted—integration.

Chalew Gebino (b. 1982), Chairman

One of five brothers, Chalew Gebino grew up in rural Ethiopia, spending his early years in a simple thatched hut without electricity. What may have been absent in a material sense was made up for by a warm family life and a rich natural world. From an early age Chalew sought out whatever limited employment opportunities existed so that he could contribute to the family finances. At the age of twelve he walked eight miles (each way) to the market to collect maize and potatoes for resale locally with his mother. Previously, he bought and sold sugar cane, working for several hours before he went to school or after he left the classroom for the day (Gebino 2021).

He enlisted in the army as a teenager, remitting almost all of his modest wages to his mother so that she could provide for his younger siblings. Serving for nearly seven years, he fought in the war against Eritrea and joined peacekeeping missions to other African countries. He later worked as an English-language teacher.

Chalew was sentenced to a six-year prison term in 2007 for his involvement in a number of armed robberies. Recaptured after an escape from court, he was brought to Isir Bet in handcuffs. The prison authorities replaced these with leg irons, which remained continuously in place for several months. During the early years of his sentence the chains on his ankles were removed and replaced repeatedly because the authorities felt that he might be planning to flee.

One year after his incarceration began, he was summoned to the administration office and told that his sentence had been increased on appeal to thirty years. Despite repeated requests he was never provided with details of the court's official decision. This was a potentially devastating blow to a man who had been despondent at the prospect of six years in custody. Chalew's response to this news was a newfound determination to find a way to sustain himself through the time ahead. (Translated into English, his name means "stay strong.") He decided to teach himself to paint, which he thought would earn him respect (if he could become a skilled practitioner) as well as money (if he could obtain commissions).

He became a successful entrepreneur, an accomplished artist, an admired leader, a deep thinker, and a voracious reader. Fluent in several languages (including English), he navigated the prison system with skill and clear strategic focus. Exuding charismatic authority, he was held in high regard by his fellow prisoners and by the prison's commander, being elected as the prisoners' chairman and spokesperson in 2012 and serving in this capacity until 2017.

Inspired by reading *Mandela: My Prisoner, My Friend* (written by prison guard Christo Brand), he translated the book into Amharic and it was circulated among the prisoners and formed the basis of many lively discussions about the relationship between a great African and his captor. The prisoners were uplifted by Nelson Mandela's courage and generosity of spirit.

His signal achievement was undoubtedly the introduction of a governance code for prisoners, the success of which would be measured by the extent to which it rendered its creator redundant. In his words: "Before we had a code, the leader's strength mattered. Now there is a system, personalities matter less. It is more civilized." The code replaced arbitrariness with clear guidance about what constituted acceptable conduct. It allowed a large number of prisoners to live in close proximity with a minimum of friction.

Chalew served eleven years before being pardoned in 2018 when, to his relief, "God opened the iron gate." (The decision to show him clemency was based on evidence of the rehabilitative gains made during his imprisonment; had his petition not been accepted he would have become eligible for parole having served two-thirds of his sentence.) He found resettlement challenging in the early days and employment difficult to secure, but with the support of a friend he obtained an acre of land and became the first English-speaking farmer in the area. For a year or thereabouts he enjoyed tending to his crops of peanut, maize, sugar cane, tomato, potato, onion, and pepper, and keeping a flock of chickens. He then put his hoe into storage and moved into office administration, which better suited his talents and where the financial rewards were greater and more predictable.

Chalew drafted the code in consultation with his executive committee (comprising vice-chairman and secretary) and the leaders of each of the dormitories. Next, there was a plenary session in the visiting area involving the heads of each of the groups into which all prisoners were organized, from both the male and female sides of prison. There were 138 of these groups for the men and another eight for the women. Each group had a chairman and a second in command. They had up to fifteen members and were known as 1–15 groups. Sometimes they picked a name for themselves, such as "peace," and viewed themselves as a team rather than a random aggregation.

The group heads were given fifteen days to discuss the code with their members and to revert with any suggestions. A new version was prepared and disseminated after these comments had been collated. Once the code had been agreed to by the executive committee and dormitory heads it was handed over to the prison's commander, who assigned a team of staff to check it for conformity with state law and prison regulations. The feedback received was incorporated into a revised draft. The final version, as distributed to the dormitories, carried the institution's official stamp on the cover.

Prisoners were invited to sign their assent and more than 90 percent did so. Periodically thereafter, the executive committee directed that various sections of the code be reviewed when everyone was gathered in their dormitory at night. These refresher sessions lasted around thirty minutes and ensured that there was an ongoing consensus about the dictates of everyday life. They contributed to the maintenance of a high degree of horizontal and vertical legitimacy.

Running to twenty-two typed pages, the code covered everything from cleanliness through acceptable conduct in the dormitories to assaults and escape attempts. It defined the parameters of permissible conduct and how they would be policed. It was devised to endure, but also to be revised; there was a specific provision for the rules to be amended if the prisoners, though their 1–15 groups, felt that this was necessary and desirable. In this way, life in Isir Bet was designed to be self-correcting. The code was sophisticated in its range, the attempt to tailor sanctions to the seriousness or persistence of breaches, and the right of appeal. This was an elaborate, and effective, exercise in consensus building and norm enforcement. It was a guide to the kind of behavior that would ease the burdens of captivity.

The challenges of cheek-by-jowl dormitory living are significant and clear rules are required regarding standards of personal hygiene, sanitary facilities, use of floor space, sleeping conventions, acceptable noise levels, and approaches to conflict resolution. Without them, irritation, irascibility, and disharmony would almost certainly ensue.

Chalew was a first-time prisoner without a criminal history. This is interesting for two reasons. First, that his code was not based on inmate preoccupations. Second, that someone without prison experience could marshal such a project through to a successful conclusion says a lot about his personal qualities. It is interesting that a charismatic leader sought to replace charisma with rational-legal authority; this was both wise and selfless. Had he decided to allow the status quo to continue and exploited it to his advantage he could have made considerable gains. Instead, Chalew sought to make himself redundant and to reduce the likelihood that another charismatic authority figure could appear and prevail.

Personalities, no matter how strong, cannot compete against a widely accepted code without risking widespread resistance and disruption. The code replaced personal whims and fiats with a set of agreed-upon protocols. Authority was to inhere in the office and not the office holder. Emotions were displaced by dispassionate considerations. It allowed a stable set of mutual expectations to be developed and reinforced; means became ends. It promoted efficiency and reliability. It made it less likely that elite groups would compete for power or seek to gain control of the internal economy with the associated opportunities for "tax" generation and personal aggrandizement.

Max Weber's characterization of bureaucracy stressed the overriding importance of rational-legal authority. Fairness was ensured by written rules, lines of accountability were clear, outcomes were predictable, and discretion was curtailed to minimize the intrusion of bias. There was little room for favoritism, and things ran smoothly because mutual role expectations were clearly specified and deeply embedded. As he put it:

"Bureaucracy develops the more perfectly, the more it is 'dehumanized,' the more completely it succeeds in eliminating from official business love, hatred, and all purely personal, irrational, and emotional elements which escape calculation" (Weber 1968: 975). The Isir Bet code replaced arbitrariness with clear guidance about what constituted acceptable conduct. This lessened the likelihood that a person who was being disciplined would attribute their treatment to any animus on the part of the prisoner leadership. The rules were to be applied without fear or favor. They allowed a thronged environment to be navigated without undue chafing or disaffection.

Constitutional Arrangements

The code comprised four substantive chapters. Chapter 1 dealt with minor offenses against discipline such as assaulting another prisoner, taking someone else's possessions, gambling, not complying with the rules around family visits, exercising outside the allocated spaces, not staying in line when food was being distributed, making noise when the television news was being broadcast in the dormitories, begging, giving medicines received from the prison clinic to family members, connecting to the institution's power supply without permission, not cutting one's hair properly, not wearing clothes, or (men) dressing in women's apparel. There was a graduated series of sanctions ranging from counseling and warnings, to physical exercise drills for ten to thirty minutes, to carrying food, to losing one's bed and being relegated to an uncomfortable sleeping space on the dormitory floor for up to fifteen days. There was also scope for a report to the institution's authorities. For example, if someone persisted in coming to the visiting hall despite not being summoned, this would be seen as an attempt to escape, and the prison administration would be informed.

Chapter 2 addressed more serious matters. These included planning or attempting to escape, not participating in group meetings, threatening or using force against the executive committee, political agitation, attempting to read the future (magical traditional beliefs were widely held), being absent from or delaying the morning and evening count, not lying quietly in bed after 10 p.m., using a cell phone, brewing or consuming alcohol, drug taking (e.g., chewing khat), damaging prison property, behaving inappropriately during visits, not obeying the institution's leaders, bringing work materials to the dormitory, engaging in sexual activity with another man, and abuse of power by anyone occupying a position of authority.

Also prohibited were ear piercing, tattooing, or other body marking, on the basis that prisoners were not allowed to change their appearance because this might compromise accurate identification in the event that they died or escaped and there was a discrepancy with their admission record. There were additional concerns about transmitting diseases and those who wore tattoos were seen as aligning themselves with men of violence. Tattooing was carried out in the prison nonetheless, especially among recidivist offenders who ripped the fabric of their clothing and styled their hair in a particular way to indicate outlaw status.

Again, there was a graduated series of sanctions ranging from counseling and warnings, to emptying the dormitory's overnight urine buckets for ten to thirty days, carrying food for ten to thirty days or digging a hole to a depth of two meters, to losing a sleeping place or workplace for up to six months (or, if the rule breaker did not have a sleeping or working place, not being granted one for six months). Some of these violations (e.g., escapes or attacks by a group on an individual) were immediately reported to the prison guards on duty and the prison administration, any early release would be forfeit, the prisoner might be placed in chains, and they could face court proceedings. In addition, they would lose their bunk and workplace had they managed to acquire same.

These punishments mattered. Someone who had, after several years perhaps, earned his place on a bunk would wish to avoid returning to a crowded floor where he would be stepped over (or, worse, upon) at night by those making their way to the urine buckets. Someone who had access to a loom and the associated earning potential would not wish to lose his job and risk plunging his family into deeper poverty. Stripping him of his workspace could be tantamount to making his family destitute if he was their primary source of support. Someone who hoped for parole or the possibility of a pardon did not wish to reduce the chances of early release through misbehavior that would be notified to the authorities.

Finally, if a particular offense set out in Chapter 1 was committed three times, it would be redefined as a serious matter and dealt with under the rules set out in Chapter 2.

Chapter 3 addressed hygiene. Prisoners were required to clean, daily, the areas where they slept, worked, and ate. Smoking was prohibited in the dormitories and allowed only in specified places in the compound. (In February 2018 the rules were changed to ban smoking everywhere, but snuff was inexpensive and its use was authorized.) Everyone was expected to play a role in cleaning communal areas. Washing clothes was permitted only in a designated area, adjacent to the shower block.

Chapter 4 dealt with education and training. The emphasis here was on attendance at school, technical and vocational instruction, and any meetings called by the executive committee or dormitory leaders as well as good behavior in the classroom and being respectful to teachers and demonstrators.

There was a right of appeal against any punishment imposed under the code and if matters could not be resolved internally the aggrieved party had three days to notify the institution's authorities of their concerns. In appraising the appropriateness of a sanction, the commander took into account the provisions of the code, which was used as a reference document. The executive committee kept punishments under review and could reconsider the issue in light of improved conduct and an acceptable apology after half of the sentence had been served. As box 4.1 shows, the principle of double jeopardy did not apply. Prisoners could be punished by the tenets of their own code and by the prison staff and, if the matter was serious enough or the victim determined enough, charges could be laid and the issue addressed by an outside court.

The code allowed for a stable and harmonious prisoner society based on enlightened self-interest and pragmatism, in combination with shared values and beliefs, rather than the search for a utopian society. It placed clear parameters around what constituted acceptable individual behavior in the interests of peaceful cohabitation. (By contrast, the Charter for Frelimo Communities that governed life on IRA-controlled wings in Northern Ireland's H Blocks was inspired by the desire to create an experimental new society based on communal and democratic principles, which might later be extended outside the prison walls.)

Box 4.1. Prisoners' Code of Conduct: Sample Offenses and Sanctions

Chapter 1, Article 12

Making noise during evening television news or when dormitory meeting is underway.

A. If prisoner is new, and interruption is accidental, counselling will be given on first two occasions.
B. If deliberate, bed place will be changed.
C. For any subsequent breaches, 20 minutes of demanding physical exercise.

Chapter 2, Article 2.3

Being member of group that assaults an individual prisoner.

A. Reported to prison staff who may place offender in chains.
B. Collect and dispose of dormitory's urine for 10–20 days.
C. Denied bed space for six months.
D. Forfeit right to apply for parole and pardon.
E. Victim may take matter to outside court.

Chapter 3, Article 3

Not participating in communal cleaning routine.

A. Counselling, warning, 10–15 minutes of demanding physical exercise.
B. Not given work opportunities.
C. Not given workplace.
D. Loss of workplace for three months.

Chapter 4, Article 8.1

Disruptive behavior in classroom.

A. Reported to relevant authority.
B. Counselling and warning.
C. Sleep on uncomfortable ground for 5–20 days.
D. School rules governing misconduct will be applied.
E. If matter is serious, legal proceedings may be instigated.
F. If behavior is repeated, will lose bed and be prohibited from working for three months.

Another advantage of the code was that it served as a training manual for those new to leadership. It reduced appeals because the sanctions for unacceptable conduct were clearly specified so expectations were set. Sometimes individuals who had contravened the rules administered the penalty to themselves before it was formally awarded, as they could anticipate the likely outcome based on scrutiny of the code's provisions.

Structure and Organization

Life in Isir Bet was complex, with many clearly defined roles and a great deal of interdependence as illustrated in figure 4.7. These were the most complicated arrangements of any of the four prisoner societies described in this book. The degree of mutual reliance worked in favor of harmony; we are less likely to be at odds when we need each other to get by.

The bureaucratic functionary is not elected but appointed either by a superior or after a competition. Security of tenure is often guaranteed. By contrast, Chalew was confirmed in office by the prison's commander after an election showed overwhelming support for him, with ninety-two of the hundred prisoner representatives who constituted the electorate (each of whom spoke for twenty members of their dormitory)

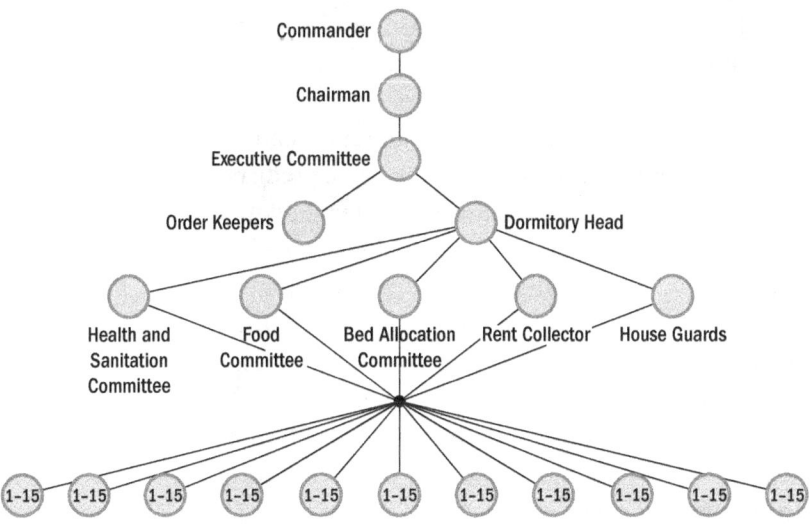

Figure 4.7. A Multiplicity of Roles.

supporting his nomination. The chairmanship was for a fixed term of two years and the commander asked him to remain on without the need for another election. This was contrary to the rules, but the consensus was that he was performing well for both prisoners and the administration. He served for a total of five years before resigning. This was the first time that the prisoners had elected their leadership team. Previously the administration had appointed the leaders. But concern that, while they certainly worked on behalf of the authorities, they were not fully accepted by the prisoner body and were exploiting their position for personal profit led to a change in the process. This is an example of the perceived deficiencies of compliance that is not normative.

Prisoners in Isir Bet were united (but not in opposition to the staff, who were few in number and largely disconnected from their daily lives). What brought them together was not ethnicity or language (of which there were a multiplicity) but rather a desire to survive the experience with family contact relatively intact. In other words, they needed to find ways to share a tightly confined space without too much conflict and to earn enough money to support themselves and any dependents.

Ethiopians are accustomed to community organization. Regions are made up of zones that comprise *woredas* (districts), which are in turn subdivided into *kebeles* (neighborhoods). Each *kebele* elects its own council, is run by a chairman and executive committee, and operates courts and a local militia (e.g., Bekele and Kjosavik 2016: 6). In terms of population size, Isir Bet would be similar to a small *kebele*. It is not surprising, in other words, that community arrangements were customized for the prison society. Perhaps the rural nature of the SNNPR, and its diversity, meant that the prisoners were predisposed to compromise and to traditional approaches to problem solving? Ethiopian society is more collectivistic than individualistic, so it makes sense that this tendency would be reflected, perhaps even magnified, in the prison. (Similarly, but malignly, in the Eastham Unit, the structural inequalities and violence of a racist society were reproduced, even exacerbated, behind bars.)

Every dormitory had a chairman. He could not be an order keeper (see below, "Order Maintenance") or chairman of a 1–15 group. The dormitory chairman was elected and stayed as long as he wished to serve and the inhabitants were happy with him. Every dormitory had a secretary who ensured everyone was present for the twice-daily counts. This person clapped his hands at 8 p.m., Monday to Friday, to call the room to silence so that all present could attend to the television news for half an hour and the main stories could be followed without interruption. It was an offense against the code to speak at this time (Ch. 1, Art. 12). Every dormitory appointed two house guards, one of whom was always present during the daytime when the dormitories were open, to make sure that the occupants' belongings were safe. They received between fifty and one hundred birr per month, depending on the paying capacity of the dormitory's members. If an item of clothing was reported stolen, and the thief was not discovered, then the guards had to pay for its replacement.

There were several two-person committees in each dormitory. These dealt with health and sanitation, food, and bed allocation. Box 4.2 summarizes the functions of the key committees shown in figure 4.7.

Box 4.2. Dormitory Bureaucracy

Health and sanitation committee
1. Checks cleanliness of dormitory as a whole and of individual beds.
2. Registers the sick and informs nurse. (Depending on nature of illness, nurse can refer patient to prison clinic or local hospital.)
3. Organizes to have mattresses carried outside for airing; sunlight believed to help eliminate bed bugs.
4. Draws up rota for 1–15 groups to clean dormitory.
5. Ensures jerry cans are hygienic enough to hold drinking water.
6. Inspects food utensils for cleanliness.

Food committee
1. Arranges for cleaning of buckets used to bring vegetarian stew to prisoners.
2. Employs prisoners to carry food from kitchens.
3. Coordinates distribution of food to prisoners with special dietary needs.
4. Organizes for water to be made available at mealtimes.
5. Saves left-over food for sale as animal feed.

Bed allocation committee
1. Assigns prisoners to bunk beds / floor space.

Each person gave five or six birr per month to the dormitory's rent collector, who paid the wages of the toilet worker who disposed of the overnight waste and maintained the communal ablutions block. (This money could be saved if the task was allocated as a punishment duty; see box 4.1.) The rent collector paid the house guards and the food collector who worked for the food committee. His final duty was to arrange a gift of fifty birr for anyone who suffered a bereavement.

The prison authorities did not participate in allocating these various roles, although if they had concerns (e.g., that an individual who was put in a position of trust was believed to be planning an escape) these could be brought to the attention of the prisoners' executive committee.

A multiplicity of committees and hierarchical administration structures are the norm in Ethiopian prisons (Special Rapporteur on Prisons and Conditions of Detention in Africa 2004: 38–43). What is different about Isir Bet, perhaps, is the democratic nature of the code; the fact that it was written down, promulgated, and diligently considered; the detailed and transparent nature of its provisions; the existence of enforcement and implementation mechanisms; the removal of ambiguity when it came to acceptable conduct; and the close liaison with prison administration. Also noteworthy were the quality of leadership among the prisoners, the extensiveness of the consultation process, the regular refresher sessions, and the scope for updating and amending the code's provisions.

Order Maintenance

One important element of the code was the creation of a body of order keepers who were identifiable by the purple hats they wore while on duty. The order keepers helped to ensure that things moved along smoothly. They nipped problems in the bud and sought to prevent squabbles from developing into antagonistic relationships. They promoted the values articulated in the code and motivated compliance. They demarcated— and patrolled—the boundaries of acceptable conduct. They had a high level of perceived legitimacy because they were members of the community that they policed and their policing role was not all encompassing. When they removed the purple hat, they returned to regular community life among their peers. The hat was a signifier of legitimacy and when it was taken off and pocketed, this indicated a change of status. A hat could be grabbed and worn by another, but the subterfuge would soon be revealed given the scale and intimacy of arrangements. These hats carried no prestige or power on the wrong heads.

The division of labor was clear. Prison staff were responsible for security. They guarded the gate, carried out the counts, locked and unlocked the dormitories, searched (cursorily) the visitors, carried the guns. The prisoners for their part were responsible for the negotiation of order within the compound. (The Eastham Unit was qualitatively different in that the BTs collaborated with staff to impose discipline and in return they received preferential treatment, including early release. There is an important distinction to be drawn between disciplinarians who do the bidding of the prison authorities and those who represent their peers.)

The order keepers were not out of place in a society where policing in rural areas is often carried out by local militias, appointed by the community leadership, that are loosely coordinated with regional and federal police and the army. According to the US Department of State (2020: 1): "Militia members serve as a bridge between the community and local police by providing information and enforcing rules." Furthermore, the existence and rootedness of community courts makes self-governance and self-policing in the prison more understandable and less contentious than it might be elsewhere. Customary and religious courts are recognized by Ethiopia's Constitution and, if both parties are agreeable, personal and family problems can be adjudicated in these forums; Muslim citizens may opt for a Sharia court (Blackburn and Matthews 2011: 169–71). This means that, outside the prison, people are closely involved in the resolution of their own conflicts. In the criminal justice arena, as elsewhere, self-reliance is a national characteristic.

Avoidance of the formal courts system is partly for reasons of affordability and partly on account of tradition. As Blackburn and Matthews (2011: 172) put it: "The customary courts of Ethiopia rely on many factors: respect for the authority of elders; kinship, honor, and accountability; and the importance of restoring community balance and familial harmony." Local dispute resolution and mediation by community elders are part of the criminal justice landscape outside the prison, where communal well-being is a priority, and this helps to explain why prisoners were content to allow the more senior among them to take charge of dispute resolution. Similarly, citizens can take on a role in policing and crime prevention in a community context (Di Nunzio 2014). Jackson et al. (2019) described the tension that exists in Ethiopia between an increasingly centralized state system and longstanding local approaches to justice where power is exercised according to tradition. The fact that hybrid scenarios exist outside the prison, with the state competing and cooperating with indigenous practices, makes it understandable that a blended approach would find acceptance within the prison.

In Isir Bet the prisoners' structures operated in cooperation with the official administration and this is illustrated in the sociogram (figure 4.7). Their code chimed with the institution's core values, which included respect for the rule of law, collaborative working, justice, loyalty, religious faith, and openness to change. The prison's stated aim was to facilitate rehabilitation so that prisoners could become law-abiding and productive citizens post-release.

Jackson et al. (2019: 131) described how elders "preside over crimes ranging from minor individual issues through to clan disputes over cattle raiding and even revenge killing, and the police frequently refer cases to them for decisions." There was a somewhat analogous process in Northern Ireland during the Troubles, where republican communities created their own policing structures to deal with antisocial behavior; this may have meant that republican prisoners were primed to organize, to self-govern, to resolve their own conflicts. The difference being that, in Ethiopia, policing is underdeveloped and not well centralized or overseen, whereas in Northern Ireland it was a very visible presence but not viewed as legitimate by a significant fraction of the population. In these societies, features of the external world penetrated the prisons. This was not the case in ADX Florence or the Eastham Unit, where the prisoners were not drawn from cohesive groups outside, meaning that the seeds of agreement did not exist inside and change required years of litigation.

The order keepers were elected as required by the dormitories. They were men serving longer sentences who had completed at least half of their time. When vacancies arose, the prisoners' leadership team asked the dormitories to put forward suitable candidates. These nominations were scrutinized by the head of the order keepers, who carried out a background check using his own records of transgressions. If the nomination was accepted the individual joined the team for as long as his services were required and he was content to continue in the role; there was no set term of office. They were assigned to a particular part of the prison where they spent the day. If a conflict developed they tried to mediate and resolve it there and then. If this was not possible they referred it to the head of the order keepers and his committee (three of them in total), who had their own office in the compound. If this committee could not resolve the matter they brought it to the prisoners' leadership team (again a triumvirate).

The advantages of being an order keeper were not pecuniary—there was no stipend, all they received for their trouble was one bar of soap per month, worth seven birr, which was no more than a token—but they had greater access to all areas of the compound, could spend longer with their visitors, and could sometimes liaise between prisoners and traders from outside who wished to buy their produce and there was a potential profit margin for them in such negotiations. The absence of formal rewards was compensated for by opportunities to benefit from the informal influence that came with their status and the associated freedom of movement. There was no obligation to act as an order keeper and if an individual preferred to prioritize education or work this was understood. There was no need to sacrifice income-generating opportunities to take on this role; a person could spend half their day at the loom and the other half wearing a purple hat. The head of the order keepers was elected for a two-year term, which could be renewed.

Before the introduction of the code there were eighty-five order keepers. Afterward sixty sufficed, despite an increase in the prison population. The order keepers outnumbered the prison guard force. They were unarmed. Before Chalew took over they carried a short plastic staff and he considered it a sign of the success of the code he pioneered that the number of order keepers could be reduced and their staves discarded. These developments made them less antagonistic and placed the emphasis on normative, and prudential, compliance rather than coercion. (There were two order keepers on the women's side; they did not wear purple hats.)

The prisoners in Isir Bet reported feeling safe. They were unsure what was meant when asked if some among them might be vulnerable by virtue of their offense status or personal characteristics. They thought a person could be at risk if he did not have an income-generating system or a family to visit him, but this was vulnerability to poverty and loneliness rather than to the threat of victimization. The head of the order keepers maintained a log of infringements. Violence was rare. During the three months preceding my third and final visit in 2018, there were six, eight, and twelve offenses respectively, an average of nine per month. In the month preceding my 2017 visit, seventeen offenses were recorded, the most serious of which were a fight that resulted in a blood injury, disrespect to the executive committee, and exercising outside of the permitted area. This is a small tally for a prison population of more than two thousand and suggests that those in custody did not have to fear for their bodily integrity. In the year before my first visit, there were no violent deaths (including suicides); the only fatality in the institution involved an elderly man suffering from consumption.

A dormitory fight between my second and third visits resulted in a death. Two (skinny) men were squabbling about who was fatter. They had been sleeping side by side. The dormitory's chairman ordered one of them to sleep on the floor. In the middle of the night the other party went to the toilet, found a piece of wood, and introduced it—with force—to his antagonist's head. Members of the dormitory seized the assailant, beat him, and tied him up. He was transferred to the worst possible sleeping position, en route to the urine buckets. In the morning the victim seemed fine and the matter was deemed to have been resolved satisfactorily. Several days later however he developed headaches and died within a month due to a brain clot. The perpetrator was sent forward to face a murder charge.

The absence of routine victimization was striking given that dormitory allocation was based on sentence length and did not take account of individual affiliations or attributes. As far as I could ascertain there were no argot terms for weak or dominant prisoners or for those who were held in disdain. The absence of a specialized language for prison violence suggests that the problem is not deeply entrenched. A comparative study of prison rape showed that if the terminology had not evolved, the associated behavior was unlikely to be embedded (O'Donnell 2004). Similarly, the absence of a disparaging or condemnatory term for those who fraternized with staff suggests that power relations were less fraught than elsewhere. The fact that prisoners played a role in their own governance might be read as a corruption of power. It is perhaps better viewed as a division of authority.

This is not to claim that no prison-specific vocabulary existed. There were some words unique to the context that indicated values and concerns. One was *mequres*, which meant food companion, a person with whom one shares one's plate. In Ethiopia, poverty is eating alone. Everybody wants *mequres*. Another word, exclusive to the prison, was *defoqa*. This described a person who slept on the ground in the dormitory. This is the fate of the tyro (or rule breaker), but everyone wishes to spend as little time as possible in this situation. Nobody wants *defoqa*.

Allocating Resources

The chairman of the prisoners and his two colleagues (vice-chairman and secretary) received a monthly stipend. The sums involved were not large, but there were ancillary advantages including freedom of movement, respect, prisoners paying for their meals, and deferring to them in the hope of preferential treatment when it came to resource allocation. Table 4.2 shows rates of pay for the various prison jobs. (To put these figures in context, the starting monthly salary for a prison guard was 1,500 birr and an unskilled male laborer earned 60 to 70 birr per day). Reflecting their status in a place where space was at a premium, the executive committee was designated its own office, with computers and printer, where it conducted its business in concert with the prison administration. Next to the office was the institution's library.

TABLE 4.2. The Going Rate (Birr per Month)

Executive committee	
Chairman	400
Vice-chairman	350
Secretary	300
Toilet cleaner	150
Dormitory guard	50–100
Food delivery to weavers	20 (per person)
Order keeper	Bar of soap

Note on exchange rate: During my visit to Ethiopia in December 2017, $1 was worth 27.30 birr.

The executive committee raised money though rental charges. A prisoner paid anything from 10 birr per month for a loom to 700 birr for a pool or billiards table (for access to which, in turn, others paid a fee per game). Shop owners and cooks paid rent also (e.g., barbers paid 250 to 300 birr). Allocation to looms (of which there were too few to meet the demand), setting of rents, and collection of dues, were all organized by the committee. These taxes were collected by a finance office. The profits of one of the prison shops (which sold raw materials to weavers as well as various other commodities) accrued to the committee; in the past this had been siphoned off by the prisoners' leaders, who became wealthy as a result.

When Chalew was elected chairman, tight financial controls were put in place, receipts were provided for any taxes paid, and stock purchased by the committee for its shop was properly accounted for. (Had he been less democratically minded and more preoccupied with personal enrichment it is possible that a less thoroughly integrated social world would have emerged despite the emphases on self-reliance and collectivism and the existence of extensive community contacts.) The committee's shop was rented out and this generated a substantial and predictable income. Under this prudent management the finances under the committee's control grew rapidly, to such an extent indeed that it could spend 567,000 birr on a pickup truck for the prison. The prisoners were proud of this contribution to the betterment of the institution that confined them. (It is impossible to imagine the men at any of the other case study institutions fundraising on behalf of their captors.)

As discussed above ("Constitutional Arrangements"), compliance had strong prudential and normative elements rather than being coerced. The group that issued commands was seen as legitimate (the prisoners elected them after all), and those subject to them obeyed dutifully (they drew up the code together after all and, having signed up to it, were honor bound to live by its dictates). It made sense to defer to the rules if one sought the opportunity to find work and to sleep in relative comfort. The obligation to obey seems to have become internalized and daily life was relatively harmonious. The final sentence in the code emphasized the importance of normative compliance: "We remind you that this rule and regulation is to be respected and thank you very much for your voluntary contribution." This contrasts with prisons where those who were to be controlled felt no urge to obey the regulations that were foisted upon them.

The formal transfer of power from keepers to kept was greater in Isir Bet than elsewhere. (In the H Blocks this transfer was officially denied.) To some extent, and reflecting the country's poverty, the prisoners in Isir Bet made a virtue of necessity. The state could not afford to provide adequate staffing levels or many material comforts so they had to fill the gaps themselves. The outcome was surprisingly benign. This was not only because of the personality of the key player (i.e., Chalew, the linchpin for the system, who was an inspirational chairman), but the widespread nature of customary dispute resolution and policing in Ethiopia also meant that prisoners were used to being self-reliant in these areas. The norms were carried into the prison from outside rather than having to be created anew.

Another reason for the success of the arrangements was the presence of a commander who was favorably disposed toward those in his charge taking responsibility for their day-to-day lives and who enjoyed an excellent working relationship with the prisoners' chairman. These factors contributed to an improvement in the quality of life for all concerned. The presence of a written code, which was signed up to after much discussion and consideration, also made a difference.

There were few uniformed staff, typically no more than thirty-five on duty at any one time, with additional clerical and administrative workers, and they seldom strayed into the compound. They entered in the morning to unlock and conduct a count and in the evening to count again and to lock the dormitory doors. Apart from this, they only stepped inside to accompany a man who was permitted to enter the female compound; (rarely) to escort a family member to a prisoner who, for reasons of ill health, was unable to come to the designated visiting area; to respond to requests for assistance after the nighttime lockup; or to buy something at a prison shop if it was better value there than in town. There was no official commissary and prisoners could trade just as they would outside, selling clothes and life's other necessities. One of the institution's shopkeepers is shown at his stall in figure 4.8. Haircuts—at five birr—were particularly cheap in the prison; this

Figure 4.8. A Prison Marketplace. Credit: Ian O'Donnell.

was appreciated by staff members who needed to eke out a modest salary. Staff were vulnerable to any contagious diseases carried by those in their custody (e.g., typhoid fever, tuberculosis, influenza), so it made sense from a public health perspective for them to try to maintain a level of social distancing.

Staff were not prevented or deterred from entering the compound by its residents but were fully occupied maintaining perimeter security, admitting visitors, providing escorts to and from court and the farm, and overseeing the busy circulating area between the prison gate and the entrance to the compound, which was traversed by prisoners going to school and workshops, by anyone entering and exiting, and by all vehicular traffic. Some of them carried firearms, and it was understood that they would shoot if anyone attempted to flee. Relations with staff were generally cordial. Insofar as I could establish, the prison's commander was seen as decent, fair, and progressive. He defined a good day as one when "no prisoner is hurt, the day is peaceful, and no prisoner goes hungry or thirsty," a modest but laudable aim.

Keeping in Touch

According to Art. 21(2) of the Constitution of the SNNPR, a prisoner "shall have the opportunity to communicate with, and to be visited by, his spouse or counsel, partner, close relative, friend, religious councilors, medical doctors and his legal advisor." The prison was a porous place. There were few restrictions on the number of visitors or how frequently they called, the only constraint being that, if a large number attended simultaneously, their allotted time had to be shortened. Visits took place every day apart from Wednesdays, which were set aside for public meetings. These involved anyone who wished to attend being addressed by the commander or an invited speaker who might provide an update on a relevant development in the criminal justice system.

Visits took place in the absence of direct staff supervision in a large hall where contact was permitted. The visiting hall was home to several market stalls where tourists would sometimes purchase souvenirs, the cost of which depended on their familiarity with local prices, their ability to haggle, and what they considered an acceptable balance between charity and extortion. The hall could accommodate up to four hundred people at a pinch and the duration of visits was adjusted to deal with demand. There was no booking system and visits lasted around thirty minutes, or longer if there was no line to get in. Visitors were given a sash to wear, which they surrendered on departure. They remained in a designated area under the supervision of the order keepers and were not permitted to stray inside the compound where the prisoners lived and worked. Visiting in Isir Bet was more permissive than elsewhere. Mekonnen (2012: 101) reported that in other prisons in the SNNPR physical contact with visitors was prohibited.

Despite the relative freedom within the compound, this was where the prisoner must remain when parents, partners, children, and friends departed. Like their counterparts everywhere, they were sequestered from the community whose laws they had violated. They were displaced citizens for the duration of their confinement. Visits were a challenge for families living outside the immediate vicinity. If a day's work had to be given up to allow the visit, and the distance to be covered on foot was substantial, and young children were brought along, this was an onerous commitment. If supplies had to be purchased and transported, this added to the burden. Making a visit could further impoverish the family. Not making it could further impoverish the prisoner.

According to Mekonnen (2012: 101): "In Ethiopia, bringing food to a partner in prison is seen as a 'woman's duty,' which husbands are reluctant to perform. And also, husbands of women who are imprisoned find it easier to remarry and start a new life when separated from their spouse, which results in the women being abandoned." In this way societal gender roles bear down more heavily on women who are deprived of their liberty. Furthermore, wives and girlfriends were more likely to visit than husbands and boyfriends (p. 105). The dislocation of being in a prison far from home was felt more keenly by the female prisoner (especially if she had children outside) who was starved of the affection and supplies that came with visits.

Homosexuality remains illegal in Ethiopia and public attitudes toward same-sex relations are almost universally condemnatory. A survey carried out by the Pew Research Center (2007: 117) found 97 percent agreement with the statement "Homosexuality is a way of life that should not be accepted by society." Intriguingly, the prisoners' code prohibited men from wearing women's clothing (Ch. 1, Art. 21.1), and anyone found engaging in same sex activity would lose their bed and face prosecution (Ch. 2, Art. 14). The fact that these activities were prohibited would suggest that they were a cause of consternation even if not prevalent.

With the exception of alcohol, drugs, tobacco, and cell phones, prisoners in Isir Bet had access to the same range of goods and services as would be available to them outside, including shops, barbers, legal and medical clinics, schools, and recreational activities such as pool, table football, and billiards. They dressed as they saw fit and possessed what they could afford to own and store. The code permitted them to keep one hundred birr on their person (Ch. 2, Art. 18) to cover day-to-day expenditure. There was insufficient space for team sports, although short games of five-a-side football were played some evenings on a patch of land between the part of the compound where the dormitories were located and the area accommodating the schools. Figure 4.9 gives a sense of the institution's spatial ordering.

The institution was home to a cohort of talented painters (O'Donnell 2019b). From early morning until late afternoon they mixed paints, stretched canvas onto frames, and sought inspiration from the work of

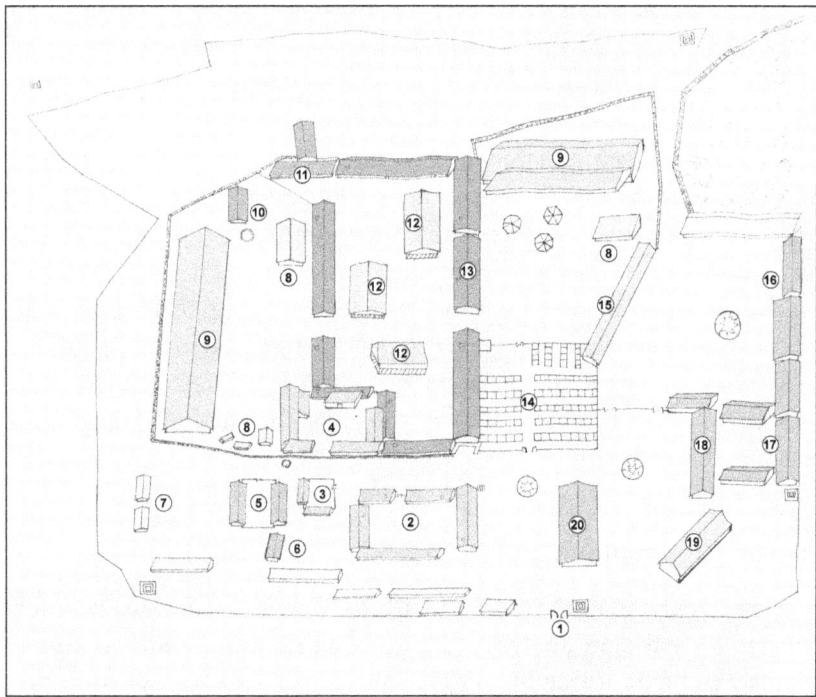

Figure 4.9. Sketching Prison Life. Map Key: 1. entrance; 2. women's compound; 3. clinic; 4. kindergarten; 5. kitchen; 6. workshop; 7. animal pen; 8. place of worship; 9. weaving hut; 10. barber; 11. ablutions block; 12. meal shelter; 13. dormitory; 14. visiting hall; 15 prisoner committee's office; 16. primary school; 17. secondary school; 18. art school; 19. administration; 20. art gallery. Credit: Tesfamichael Yohannes.

others and their own imaginations. Their art was characterized by spontaneity, color, emotion, and the human drama. There were opportunity costs associated with these endeavors, as every day spent painting was a day when money could not be earned working as a weaver, fishing-net maker, or service provider of one kind or another. While the painters benefitted from the occasional commission, their activity derived from something deeper than the potential profit associated with sporadic sales.

During the day, when the dormitories were vacated, their occupants were free to move about, to work, and to socialize. They could choose where, how, and with whom to spend their time. Friendship groups could take meals together, sit and talk, walk around the compound and, depending on the nature of their employment, perhaps even work side by side. They were not reduced to weak, dependent creatures who must ask permission to do anything. They were not caught up in a web of rules that had been designed by the authorities to control every aspect of their behavior and where decisions could be made about them, but rationales withheld. The loss of autonomy was not as pronounced as for their counterparts in the US and UK. There was no enforced deference or childlike helplessness. Even so, they had to return to their dormitories at the prescribed time and could not leave before the morning unlock. The prison *injera* was served at the same time every day so, if they were not buying their food from one of the cafés, they had to arrange their schedule accordingly.

Lessons from Ethiopia

I am not applying European standards to African prisons, which might lead to a dystopian analysis, emphasizing failures to meet minimal human rights requirements, especially in the crowded dormitories. I found that while the conditions of confinement were poor, the lived experience was rich. Many of the men—but not, as alluded to above ("Women and Children"), the women—followed active, purposeful lives. The opposite is often the case in prisons in the Global North.

Subpar prison conditions do not imply an impoverished social life. Isir Bet was harmonious and convivial despite the crowding and poverty. ADX Florence was life stripped to the bone, despite the generous resources available to the BOP. Consider that the 2020 budget for the BOP came to $7.78 billion (US Department of Justice 2020). This was more than half of the total planned expenditure for the Ethiopian government in the same year of 476 billion birr ($12.85 billion at exchange rate on October 9, 2020), which in addition to covering prisons, courts, and police dealt with transportation, education, debt repayments, health, defense, irrigation, agriculture, and all of the costs associated with the infrastructure of a rapidly growing state (Cepheus Research and Analytics 2020: 11). Highly integrated prisoner societies tend to have dependable community supports, whether because they are political and have an organization behind them (like the H Blocks), or they need family to keep in touch for survival (like Isir Bet). This helps them to withstand significant deprivations.

I was repeatedly struck by the ease with which prisoners got on with their lives, the air of industry and productivity, and the freedom of movement within the compound. There was full (respectful) contact during visits, the prisoners could see the sky and breathe fresh air, they were close to town and could occasionally avail of a day out (subject to being in a position to pay the accompanying staff's wages). They hoped for a pardon and had a reasonable chance of success in this regard. Yilma and Roberts (2019: 320) referred to a report from a government minister in September 2018 that noted how "in the previous two years, approximately 40,000 prisoners had been released in this way by executive decree." This is a sizable number in a country where the daily average prison population in 2010 was 105,000 (p. 319).

While not wishing to paint an excessively rosy picture, what I saw in Isir Bet was a long way from the lethargy, despair, and cruelty that can characterize prisons in the US, and from the horrors of arbitrary detention, torture, and extrajudicial executions that are too often the response to political opposition in Ethiopia.

In a report on Ethiopia, the Special Rapporteur on Prisons and Conditions of Detention in Africa (2004: 38) observed:

> The relationship between the prisoners and the prison authorities is good. There is an impression that prisoners believe that the conditions under which they are living is the best the government can offer and as such are contented with their conditions. Maybe this belief is informed by the general level of poverty in the country. Prisoners are also under the impression that whatever improvements that can be made to their living condition is not within the competence of the local prison administration but rather the government.
>
> ... there were very little complaints about the prison administration. The majority of the complaints—delays in trial, pardon, clemency, no mattresses etc were directed against government.
>
> ... the prisoners are generally happy with the way they are being treated. One reason for this it would seem, is the fact that the prisoners are virtually responsible for their wellbeing while in prison. This is done through the prisoners' committees.

In other words, in addition to having a great deal of autonomy in how they dealt with their own affairs, the prisoners appreciated that, in a country where poverty was deep, expectations had to be trimmed accordingly. I would concur with the special rapporteur's assessment. The Eastham Unit and ADX Florence were different on both scores: the men they incarcerated had little autonomy and they lived in the world's biggest economy, so their treatment had more to do with policy choices than limited resources. The implied message is clear.

Some of the men held in Isir Bet earned considerably more than their counterparts at liberty and most tried to do about the same. Because it was a cash economy they could convert their income into goods that they consumed inside or sent outside. Things were very different for the wealthy prisoner in ADX Florence who, at best, might risk hoarding candy from the commissary. Other than a young child, perhaps, no one would be considered rich in a community setting for having several bags of candy.

The peace established between custodians and captives—and among captives—is always vulnerable to a descent into turbulence. Isir Bet descended into a period of instability in July 2018, two months after my final visit. One man was shot trying to escape and died later in the hospital. Another was killed by his fellows. The local police were called to reinforce prison staff and they used tear gas to subdue large crowds of stone-throwing prisoners. There were multiple stabbings, fires were set, and property was destroyed, including the prison's health center, which had been a boon in a place where HIV/AIDS and other serious illnesses are common. Similar protests took place at other prisons around the country (Abiye 2018).

This disturbance did not flow from an attempt by staff to (re)assert their authority. As we have seen, the degree of self-government was high, and it is unlikely that, even if it deemed it desirable, the state could afford to provide sufficient finances to enable the levels of surveillance and control that are common in prisons across the Global North. Allowing prisoners to organize their own affairs was less an abdication of responsibility by the authorities than a pragmatic response to limited resources. What then explained the riotous behavior?

It had its roots in political developments that were external to the prison. A newly elected prime minister, and future Nobel Peace Prize winner, Abiy Ahmed, was introducing radical reforms across the public service, and prisoners' hopes of a general amnesty were suddenly raised. Staff shared the view that wide-scale releases were imminent and were congratulating potential beneficiaries on the imminent restoration of their freedom. When they were equally suddenly dashed by a public announcement that early release would be limited to those who had been jailed for opposing the government, widespread frustration was translated into a wave of violence. This is an example of delegitimation (see box 1.1), in that the prisoners withdrew their compliance because of a perception that the state had reneged on a promise to grant a general amnesty. Even with a code, then, the social system of the prison was not immutable; it could not withstand a shock of such magnitude. Peace is fragile in prisons and hope can be evanescent; neither is guaranteed.

Another factor may have been the resignation of Chalew Gebino several months previously, having led the compound for five years in close cooperation with the prison's commander. That he was no longer in a position of leadership meant that a potential restraining force was absent. During his tenure, Chalew worked hard to maintain the prison's equilibrium. The détente that followed the breakdown in order required careful navigation by all concerned. A large number of pardons to celebrate the Ethiopian New Year on September 11, 2018, came too late to prevent the carnage but may have done something to dispel any lingering sense of bitterness and despair. Stability returned. Time will tell at what price and whether the prison's carceral geometry was affected (see figure 1.1). It is possible to imagine a shift (downward) in integration and a corresponding shift (upward) in regulation (although any movement in this direction is likely to be muted in light of prevailing financial constraints).

Coda

Tertsakian (2008) studied life in Rwanda's prisons after the 1994 genocide, where it was not uncommon to be detained for a decade without trial, and in some cases without even knowing what charges had been laid. Progress was slothful on account of corruption, bureaucratic inertia, an enormous backlog of cases, and indifference to the plight of the *génocidaires*. The scale of incarceration was greater in Rwanda than in

Ethiopia, the crowding was more intense, the conditions were inferior (some prisoners spent so long standing in muddy yards that they developed trench foot and their legs were amputated; others died where they lay), the alleged crimes were graver, and the socioeconomic mix was more varied. Notwithstanding these differences I would concur wholeheartedly with her observation: "The world of the prisons is held together by a dense web of contradictions. It is a world of extreme suffering, misery, egotism, harshness and despair. It is also a world of energy, hope, creativity, humour and inspiration. Amidst the bodies squashed up against each other, the ragged clothes, the hollow faces, the stench of sweat and dirty water, there is calm beauty and there is dignified resilience. The whole of humanity can be found there, living, breathing, thinking, remembering, acting, waiting and dying" (p. 17). Even in the most appalling circumstances, then, people whose liberty has been denied can find ways to organize their lives that allow most to survive and some to thrive.

5

ADX Florence, Colorado

You have the right to expect that as a human being you will be treated respectfully, impartially, and fairly by all personnel.
—Federal Bureau of Prisons, 2008, *Admission and Orientation Handbook*, Attachment D, p. 2, para. 1

A person's sense of self is created and maintained through interaction with others. How we see ourselves reflected in our relationships helps us to understand who we are and what makes us unique. Intimate attachments are necessary for individual flourishing and even the most robust identity needs reinforcement from time to time to prevent it from becoming undermined. In isolation, without the mirroring effect of others, the personality—what Cooley (1902: 184) memorably termed the "looking-glass self"—can threaten to splinter. This is terrifying, especially when not anticipated. For the person whose sense of self is fragile at the outset, the cauterizing of relationships is especially troubling.

We require the steadying effects of other people to be fully human. We need to be reminded that we exist, that there is a place for us, and that we have a residual value as human beings that can never be extirpated no matter what we have done or endured. It is not just the presence of others that is necessary—all captives have their captors—but the proximity of allies and confidants. Solitary confinement is inhumane because it mocks and degrades human relations, nowhere more emphatically than at ADX Florence.

Meaningful engagement is difficult to attain when prisoners are only entitled to "expect" respectful, impartial, and fair treatment (an expectation that, as we shall see, is often dashed), and when respect, impartiality, and fairness do not preclude extreme harshness (which is integral to the arrangements in place at ADX Florence). In fact, it might be argued that the attempt at pared-back equity encapsulated in the chapter's epigraph rules out any softening of an often brutal regime. It pushes mercy to the margins. Transparency and consistency in administration have human consequences that are not always benign.

The promotion of impersonal, unyielding even-handedness signals a profound rupture from the ebullient confidence expressed by the National Prison Association, forerunner of the American Correctional Association (ACA), in the principles promulgated at its first congress in 1870, several of which are excerpted in box 5.1. The emphasis here is on the inculcation of hope and self-improvement, and the avoidance of degradation and coercion—noble sentiments for prison systems whenever and wherever they are found.

Box 5.1. Correctional Confidence. From Wines (1871: 541–43)

II. [T]he supreme aim of prison discipline is the reformation of criminals, not the infliction of vindictive suffering.

IV. Since hope is a more potent agent than fear, it should be made an ever-present force in the minds of prisoners.

V. The prisoner's destiny should be placed, measurably, in his own hands; he must be put into circumstances where he will be able, through his own exertions, to continually better his own condition.

XII. A system of prison discipline, to be truly reformatory, must gain the will of the convict. He is to be amended; but how is this possible with his mind in a state of hostility?

XIV. The prisoner's self-respect should be cultivated to the utmost.... There is no greater mistake in the whole compass of penal discipline, than its studied imposition of degradation as a part of punishment. Such imposition destroys every better impulse and aspiration. It crushes the weak, irritates the strong, and indisposes all to submission and reform. It is trampling where we ought to raise.

XV. In prison administration, moral forces should be relied upon, with as little admixture of physical force as possible, and organized persuasion be made to take the place of coercive restraint, the object being to make upright and industrious freemen, rather than orderly and obedient prisoners.

The ACA (2019) has periodically updated these standards and claims to cleave to "the spirit of our founders by ensuring that these principles continue to guide sound corrections practices, make our philosophy and aims clear, and inspire cooperation and support from leaders of local, state, national and international communities and organizations." The principles are so feebly enunciated in ADX Florence (as indeed they were in the Eastham Unit) that it is difficult to see how they illuminate practice in any meaningful way. ADX Florence epitomizes the shrinking scale of ambition for prisons, and the truncation of aims, that have characterized recent years (O'Donnell 2016). At its most extreme, the modern experience of incarceration is harm unmitigated by benevolence. It is what remains when optimism has evaporated and been replaced by institutional despair tinged with profound indifference.

As previously noted, each epigraph sets out a statement of purpose that pertained during the decade of interest, and then contrasts this with the reality. In ADX Florence, minimal expectations were the order of the day, but the intrinsically disrespectful nature of solitary confinement meant they remained elusive. This is an example of prison life where an extremely high level of regulation is combined with a vanishingly low level of integration (see figure 1.1). The time frame is 2001 to 2011, when John Jay "Jack" Powers languished in the prison's control unit.

"Alcatraz of the Rockies"

ADX Florence is where prisoners are exiled within the BOP. The highest-security prison in the United States, it opened in 1994 to replace United States Penitentiary (USP) Marion, which had replaced USP Alcatraz. It is for those deemed to be violent, predatory, disruptive, or escape prone. A person may be sent there if his crime or profile is deemed to create a sufficient security risk. For this reason, some terrorists have been assigned to the facility in the absence of a record of institutional misconduct (Amnesty International 2014: 18). It also holds a small number of men from state systems who are believed to present a risk that cannot be managed locally. This is purported to be administrative rather than punitive segregation, although the niceties of this distinction must be lost on many who find themselves isolated there, for whom the grind of daily existence is not alleviated by the choice of nomenclature.

Dowker and Good (1993: 97) described how the location selected for the prison was an "economically devastated community," which raised the funds to purchase the land upon which the facility would be built in order to provide employment opportunities and stimulate economic development. One local poll indicated an approval rating of 97 percent for the initiative and the decision to commence construction was greeted with widespread jubilation. The fact that the prison was to be located close to a former uranium-processing facility, the waste from which contaminated the local air and water supply, did not stop the development (Perkinson 1994: 126–27). Despite the efforts that residents made to secure the prison, its economic benefits were less than they had hoped for (Williams 2011: 47, 86–87).

The legitimacy gulf at ADX Florence is too wide to bridge. Those selected for this treatment—believed to be the worst of the worst—have come to the end of the line and are deemed to pose an uncommonly high threat and to deserve the tightest control, regardless of how they might perceive the situation. Robert Hood, warden of the facility from 2002 to 2005, described it in a television documentary as "a clean version of hell" (*60 Minutes* 2007). Garrett Linderman, who had served time there, was interviewed for the same program from his cell in a prison in Washington State. He described ADX Florence as "the perfection of isolation, painted pretty."

Table 5.1 shows that the population of ADX Florence stands apart in terms of offense seriousness, age, sentence length, and the extent to which its members are at odds with other prisoners. In addition to a preponderance of lifers, the average determinate sentence was much longer than elsewhere in the BOP (twenty-nine years compared with ten years). Once people arrive, they stay for quite a while. A snapshot in November 2013 found the average length of time in ADX Florence was 1,376 days (CNA 2014: 58; this contrasted with 76 days at special housing units operated in other locations by the BOP). This is a glaring repudiation of the UN prohibition on any period of solitary confinement in excess of 15 consecutive days (United Nations 2015: Rules 43 and 44). Fewer than one in ten of the men at ADX Florence are held in step-down units where they enjoy a limited amount of social interaction, having already experienced prolonged and extreme isolation in general population.

TABLE 5.1. Older and Bolder. Percentages may not total 100 due to rounding. Source: CNA (2014: 52–57)

	ADX Florence (%)	Other BOP facilities (%)
Gender		
Male	100	93
Female	0	7
Age		
Up to 35 yrs	19	41
36 yrs +	81	60
Race		
White	59	60
Black	38	37
Other characteristics	4	4
Offense (selected)		
Homicide/aggravated assault	32	2
Drugs	12	47
Burglary/larceny/robbery	31	7
Other characteristics		
Life sentence	39	2
Gang member	57	8
Requires separation from specific other inmates	96	40

Perkinson (1994: 124–25) described the prison the year it opened in the following terms:

> an imposing triangle of X-shaped cell blocks, surrounded by double 20-foot fences interwoven with 10 rows of razor wire. Two perimeter roads, 8,000-watt lights, microwave sensors, anti-escape trip wires, and six sniper towers separate the ADX from the other facilities [that share the 640-acre site]. Prisoners are unlikely ever to reach this dead space since the prison walls themselves serve as the primary perimeter, containing the limited recreation areas and everything else. Guards and visitors enter the prison through a tunnel.

Figure 5.1. A Place of Despair, Seen from the Air. Credit: Esri World Imagery.

Figure 5.1 shows this isolated (and isolating) fortress from the air. If the US is an outlier in terms of penal severity, then ADX Florence is the outlier's outlier.

It is worth noting at this juncture that the numbers in solitary confinement are dropping across the US (Correctional Leaders Association and Arthur Liman Center for Public Interest Law 2020: 89). There seems to have been a shift from seeing isolation as the solution to prison security to regarding it as a problem in its own right that needs to be addressed. The national trend is reflected in ADX Florence, where numbers were fairly stable between 2004 and 2014, averaging 425 (CNA 2014: 20), but by 2021 had fallen to 332. This is one-quarter of 1 percent of the federal prison population (Federal Bureau of Prisons 2021b).

ADX Florence is defined by the stripping back of human engagement to the point of virtual invisibility. It is also characterized by a lack of external scrutiny. These factors are not unrelated. Prior to 2002 some journalists had regular access to the facility and Amnesty International visited in 2001, but from January 2002 to May 2007 every media request for a tour of the facility or an interview with a prisoner was denied (Amnesty International 2014: 42, note 13). A restricted tour was permitted to selected media outlets in September 2007 following a brief visit by Human Rights Watch several months previously, and then the shutters came down again. Since 2013, the UN Special Rapporteur on Torture and Other Cruel, Inhuman or Degrading Treatment or Punishment has made several requests for an invitation to visit, but these have not been granted. Similarly, my own application in October 2019 was peremptorily denied.

For two days in April 2017 the District of Columbia Corrections Information Council (2018) toured the control unit, the special housing unit (SHU), one general population unit, and two step-down units but was denied access to Range 13 (see below, "Shrinking the Shrunk") and did not visit the special security unit (SSU). The SSU was excluded from an independent review of restrictive housing (CNA 2014: 19). There have been visits by arms of the state that focused on specific aspects of ADX Florence's functioning such as mental health (Office of the Inspector General 2017), compliance with the Prison Rape Elimination Act (Bradshaw 2016), and adherence to policies relating to segregated housing (US Government Accountability Office 2013).

Home on the Range

ADX Florence can house up to 490 men in nine units. The cells in the general population units, where most are held, measure eighty-seven square feet with a sally port (vestibule) measuring another seventeen square feet. They have double sets of sliding metal doors (an inner one with bars and an outer one of solid steel, known as a boxcar door).

The double doors increase the isolation because prisoners do not have a clear view of what is going on outside their cells. Meals are pushed through a slot in the inner door and consumed alone.

The cells are arranged in a linear design down one side of a hallway (called the unit range), which prevents their occupants from seeing each other. The solid exterior door has a window (five inches by eighteen inches) that looks out onto the range and there is another window, similarly oriented, to the side of the door measuring forty-eight inches by twelve inches. There is a window in the external wall (five inches by thirty-eight inches). There is a sink, toilet, and automated shower, all made from stainless steel. The shower stall measures three feet by three feet. A concrete slab serves as a bed upon which a thin mattress is placed. A concrete stool, desk and shelf complete the furnishings.

In an official response to a petition to the Inter-American Commission on Human Rights, Sullivan (2016) described how everyone who was not in disciplinary segregation had a thirteen-inch color television in his cell with twenty-four-hour access to a selection of fifty-two broadcast channels, radio stations, and closed-circuit institutional programming such as psychology, religious services, and education. The televisions and outside channels were paid for out of profits made on sales from the inmate commissary (US Department of Justice 2016: 40). One of the channels utilized to provide in-house bulletins also showed the date and time.

In a further comment on in-cell entertainment the District of Columbia Corrections Information Council (2018: 32) reported: "Inmates also have access to movies from Netflix and DVDs, which are restricted to PG-rated and presented through the CCTV. . . . The Recreation Department has two channels that play music and present wellness information and programs, including programs for step aerobics and yoga." The image of hardened criminals, supposedly the worst of the worst of the US penal system, sitting in their isolation cells watching children's movies, or doing step aerobics, is as preposterous as it is depressing. It is difficult to imagine a greater contrast with the buoyantly optimistic principles set out in box 5.1. Or, indeed, with prisons elsewhere. In Isir Bet, for example, inmates were free to watch whatever was available on the satellite subscription package availed of by their dormitory. European football and US crime dramas were popular.

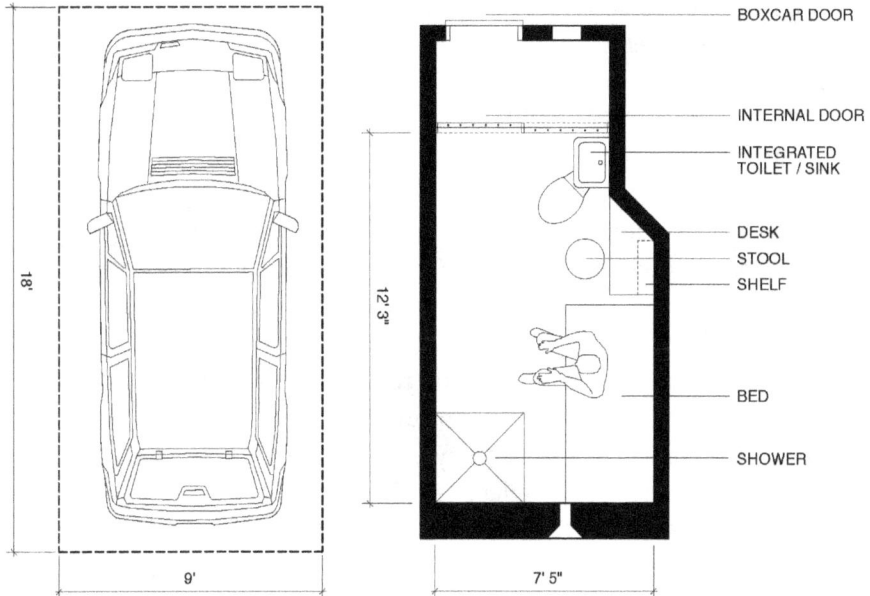

Figure 5.2. Parked in Solitary.

The facility's former warden Robert Hood told the *New York Times Magazine* that he used to inform prisoners who complained about the starkness of their surroundings: "This place is not designed for humanity" (cited in Binelli 2015). The parameters of daily living are almost unfathomably tight. Consider that a standard car parking space in the US measures 9 feet by 18 feet. This is almost double the living area for anyone held at ADX Florence (162 square feet compared to 87 square feet; see figure 5.2) and the occupants of these tiny dwellings spend at least twenty-two hours a day there, often for years, sometimes for decades. Those who support this method of penal treatment would do well to think about the spatial dimensions of confinement next time they pull up at the grocery store. That these cramped conditions exceed the ACA minimum standard of 80 square feet for a restrictive housing cell (US Department of Justice 2016: 389) is a sad reflection of the lack of ambition that characterizes penal treatment.

The men in general population get ten hours out of their cells per week for exercise: two hours per day for five days (CNA 2014: 195). This alternates between indoors and outdoors. Exercise is taken indoors in a windowless cell (14 feet by 10 feet) with a single chin-up bar that is euphemistically referred to as a "gym," or outdoors in an individual cage (20 feet by 12 feet) in the recreation yard, accurately described as a "dog run." They are allowed to play with a football outdoors and a handball indoors (solo, of course). The District of Columbia Corrections Information Council (2018: 33) described the outdoor recreation space for the general population as "a large, deep, concrete area with a caged ceiling and five individual cages for each unit. . . . Inmates are confined to separate cages but are able to see and speak with a limited number of other inmates."

Each month they may receive up to five social visits. If family and friends can afford to make the trip (unlikely given the prison's remote location), there is no contact as they are separated by a plexiglass barrier and communicate using a telephone. Every time they leave their cells they are placed in handcuffs, leg irons, and a belly chain ("Martin chain") and accompanied by two guards. A black box covers the handcuffs to prevent tampering (CNA 2014: 176). The hand restraints are removed after the individual is secured in the non-contact visiting booth; the leg irons remain in place.

Shrinking the Shrunk

There are even more restrictive environments than general population. While the cell layout is the same in the SHU and control unit as it is in general population, outdoor recreation is taken alone, with no one else visible, in a small roofless bunker (see figure 5.3). The outdoor recreation area for Range 13, a four-cell wing of the SHU, accessed via a remotely operated door adding yet another layer of depersonalization, was described by one of its regular users as "a concrete pit surrounded by high, featureless walls on all sides. It felt like being inside of a deep, empty swimming pool. I couldn't see any of the mountains, even though I knew they had to be close by. I also couldn't see a single tree, blade of grass, or any sign of nature" (Silverstein 2011: para. 189). Thomas Silverstein arrived at ADX Florence in July 2005, having already spent twenty-two years in solitary confinement, and he was placed on Range 13. There was one other person held there at the time and Silverstein was relieved to be able to shout occasional comments to him. However,

Figure 5.3. Recreation Yard (Control Unit). Credit: *Bacote v. Federal Bureau of Prisons.*

even this level of "conversation" was deemed unacceptable, and a solid steel door was erected in the hallway so that previously muffled sounds became inaudible.

Silverstein had been placed on a "no human contact" order after a lethal attack on a corrections officer in USP Marion on October 22, 1983 (O'Donnell 2014: 158). Between then and his death on May 11, 2019, aged sixty-seven, he spent 12,985 consecutive days (thirty-five years, six months, and nineteen days) in solitary confinement, interrupted only by an interlude when he was at large for a few days in USP Atlanta in 1987, in the context of a riot during which other prisoners opened his cell. He never ate a meal in company, touched another human being with affection, shared his recreation time, or idled an hour away in companionable silence. The last fourteen years of this stretch were spent at ADX Florence. Silverstein holds the record for long-term isolation in the US federal prison system. Hopefully it will never be broken.

Range 13 cells are slightly different to those occupied by men on the control unit or among the general population in that restraint

Figure 5.4. Cell (Range 13). Credit: Federal Bureau of Prisons.

points are fixed to the bed and adjacent wall (prisoners in other parts of the facility must be removed from their cells if they are to be tied down), there is a different floorplan (the toilet is positioned beside the shower), alternative fenestration, and shelves that are fabricated from metal rather than concrete. Figure 5.4 shows these forbidding internal arrangements.

Edgar Pitts (2020), a control unit veteran, described how being tied to the bed was physically and psychologically damaging:

> To be four-pointed is to be rendered helpless; to be four-pointed for no reason is to be rendered hopeless. It is the ultimate enforcement of the power of those who have been given control over us. . . . To be four-pointed is to be strapped by the hands and feet to a bed, then left in that helpless condition to think and hear your thoughts reverberate in your head, to worry and to turn your worries into a reality, to get angry and to be consumed by your anger, to feel sorrow and to feel cornered by your sorrow, to urinate and defecate on yourself, and to

be rendered hopeless. This is more than a time-out for adults. This is a method to break and control the human spirit.

Every time a man on Range 13 lies on his bed, he is reminded of this possibility.

Each cell has a light with three settings (dim, medium, and bright) that its inhabitant can adjust as required. The lights in the hallway are permanently on, so the cells are never fully dark given the windows in the door and wall. Silverstein (2011: para. 182) noted that the sally port was constantly illuminated when he was on Range 13 so even if he dimmed his cell lights it was far from dark.

The control unit and Range 13 are the most restrictive parts of this most restrictive of prisons. There is no contact with other prisoners and only minimal contact with staff. The control unit provides housing for men who are considered to be unable to function in a more permissive environment without posing a threat to others or to the institution. They are assigned there "for fixed terms for serious offences, usually committed in other prisons, after a hearing which is similar to a disciplinary hearing ... and may be extended if further offences are committed while the prisoner is in the Unit" (Amnesty International 2014: 27). Jack Powers (see figure 5.5) was sent to the control unit for sixty months for escaping but ended up spending twice as long. Prisoners have access to television and the same in-cell programs as are available to those on general population units. But they get less exercise: seven hours per week. Three to five staff members escort each person to recreation and shake down his cell every time. What is available to them when allowed outside consists of a half dozen "narrow, empty concrete spaces" (District of Columbia Corrections Information Council 2018: 33).

Men in the SHU, who are sent there for indiscipline, are denied televisions and radios and the time spent there is generally shorter than on other units, although it can be extended for repeated infractions. They get five hours out of cell per week (US Department of Justice 2016: 45). Their outdoor recreation area is similar to that available to the men in general population but with the difference that only one person from the SHU is allowed outside at a time. Anyone in the SHU on administrative detention has a television but is limited to in-house programming.

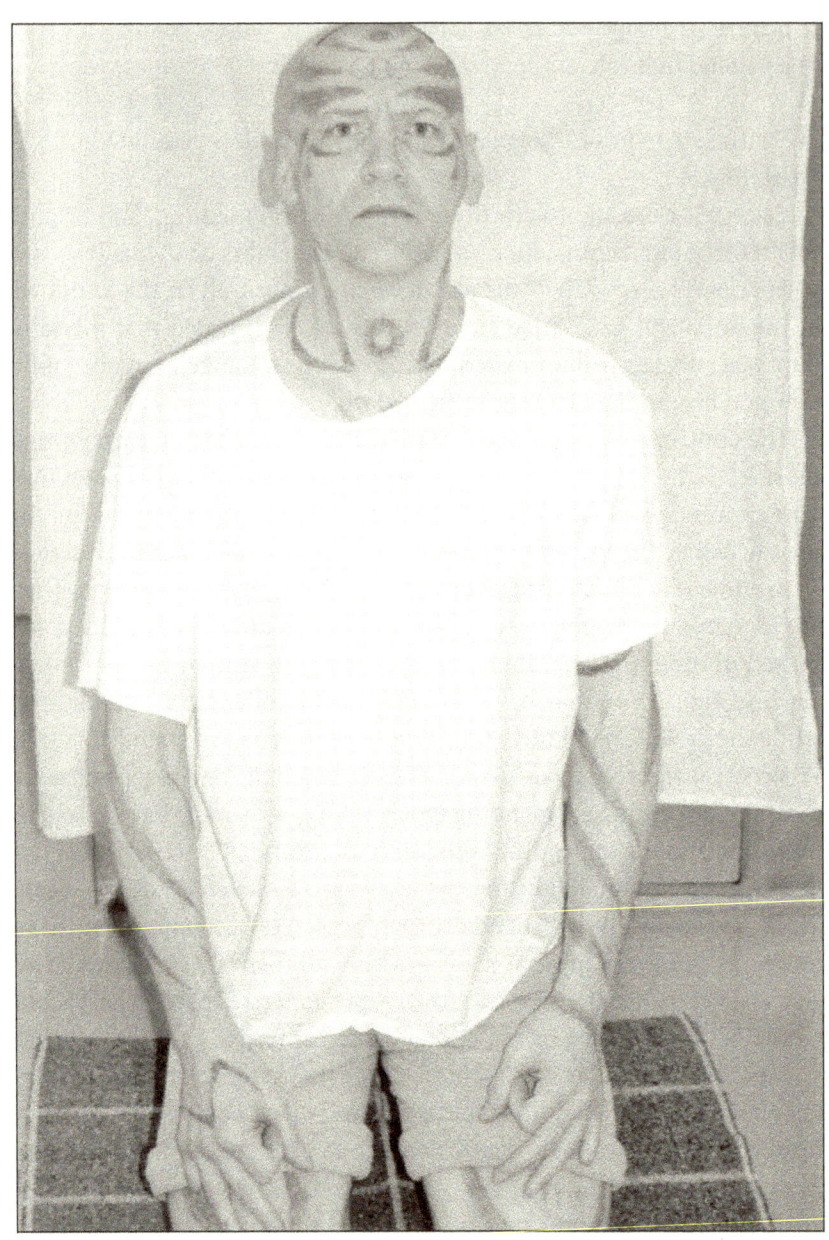

Figure 5.5. Jack Powers in 2012. Credit: Jack Powers.

According to the District of Columbia Corrections Information Council (2018: 32), control unit residents get two fifteen-minute phone calls per month and those in the general population get up to three. All calls are monitored and they must be paid for. The cost for what is invariably a long-distance call is $3.45. For those who can afford it, this is too little time to maintain family ties. Telephone access can be revoked as a punishment. Literate prisoners can send and receive letters. All incoming and outgoing correspondence is inspected.

Men on the control unit are allowed to receive up to five visits per month (US Government Accountability Office 2013: 9). Full restraints (hands and legs) remain in place for the duration of any visit even though the prisoner is held in a secure booth without any opportunity for physical contact. It is hard to imagine that he poses a threat to his visitor, making the level of chained immobilization seem greatly disproportionate. What would be seen as exceptional measures elsewhere have become normalized in ADX Florence.

As for the dress code, the regulations were prudishly specific during the decade of interest:

> All visitors entering the institution for a visit will be appropriately attired. Visitors may not wear shorts, mini-skirts, sheer or tight fitting clothing, excessively short or low cut clothing, backless clothing, halter tops, or sleeveless clothing. Dresses, blouses or other apparel of a suggestive or revealing nature may not be worn. Female visitors must also wear a wireless brassiere and undergarments. (Federal Bureau of Prisons 2011a: 3)

The requirement to "wear a wireless brassiere and undergarments" was removed in 2014, but all the other strictures remained in place (Federal Bureau of Prisons 2014a: 1).

Contrast this regime with Isir Bet, where access was easy and contact was uninhibited but respectful, and even the H Blocks, one of the highest-security prisons in Europe, where there was a lot more laxity for men who posed a serious threat to the state. Indeed, the majority of republican activists in the H Blocks who had served more than twelve years were allowed home for five days at Christmas and for a couple of weeks during the summer so that they could maintain, and nurture, family and community ties (Gormally et al. 1993: 102). They never failed to return to custody, whereupon they dedicated themselves to escaping. That extending such a privilege to the terrorist prisoners in ADX Florence would be considered breathtakingly unlikely (to say nothing of reckless) says a great deal about how they are viewed.

Distorted Thinking

The closest contact that prisoners in the general population could have was if their outdoor recreation time happened to coincide with that of a friend, their cages were adjacent, and they could surreptitiously arrange a "finger shake" by simultaneously pressing the metal mesh around their enclosures so that their flesh was in contact. This could not be done openly for fear of being cited for a Code 409 violation (see table 5.4) and even this possibility was removed from those on the control unit or SHU, who always exercised alone. A caring touch is emolliative and reparative. It is part of being human, of demonstrating companionship and empathy. To rule it out is gratuitously callous. This is a stripped-back existence, by any measure.

Prisoners could attempt to converse with the occupant of a contiguous cell by blowing the water down the pipes of their sink or shower and then speaking into the drain, literally plumbing the depths of conversation. They could also talk via the ventilation system. Yelling through the vents to a neighbor who remains out of sight is not the kind of communication that promotes contented companionship. By its nature it is conversation without adornment, a way of transmitting gobbets of information rather than allowing a free flow of thoughts and ideas and building rapport. Even speaking through the drains was a limited device due to toilets flushing and showers running and guards relocating prisoners if they felt they were developing neighborly relationships.

Contact with staff was terse, tense, and ritualized. Food trays were delivered and collected. Handcuffs, leg irons, and Martin chains were secured in place. Post and commissary items were delivered. Head counts were conducted. There was virtually no casual communication. Why would correctional officers engage in social niceties with the worst of the worst? These were men to be addressed with chains and batons rather than kindness and banter. They were foes to be vanquished rather than allies to be recruited. Some, of course, lived up to their reputations, confirming and consolidating the official view of them as desperate and dangerous. Verbal communication was short and stylized. Written communication comprised disciplinary reports or responses to grievances raised and remedies applied for. There was none of the cut and thrust, the chat and backchat, that can give a conversation spice. By even the most flexible measure this does not constitute meaningful engagement.

Lack of social contact has additional repercussions for anyone whose religious faith demands congregation. IRA men went to Sunday Mass in the H Blocks and weekly services were packed to capacity in Isir Bet. The spiritual needs of Christians and Jews were catered for at the Eastham Unit. But in ADX Florence, believers pray alone in their cells. This is particularly problematic for Muslim men who are required to attend Friday prayers to worship together and listen to a sermon. The only exception is if they are traveling, a bitter irony at ADX Florence, where their sphere of movement is so tightly circumscribed that a few feet back and forth in their solitary cells is as much of an expedition as can be hoped for.

Despite the foregoing, the BOP does not recognize the term "solitary confinement" or acknowledge that anyone in its custody is so confined, preferring to think of "restrictive housing" (Office of the Inspector General 2017: 15). As far as the BOP is concerned, solitary confinement does not exist because: "BOP staff frequently visit inmates held in single-bunked cells alone . . . regularly interact with inmates during their required monitoring rounds and while providing meals" (US Government Accountability Office 2013: 12). The façade that solitary confinement does not exist is maintained despite the fact that men spend at least twenty-two hours per day in single cells, some for many years.

According to Sullivan (2016: 20): "Inmates at ADX have many opportunities for social interaction and thus are not held in 'solitary confinement' as that term is commonly used." For Sullivan, as for the BOP, solitary confinement is a misnomer. The fact that prisoners can communicate with the occupants of adjacent cells (lungs and plumbing permitting); make a limited number of telephone calls each month; send and receive (censored) correspondence; converse with the occupant of another cage if they are in general population, happen to be in the recreation yard simultaneously, and get along; and have occasional non-contact visits if their families have the time and money to make the long and arduous trip to the Rockies, is proof that they are not in solitary confinement. In addition, he argued, they were regularly visited by staff (even if these encounters were generally perfunctory). What might be a swirl of social activity for supporters of ADX Florence is a profound lack of sincere human engagement for a neutral observer.

Sullivan (2016: 18) is a master of overstatement and omission, giving the following halcyon description of life in what the prison's former warden described as a hellish environment:

> Inmates who choose to go outside for recreation have access to sunlight and fresh air. Generally, the areas contain pull-up bars, and inmates are allowed to use handballs and soccer balls. Inmates may request instruction in aerobic exercise from ADX Florence recreation staff, who have training in aerobic exercises that can be performed in the individual recreation areas. Inmates have access to wellness programs, weekly leisure games via the ADX Florence closed circuit television system, a creative arts program offered in a group setting, weekend "brain teaser" games, arts and crafts, a weekly movie program, and special holiday activities. Inmates may also subscribe to periodicals; may borrow leisure reading materials from the institution's library; may take high school equivalency, Adult Continuing Education, and correspondence classes; may paint, draw, or crochet; may participate in a weekly bingo game; and may participate in art, essay and poetry contests. Inmates may make purchases from the commissary, including food items and additional toiletry and other items, beyond the standard items provided to them free of charge.

The same text appears in a report from the US Department of Justice (2016: 39–40), so it is reasonable to see this as a settled official view. A more accurate assessment, and one that is more closely aligned with firsthand accounts and objective analyses, is that of Rovner (2018: 464), who declared: "There may be no prison in the country where the conditions are more draconian—and more hidden—than ADX." The educational opportunities are paltry compared with Isir Bet, where teachers visit the compound to deliver the national curriculum, and the H Blocks, where some republican activists worked toward graduate degrees. It is difficult to imagine how individual autonomy could be any more thoroughly constrained.

The District of Columbia Corrections Information Council (2018: 24) reported: "Staff members at Florence ADX are required to wear slash-resistant vests when around inmate populations. Additionally, the facility is the only BOP institution that permits staff to carry lethal weapons. Staff reported to the CIC that, to date, lethal weapon discharge had never occurred." Perhaps the fact that there had been no need to discharge a firearm since 1994—almost a quarter of a century without a bullet fired—suggests that the threat may be exaggerated? Nonlethal force was not uncommon and, according to the same report, between March 2016 and February 2017, "there were 73 instances of chemicals use on inmates, 47 instances of use of force by staff toward inmates, and 96 instances of restraints being placed on inmates" (p. 24).

For such a small institutional population, this is a relatively high level of gassing, beating, and tying down. In addition, there will have been occasions when handcuffs were tightened with a little too much zeal, or staff who were escorting prisoners or extracting them from their cells did so with incivility and undue roughness. There will also have been times when maltreatment did not result in an official notification. Despite their extreme isolation, then, prisoners were still vulnerable to staff violence. If force betokens failed authority, then ADX Florence is perpetually failing.

Looking at assaults on staff over the same twelve-month period, "there were 42 instances of assault on staff with no weapon, 40 attempted assaults on staff with no weapon, and one assault on a staff member with a weapon" (District of Columbia Corrections Information Council 2018: 24). One wonders about the seriousness of these attacks. An attempted assault without a weapon by a caged or shackled inmate against a far superior guard force can hardly pose a significant risk of harm, and on the one occasion where a weapon was deployed we are not told what it was or whether it caused injury. There were seven cases of inmates assaulting other inmates. In other words, prisoners were much more likely to be on the receiving end of violence dispensed by staff than by their peers.

When correctional officers rely upon handcuffs, leg irons, Martin chains, tasers, batons, shields, pepper canisters, and firearms, it is hardly surprising that they come to view those whose lives they oversee as being less than human. Otherwise, why would such overwhelming coercive power be required? What is the point of trying to cajole and persuade, let alone to empathize, when any debate can be won with the release of a spray or a call for (body armored) reinforcements? Sullivan (2016: 3) reported that the ratio of (more than three hundred) staff to (just over four hundred) prisoners was the best anywhere in the BOP. With such a generous level of staffing, prisoners are unlikely to gain the upper hand in terms of numbers or weapons.

When staff treat any interaction with prisoners as potentially hazardous, and when prisoners can be preoccupied with violent fantasies regarding staff, encounters are charged and anxiety-provoking for both sides. Toch (2001: 382) described the resulting atmosphere as "a climate of trench warfare" where staff "view their charges with trepidation or contempt," as people who must be caged or trussed, or sometimes both if they are placed in four-point restraints and tied to a bed in a tiny cell. It requires singular resourcefulness for a prisoner to behave with dignity in such an environment. The same is true, to a lesser extent, for staff.

Uncle SAM Twists the Screw

Special administrative measures (SAMs) entail an extra level of dislocation. SAMs are rare and can be imposed only by the US attorney general, typically for reasons related to national security. The majority of those subject to this additional layer of restrictions are Muslims. Most sentenced prisoners with SAMs are held at ADX Florence's SSU (also known as H Unit). They often have terrorism and religion in common so might be a more cohesive group than the other prisoners in the complex, even though they come from disparate locations ranging across Europe, the US, and the Middle East.

The earliest SAMs date from 1996 and, according to the Center for Constitutional Rights and Lowenstein International Human Rights Clinic (2017: 4), they were targeted at individuals who were believed to be orchestrating violence from within their prison cells. Their usage increased after the terrorist attacks on the US on September 11, 2001, with the number of individuals under SAMs jumping from sixteen in November 2001 to fifty-one in June 2017 (p. 2). The US Department of Justice (2016: 38) reported that in November 2015 there were thirty-four international terrorists held at ADX Florence along with ten domestic terrorists, nineteen members of Al Qaeda, three of Gama'a Al-Islamiyya, and three of the Taliban. Not all were under SAMs.

SAMs can remain in place for a long time. A count in 2013 found that thirteen men had lived under them for more than a decade (Center for Constitutional Rights and Lowenstein International Human Rights Clinic 2017: 11). We do not know how much they have suffered because they—or anyone who has dealt directly with them—cannot speak out, for fear of prosecution. No one is likely to organize rallies on their behalf, in the US at least. However, it seems reasonable to assume, given what we know about the harms of solitary confinement, that the aggravated version experienced by those under SAMs is likely to have even more malign consequences.

According to the Center for Constitutional Rights and Lowenstein International Human Rights Clinic (2017: 1):

> SAMs are the darkest corner of the U.S. federal prison system, combining the brutality and isolation of maximum-security units with additional restrictions that deny individuals almost any connection to the human world. Those restrictions include gag orders on prisoners, their family members, and their attorneys, effectively shielding this extreme use of government power from public view. . . . They prohibit social contact with anyone except for a few immediate family members, and heavily regulate even those contacts. And they further prohibit prisoners from connecting to the social world via current media and news, limiting prisoners' access to information to outdated, government-approved materials. Even a prisoner's communications with his lawyer—which are supposed to be protected by attorney-client privilege—can be subject to monitoring by the FBI [Federal Bureau of Investigation].

A single fifteen-minute telephone call per month is permitted to an approved immediate family member. This is monitored and recorded by the FBI. Visits are rare and very tightly controlled. Three sheets of writing paper are provided per week for a letter to a single recipient (at the discretion of the BOP) that is forwarded to the FBI, where it is analyzed and copied before being sent on, sometimes several weeks after it was written. This is the total extent of contact with the outside world. Stahl (2019: 16) reported: "The ADX was allowed to take 60 business days to mail out a letter in Arabic and 60 days to process an incoming one," so if a son wrote to his father in the Middle East in January, allowing some additional time for the vagaries of international postal systems, he might not hear back until the summer.

Within the institution, communication with other prisoners is prohibited. They do not have showers in their cells so shouting into the drain is not an option. They can put their heads into the toilet bowl, roar, and hope that the pipes carry their voice, but this is humiliating. If the imam visits to provide spiritual guidance this must be offered in the presence of an FBI agent or a BOP official. Newspapers and magazines are made available after they have been heavily redacted and long delayed, making it impossible to keep abreast of current affairs. A review of restrictive housing carried out for the BOP excluded anyone under SAMs at ADX Florence (CNA 2014: 3). They inhabit a dark site within a famously opaque prison.

SAMs intensify the experience of solitary confinement by stripping away to the point of absurdity the already limited opportunities for social interaction and community connection. Prisoners in the SSU have the same paltry out-of-cell time as those in the general population (i.e., ten hours per week of solitary exercise in an empty room or an outside cage). They can go years without being touched by anyone other than a prison guard.

According to the Center for Constitutional Rights and Lowenstein International Human Rights Clinic (2017: 6): "When first placed under SAMs at ADX Florence, Nidal Ayyad was limited to five hours of exercise per week, and recreation, as well as showers, were cancelled any time a lieutenant and two officers were not present. Also at ADX, SAMs prisoner Mahmud Abouhalima was only permitted to go to inside or outside recreation if he submitted to a strip-search by three staff and a lieutenant, both on the way out to recreation and on the way back to his cell. He refused recreation under such degrading circumstances. As a result, SAMs prisoners in the H-Unit at ADX often go days without leaving their cells." While strip searches are demeaning for everyone forced to undergo them, the offense against modesty carries extra pain for the devout Muslim.

SAMs are a layer of misery on top of solitary confinement. Living under them is the zenith of penal regulation and the nadir of prisoner integration. After Range 13 and the control unit, this is the most extreme microenvironment within the penal tundra that is ADX Florence. Sometimes the men there protest the only way left to them, by attempting to reclaim sovereignty over their own bodies and what they ingest, but even such actions elicit a cruel response.

Stahl (2019: 13) showed that correctional staff were relentless in their chaining of prisoners who tried to resist through fasting. On November 11, 2015, after 34 days without food, a weak and emaciated Mohammad Salameh was placed in leg irons and handcuffs by a team of five officers dressed in riot gear. Having been extracted from his cell he was brought to the medical observation room, strapped into a chair, and handcuffed so that a feeding tube could be inserted into his nose. Convicted in 1994, Salameh was transferred to ADX Florence in 2002 and moved to H Unit under SAMs in 2005. During eleven years in this situation, he went on hunger strike eight times and endured 220 force feedings over a total of 428 days. The first hunger strike took place soon after his move to H Unit and lasted 89 days during which he was force fed 78 times. He reckoned that others had been force fed even more often, a scandal that has not become public because of the onerous restrictions on their ability to communicate with the outside world. He was eventually moved from ADX Florence to USP Big Sandy in Kentucky and is scheduled for release in 2067 by which point, if still alive, he will be one hundred years old.

Salameh was resolute and Stahl reported how he "conveyed his determination to keep protesting with a line from a poem he translated from Arabic: 'Make me drink the bitter cup, but with dignity'" (p. 17). He accepted that the SAMs would not be removed, and that he would die in prison; his request was for a second monthly telephone call and some additional outside recreation time. That such modest requests necessitated such drastic action says a great deal about the deprivations prisoners must endure and the vigor with which the rules are enforced.

Sometimes, despite the considerable odds, the men on the SSU protested together. According to Stahl the biggest coordinated action took place in 2009 when, over a period of time, ten of them were refusing food: "It started after Barack Obama's inauguration, when a prisoner on the unit requested a copy of his memoir *The Audacity of Hope*, along with some Islamic texts. The books were denied on national-security grounds" (p. 17). The individual whose request was turned down went on hunger strike with two others and soon the numbers grew. To protest against the inhumanity of their isolation the prisoners decided to embark on a campaign that, if taken to its conclusion, would render the issue moot. Stahl estimated that, between 2005 and 2016, as many as two-thirds of SSU residents participated in hunger strikes and there were hundreds if not thousands of forced feedings: "With assistance from lawyers, they won concessions, including more telephone calls, more recreation time, fewer restrictions on outside media, and the ability to conduct no-contact visits unshackled" (p. 20).

The SSU is predominantly Muslim, but men of other faiths and none are held there under SAMs, including spies and gang leaders. As noted above ("Distorted Thinking"), for Muslims, not being able to coordinate their prayer is a particular burden. If funds permit, they can buy a prayer rug ($13.65) and kufi ($8.00) from the prison commissary (Matevousian 2018a). But they can never roll out their rug and bow toward Mecca alongside a fellow believer. Prerecorded religious programming is available via the in-cell television, including religious movies and sixteen hours of Qur'an recitations. Some books are available. If a man is approved by the head chaplain for a religious diet he will receive one ceremonial meal per year (District of Columbia Corrections Information Council 2018: 37).

In some respects, being under SAMs is worse than what Thomas Silverstein endured as those forced to submit to such treatment cannot tell anyone about it. At least Silverstein could litigate and his lengthy and informative affidavit has become part of the record (*Silverstein v. Federal Bureau of Prisons*, 2011). In addition, a website (https://thomassilverstein.net) and a blog (http://tommysilverstein.blogspot.com) were maintained on his behalf and his artworks (e.g., figure 5.6) and letters were circulated. Silverstein's writings and drawings suggest an organized mind. That such an articulate account could be written by a man who was held in isolation for so long is a striking instance of the human capacity to endure adversity.

Psychological Disintegration

The coercive power of "no touch torture" (McCoy 2006: 7) was recognized by the Central Intelligence Agency (CIA) in the mid-twentieth century. Part of its attraction was that it was swiftly and brutally effective and left no physical trace. It had long been known that physical pain, however extreme, could be met with heightened resistance. But the will of even the most determined individual soon unraveled when they were exposed to techniques such as sensory deprivation, isolation, temporal disorientation, extremes of temperature, unpredictable combinations of silence and noise or darkness and light, and the maintenance of natural postures for unnatural durations (e.g., standing with arms extended to either side for an hour). The cumulative impact of these techniques was the disintegration of personal identity and the tantalizing prospect—to the torturers at least—that the individual's belief systems could be altered—that, using the language of the Cold War, they could be "brainwashed." This possibility was attractive to the CIA, which was searching for interrogation methods that would leave the body intact, but the mind disorganized and vulnerable.

In an examination of why psychological approaches could have such a devastating impact, leading to patterns of reaction that were akin to those found in psychoses and in disorders with an organic origin, Doerr-Zegers et al. (1992: 180–83) argued that the answer was to be found in six facets of the phenomenology of the torture situation:

(1) asymmetry of the relationship
(2) anonymity of the torturer
(3) "double bind" of suffering or denouncing others
(4) falsehood and lies, ranging from reason for imprisonment to "mock executions"
(5) distortions of space signifying "displacement, trapping, narrowness and destruction"
(6) temporality "characterized by some unpredictability and much circularity, having no end"

Many of these conditions are found in ADX Florence. The asymmetry of power is extreme; staff and prisoners view each other in stereotypical ways and while the former are not anonymous, they present as distant, uninterested figures, whose personal lives are kept secret; to move on, prisoners may have to "debrief," or divulge information about their associates, which is seen as a betrayal of inmate solidarity; the entry route is not clearly charted and those forced to endure it feel that their segregation is thinly disguised punishment motivated by malice rather than credible evidence; the spaces of confinement are distinctive and tightly confining; the temporal dimension of existence is monotonously circular, the routine disturbed by occasional, and unpredictable, cell searches and extractions, and the length of time to be spent there is often unclear. Following the logic set out by Doerr-Zegers et al. (1992), then, the environment at ADX Florence—especially on the control unit and for the handful of men on Range 13—is well organized to breach the prisoner's existential defenses. It is, in other words, a site that could have been designed for "no touch torture" and as such it is not altogether surprising that those who reside there sometimes display the patterns of personality breakdown exhibited by torture victims.

Silverstein's drawing of a nail being driven through a hand (figure 5.6) was completed before his transfer to ADX Florence. It is not a representation of himself as a martyr, as someone who is in any way Christlike (although this is how it might first seem). Rather it illustrates pointless pain, suffering without the prospect of salvation, misery without relief, agony for its own sake. It shows the crucifying nature of prolonged isolation, which the artist described as "a slow constant peeling of the skin, stripping of the flesh, the nerve-wracking sound of water dripping from a leaky faucet in the still of the night while you're trying to sleep. Drip, drip, drip, the minutes, hours, days, weeks, months, years, constantly drip away with no end or relief in sight" (cited in Prendergast 2007). These are some of the human consequences of "no touch torture" as it plays out in the solitary confinement cell.

For most of those held at ADX Florence, the quantity and quality of interaction with staff is minuscule, and usually takes place at the cell door. Silverstein (2011: para. 224 and attachment A) recorded "each and every contact" with staff members during the month of December 2010. He timed these exchanges on his watch and immediately afterward logged the precise duration and noted the reason for the contact. Many took no more than a few seconds, such as asking if he wanted access to recreation or a newspaper with his food tray. On Christmas Day his interaction time totaled twenty-six seconds, beginning with two seconds at 6:04 a.m. when his breakfast was delivered to his cell door. Most of the contact with staff involved his tray being delivered and collected and

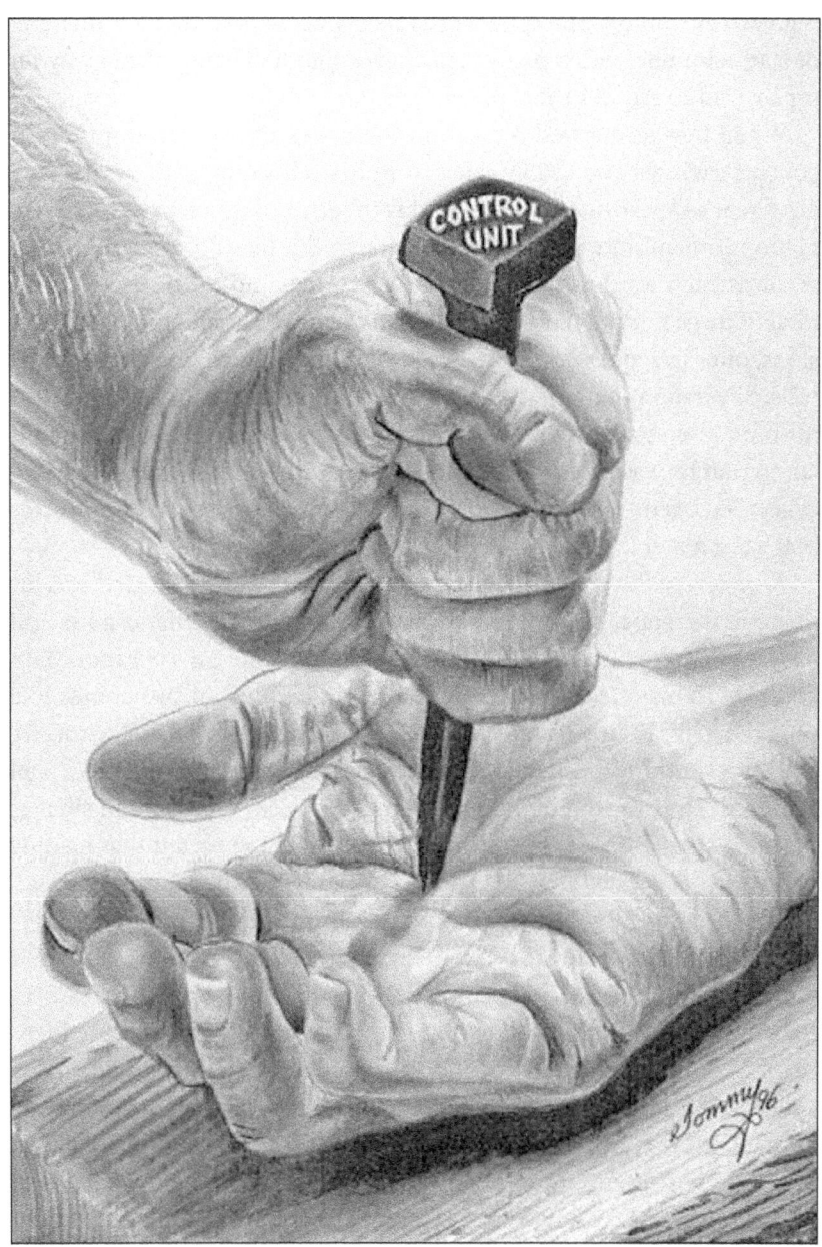

Figure 5.6. Crucifying Aloneness. Credit: Tom Silverstein (1952–2019).

regular cell counts. The only words he spoke were to thank a member of staff who returned a pair of spectacles that had been taken away for repair, and to request toilet paper.

When he was allowed recreation there was an additional minute of contact each way on the journey from his cell to the gym or dog run. New Year's Day 2011 was a bumper day in terms of contact as he had recreation (one minute each way) and time in the "law library" cell (thirty seconds each way) as well as the usual counts and meal deliveries—a total of three minutes and twenty-seven seconds. He spoke on two occasions, once to request access to the law library and again to ask for toilet rolls. Silverstein's experience was extreme given that he was subject to a no-human-contact order. Unlike the other men held on a general population unit he was never allowed to interact with his peers in the outdoor cages. But even the other general population prisoners had life worlds that were massively restricted by any objective yardstick.

A review of Silverstein's log suggests his interaction with staff was little more than one minute per day on average. Like the others on his unit he was permitted to make two fifteen-minute phone calls per month. In addition to his one-minute daily interaction with staff this comes to a total of twelve hours of conversation per year. Such enforced taciturnity does not amount to meaningful engagement even by the most frugal standard. His time out of cell (ten hours per week) was spent in silence, pacing a small bunker. The prison's remote location meant that he only had two social visits over a period of five and a half years (para. 222). This is life at its most attenuated and impermeable.

Denied human connection, Silverstein relied upon drawing and painting to maintain a sense of self. As he reflected on this process: "In the absence of human contact, my art had become central to my identity. It was almost the only way I knew I was alive, that I existed. No one spoke to me, but I felt that I was able to communicate that I was a living human being by making art. Without it I felt like a part of my soul had been taken from me" (para. 123). Figure 5.6 shows how he managed to communicate a profound sense of loneliness combined with a steely determination to carry on.

Life at ADX Florence is almost totally devoid of contact that is worthwhile in a social sense. Added to severe restrictions on movement and highly limited sensory input this extracts a considerable psychological toll. An occasional brief exchange—whether gruff words or banal pleasantries—while a food tray is pushed through the slot in a cell door or a person is being escorted, in shackles, to an exercise cage is not the kind of conversation that nourishes an individual. When prolonged, the consequences of such a situation are dismal:

> The prisoner and the cell become locked in a melancholic embrace, with the restrictions of the physical environment finding behavioural expression in a severely limited repertoire of movement, emotional constriction, and poverty of speech. The solitary cell becomes part of the fabric of the prisoner's personality. It confines the body and trammels the mind, smothering individuality and making it difficult for the person subjected to it to retain the sense of uniqueness that is central to being human. It shrinks the core of personhood to an unadorned minimum and whether the prisoner looks inward or outward they are confronted by a vista that is uniformly bleak. (O'Donnell 2014: 78–79)

Perkinson (1994: 125) described ADX Florence as "a chamber of sensory deprivation, designed to press inmates to the brink of insanity by its very architecture." The isolation was deepened by the availability of technology that allowed arm's-length surveillance. Cameras, computers, motion detectors, electronic doors, and a range of lethal and nonlethal weapons all meant that the security which had formerly been delivered through human contact was now administered remotely. Technology displaced the kind of "dynamic security" that saw safety in the cultivation of strong relationships and easy rapport. This allowed a studied indifference to be paid to prisoners, reinforcing their status as socially redundant. It also diminished correctional officers' interpersonal skills and mastery of "jail craft," which are usually core elements of their occupational identities. This extra distance was appreciated, with Coid (2001: 294) finding that staff working at ADX Florence felt in control and safe; their working lives were "relatively stress-free." The benefits that accompanied draconian treatment made any mitigation of the regime highly unlikely.

In the convivial surroundings of the H Blocks and Isir Bet and the forced congregation of the Eastham Unit, there was no need to devise ways to deal with profound and enduring aloneness. But how do people cope in a disintegrated society where the ingredients are in place for the destruction of the personality and they cannot fall back on the collective for support? In a previous book, I explored a variety of ways that time could be rendered less abrasive (see O'Donnell 2014: 222–55). They are listed below in descending order of popularity and ascending order of importance. They are important for prisoners everywhere but take on added urgency for anyone who cannot assuage the pains of confinement with human company.

Rescheduling	Using different intervals to gauge time's passage.
Removal	Keeping busy through work or exercise.
Reduction	Shortening the day by sleeping or taking drugs.
Reorientation	Resetting temporal horizons to focus on the present.
Resistance	Fighting or litigating.
Raptness	Mastering an activity like creative writing, craftwork, or painting.
Reinterpretation	Reimagining and recasting the situation.

Some of these approaches are difficult to adopt in ADX Florence given the limited opportunities for removal and raptness, the likely disciplinary response to resistance, the practical problem of rescheduling when the duration of stay is uncertain, and the lack of access to the kinds of substances that enable reduction. But there is some scope for reorientation and reinterpretation (see O'Donnell [2018] for an exploration of how prisoners on death row, most of whom are held in solitary confinement, tussle with time).

Going to Law

Bacote v. Federal Bureau of Prisons (filed June 18, 2012) became *Cunningham v. Federal Bureau of Prisons* (filed May 24, 2013; second amended complaint June 15, 2015) when Michael Bacote asked to withdraw from the lawsuit, feeling that he had not been kept informed of the details of the files submitted in his name, and expressing unhappiness that the lawyers taking the case were going to seek recovery of their fees from the court rather than operating on a pro bono basis (Bacote 2012).

TABLE 5.2. Out of Sight, Out of Mind (in Both Senses). Calculated from address details in *Cunningham v. Federal Bureau of Prisons* (2013: paras. 133–236)

Plaintiff	Previous address	Distance to ADX Florence (miles)
Harold Cunningham	Washington, DC	1,700
Carlton Dunbar	Arlington, Virginia	1,700
John W. Narducci	Hartford, Connecticut	1,940
Jeremy Pinson	Oklahoma City	580
Jack Powers	Tampa, Florida	1,820
Ernest Norman Shaifer	Washington, DC	1,700
Marcellus Washington	New Jersey	1,800

Table 5.2 lists the plaintiffs in the *Cunningham* case when it was originally filed and the distances from where they were living prior to their incarceration to their isolation cells in the Alcatraz of the Rockies. These distances are so vast that covering them with any degree of regularity would put even the most financially and emotionally secure relationship under severe pressure. Added to this is the fact that even if the arduous journey is made, all that awaits is a visit where contact is prohibited and the parties view each other through a thick screen—hardly the circumstances for strengthening ties of mutual affection. For those with families overseas even the rare trip to a secure visiting box is out of the question. Given how widely scattered were their places of origin, the men in ADX Florence had no preexisting social networks to fall back upon.

Contrast this with the IRA prisoners in the H Blocks, many of whom came from Belfast, a mere 13 miles away, and could enjoy plentiful open visits. Laurence McKeown hailed from a rural area in Northern Ireland, but the distance from home to the H Blocks was only 25 miles. Many knew each other outside, either personally or by reputation, and it was not unusual for them to be linked by deep familial and community ties. They were united in background as well as in political outlook. Compare this with the 1,820 miles to Florence, Colorado, from Tampa, Florida, where Jack Powers had been residing at the time of his arrest. The degree of spatial dislocation for those held at ADX Florence is spectacular. Incarceration there involves a doubling down of marginalization;

prisoners are held at a remove from their families and communities as well as from their peers.

The *Cunningham* lawsuit prized open the closed world of ADX Florence, exposing a terrifying vista:

> Many prisoners at ADX interminably wailed, screamed, and banged on the walls of their cells. Some mutilated their bodies with razors, shards of glass, sharpened chicken bones, writing utensils, and whatever other objects they could obtain. A number swallowed razor blades, nail clippers, parts of radios and televisions, broken glass, and other dangerous objects. Others carried on delusional conversations with voices they heard in their heads, oblivious to reality and to the danger that such behavior might pose to themselves and anyone who interacts with them. Still others spread feces and other human waste and body fluids throughout their cells, threw it at the correctional staff, and otherwise created health hazards at ADX. Suicide attempts were common; many have been successful. (*Cunningham v. Federal Bureau of Prisons* 2015: para. 5)

The testimonies collected for this litigation vividly illustrated how the fragmentation of prisoner society had massive individual consequences and these were exacerbated in a system where discretion around rule application was so limited. Members of the so-called caring professions allowed themselves to be captured by the "ecology of cruelty" (Haney 2008: 958) within which they worked to the extent that a psychologist accompanied a team clad in riot gear to participate in the "violent" cell extraction of an individual who had attempted suicide by hanging (*Cunningham v. Federal Bureau of Prisons* 2015: para. 79). Other psychologists seemed to see themselves as correctional staff first and mental health professionals second, and they "performed prisoner escort duty within the prison while armed with weapons, openly brandishing those weapons in the presence of prisoners; worked shifts in the prison's gun towers; appeared at the doorways of prisoners brandishing clubs in an aggressive fashion" (para. 85). These were hardly activities likely to promote a strong therapeutic alliance with potential clients. The demarcation lines were clear—it was us against them and we must maintain a united front.

One Man's (Horror) Story

Jack Powers, one of the lead plaintiffs in *Cunningham*, was forty years old when he arrived at the control unit in 2001, a mature adult with no history of mental illness or self-harm. His problems began when he testified against other prisoners and thereby placed his safety in jeopardy (see pen portrait). Fear and post-traumatic stress disorder (PTSD) escalated, and the control unit undid him. He was retained even longer in the environment that was causing him such distress because of his response to its demands and the devastating toll it took on his body; it fanned his PTSD into a psychological inferno.

Powers (2021a: 22) poignantly described creating a simulacrum of life in cell 208 during the early phase of his time in the control unit:

> I am trying to make it the best way I know how. I study and write and exercise. I have begun to practice yoga meditation through a correspondence course. The black mastic around the window makes excellent ear plugs. I save pats of margarine and, when I get enough, put them into a plastic bag and fill it with hot water. The oil then comes to the top, and I put a hole in the bottom of the bag and let the water drain out. The oil I use to make a candle, and I use the candle at night when I meditate. I folded my blanket and use it to sit on while I gaze at the candle and try to clear my mind. Sometimes I hold small pieces of bread over the flame and make toast.

John Jay "Jack" Powers (b. 1961), Survivor

Jack Powers grew up in New York, leaving home at fourteen and later serving time for burglary. After his release he married and moved to Michigan where he set up a construction company and beauty salon. The businesses failed and Powers turned to bank robbery to generate an income. Convicted in the Sunshine State in 1990, he was sentenced to forty years in federal prison.

Four years into his sentence one of his friends was stabbed by members of the Aryan Brotherhood (AB). Powers carried the bleeding man to the prison hospital, where he succumbed to his injuries. Later he testified at the trial and three AB gang members received life sentences. Powers understood that cooperation would earn him a sentence reduction, but by 1999 he had still not received any such discount. Believing he was to be moved out of protective custody, which he felt would place him in danger, he escaped and went to New York to visit family members. He was arrested after two days. In June 2001 he was convicted of escaping and given an additional prison term of forty-five months.

Now deemed a flight risk, he was transferred to ADX Florence in October 2001 to spend sixty months on the control unit. He was threatened by AB members as soon as he arrived, the post-traumatic stress disorder that he developed in the aftermath of his friend's murder intensified, and the other prisoners treated him as a snitch and avoided him.

Over the next decade, Powers unraveled. He committed savage violence against his body, cutting off his earlobes, slashing his Achilles tendon, biting off one of his fingers, and removing a testicle. One night in 2010 he covered his body with tattooed stripes by rubbing the ashes of carbon paper he had burned into thousands of tiny cuts that he made with pieces of broken glass. Describing this transformation, Binelli (2015) wrote: "The smirking, shaggy-haired young bank robber who entered the federal prison system in 1990 no longer existed, and the man who replaced him looked like something out of a nightmare." He remained on the control unit until March 2011.

Jack Powers is a skilled wordsmith. He has written several books, including *The Manual Program: For Personal Growth* and *ADX Supermax: The Alcatraz of the Rockies*. Both are deeply humanistic texts. *The Manual Program* is a guide to authentic living that provides a thirty-day cycle of instructions that, once concluded, is repeated indefinitely. The instructions are prompts to examine facets of experience such as humility, self-control, kindness, introspection, and acceptance. Each is illustrated with two vignettes and accompanied by a suggested practice. Before the daily instruction is read, the individual completes a period of diaphragmatic breathing to ensure that their mind is clear and their body relaxed. Nowhere in the book is prison mentioned, and readers will not learn anything of the author's biography. This is not a manual by a prisoner, for prisoners; it is by a person, for people. It is a self-help guide wrought from the most arduous personal experience. (Powers recalls receiving a copy of the *Philokalia* from a chaplain and being struck by the wisdom therein; the influence of this Eastern Orthodox spiritual text shines through *The Manual Program*.)

ADX Supermax is more personal. It is a profound and subtle reflection on hopelessness, pain, and endurance—an account of how despair can be vanquished, and extreme adversity overcome. This book took courage to write and it will be read with sadness, but also with profit, by anyone who cares about the cruelty that is inherent in imprisonment. It is the autobiography of a man who unraveled but (eventually) managed to weave the threads of his life together to create the fabric for a new existence. There are echoes of the medieval anchorite, confined to a tiny space, dead to the world, mortifying his flesh, but somehow finding the wherewithal to carry on and to hope for salvation and, in the process, inspiring others. If Powers had a motto, it might be Ovid's "Perfer et obdura; dolor hic tibi proderit olim" (Be patient and tough; someday this pain will be useful to you).

Jack Powers regained his liberty in September 2021.

Powers is an emblematic case because he was not mentally ill prior to his arrival at ADX Florence and then descended into florid madness and self-harm, including serial mutilation and extensive self-tattooing (see figure 5.5 for a photograph taken the year after he returned to the general population). He gave an evocative and hard-earned description of what life felt like in ADX Florence in his comment: "My experience at the ADX was like being chained to a chair in a dark room where someone comes by every 20 minutes or so and slaps you in the face" (Powers 2014). This was torturous—and tortuous—treatment. Table 5.3 catalogs Powers's descent into madness.

Powers was moved from the control unit to the United States Medical Center for Federal Prisoners (MCFP), Springfield, Missouri, for several months in 2002, 2005, and 2009. Each time he was returned to the control unit afterward. He spent much longer there than originally intended because his mental illness prevented him from complying with the regulations necessary for forward momentum. The response to his self-harm was often a disciplinary one—he was placed in restraints or on report. When he eventually left the control unit it was to the marginally better—but still isolating and oppressive—conditions of general population in ADX Florence.

Powers's difficulties did not end when he left the control unit. The terrible self-mutilation continued and in March 2012, in an echo of how

TABLE 5.3. Jack Powers: Timetable of Trauma. Excerpted from *Cunningham v. Federal Bureau of Prisons* (2015: paras. 383–418)

1990	Imprisoned for armed robbery
1994	Witnessed murder of friend by members of Aryan Brotherhood
1997	Diagnosed with post-traumatic stress disorder
1999	Escaped from prison and remained at liberty for two days
2001	Transferred to control unit at ADX Florence
2002 (July)	"rammed his head into the metal door jamb of his cell"
2005 (Oct.)	"severely lacerated his scrotum with a piece of sharp plastic"
2006 (Apr.)	"broke the glass on his television set, which he used to cut himself"
2006 (July)	"amputated his testicle"
2007 (Sep.)	"bit off his finger"
2008 (Apr.)	"inserted a staple into his forehead"
2008 (Dec.)	"amputated one of his fingers, tore out the stitches used to close the wound, and then swallowed a toothbrush"
2009 (Feb.)	"cut a triangular flap of skin out of his face and inserted several staples into it"
2009 (July)	"cut his wrist, bled all over his cell, and was found unconscious and unresponsive"
2009 (Dec.)	"bit off his pinkie"
2010	"covered most of his body with tattoos . . . by slicing thousands of tiny slits into his skin with a razor blade and rubbing carbon paper dust into the slits"
2010 (Dec.)	"amputated his scrotum and attempted to suture the wound himself"
2011	Transferred to general population at ADX Florence
2012 (Jan.)	"sliced off his earlobes, using pencils as tourniquets"
2012 (Mar.)	"sawed through his Achilles tendon with a sharp piece of metal, nearly severing it"
2012 (May)	"again mutilated his genitals"
2013	Transferred to USP Tucson

prisoners in Texas harmed themselves to avoid going back to the fields, he sawed through his Achilles tendon. Even if the damage is the same, there is a world of difference between deciding to wound oneself in an attempt to bring about a temporary pause from a chronically unpleasant work environment and the same behavior being exhibited in the context of profound and debilitating psychological distress. (This is not to ignore the adverse mental health consequences of being overworked, undervalued, and unpaid.) Powers went to the MCFP again in 2013, before being transferred to USP Tucson. There was an emergency airlift from Tucson to Springfield when he drilled a hole in his skull, exposing his brain (*Cunningham v. Federal Bureau of Prisons* 2015: para. 414). He later inserted shards of metal into his brain through this hole. The self-trepanation followed his placement back in solitary confinement and the withdrawal of his psychotropic medication. This is the chronology of a man falling apart and the legacy of ADX Florence. Further horrific self-injury occurred at various locations for several more years; without proper support and medication the consequences were predictably awful. Table 5.3 is limited to the damage done during Powers's time at ADX Florence, most of which was spent in the control unit.

Reading the account set out in *Cunningham* it seems that each move to the MCFP was preceded by a bout of serious self-injury that had been precipitated by a weakening of already fragile social bonds or a realization that there was no one who could be depended upon (two sides of the same coin). Things deteriorated when he returned from a hospital stay and his medicine was discontinued. Scared and without allies Powers could not cope with the threats being issued by the occupants of adjacent cells who believed he was an informant. When he eventually made a friend, Jose Vega, with whom he could converse via the air vents, his interlocutor committed suicide. In the psychologically arid environment of ADX Florence, where prisoner bonds are severely fractured from the outset, and the degree of social separation is such that it is virtually impossible to form them from scratch, the loss of a friendship, even one forged through ventilation pipes, is a crushing blow. Vega was shackled at his wrists and ankles while staff attempted to resuscitate him. The chains remained in place while his body lay on a slab in the mortuary awaiting an autopsy (Cohen 2012). Even in death he was allowed no dignity.

Powers's self-harm signaled that the system could not inflict any damage in excess of that which he was prepared to cause himself; its ferocity was in proportion to the tightness of his confinement and his determination to retain some ability—however pernicious—to direct his life course even if by so doing he risked obliteration. The penal system did its worst, he trumped this and, through a large measure of good fortune and medical attention, survived to tell the tale. In more forgiving circumstances such signaling could reasonably expect to elicit sympathy and even reflection on possible causal factors and how they might be ameliorated. In the austere environs of the control unit at

ADX Florence at the time, such a repertoire of responses was nonexistent. The regime proved deaf to cries of despair and blind to a body in pain. By any measure this constituted an inhumane degree of imperviousness to suffering.

In an article written for the *Colorado Independent*, Powers (2013) recalled: "The world outside is like another planet. I feel like I am trapped within a disease." The damage wrought by the profound aloneness that had been forced upon him for so long took time to repair.

This is an extreme example of what isolation can do to a man, in a world characterized by little engagement with his fellows (low integration), unbending rule enforcement by a large guard force (high regulation), and single-ply legitimacy (the regime was legally valid but not based on shared beliefs and values, and the consent of prisoners was neither expected nor sought). From the perspective of the captive population, legitimacy lacked a horizontal component and its vertical aspect was, at best, thinly present. Prisoners who were not seriously mentally ill may have accepted that they were lawfully held in the institution and been aware of the framework of rules within which they were required to order their lives. However, they could not accept its inherent inhumanity, the uncertainty about how long they would spend there, the lack of clarity about how to move on, the disproportionately harsh treatment that they were expected to endure, and the wide range of behaviors that met with a disciplinary response.

Vignettes of Pain

Powers was not unique. There are numerous examples in the original filing of *Cunningham* of distressed men sitting mute in their cells for months on end, or howling incoherently, or eating their feces, or inflicting the most horrendous violence upon themselves. This mental illness was not hidden, as the following excerpts show.

> David Baxter: "has engaged in horrific self-harm, including slashing himself with sharp objects, swallowing razor blades and sharp pieces of metal, and carving a large circular design covering most of the left side of his face, apparently using a staple or other sharp object to gouge out pieces of skin." (para. 88)

Jaison Leggett: "used a razor blade to cut an artery in his leg. . . . When BOP staff attempted to stop him from cutting his leg any further, Mr. Leggett swallowed the razor blade. He was subsequently transferred to the MCFP Springfield, where his leg was amputated. (para. 254) . . . [B]ecause of continuing pain caused by the improperly fitted prosthetic, Mr. Leggett damaged his prosthetic leg and swallowed some of its metal parts. The BOP has refused to replace Mr. Leggett's prosthetic leg, instead forcing him to crawl around on the floor of his cell." (para. 257)

David Shelby: "heard a voice, which he took to be God's voice, commanding him to eat his finger. In response, Mr. Shelby amputated his left pinky finger approximately 1/2 inch from where the pinky joined his hand, and cut the finger into small pieces, which he added to a bowl of ramen soup and ate. ADX staff discovered him bleeding in his cell, and one ADX staff member asked him how his finger tasted." (para. 284)

Jonathan Francisco: "has not spoken a word to anyone in the nearly 18 months since arriving at ADX; rather, he spends all day, every day, staring at the wall of his cell. He frequently defecates on the floor of his cell or on a food tray, and smears his feces on himself, his cell or his other surroundings. He ignores other prisoners' attempts to help him, does not communicate with staff, and makes no effort to maintain his health or hygiene. As a result, he lives in squalor, rarely eats and is showered only when ADX staff members force him into a shower enclosure." (para. 322)

This is what can happen to human beings when denied company over an extended period. The consequences are particularly catastrophic for those who were vulnerable beforehand. Seriously mentally ill prisoners were not supposed to be assigned to ADX Florence according to BOP policy. But they were, and they paid a terrible price.

The program specification for control units stated that a referral may not be made: "If the inmate shows evidence of significant mental disorder or major physical disabilities as documented in a mental health evaluation or a physical examination" (Federal Bureau of Prisons 2001: 6). Powers may not have met this standard when he was sent to the control unit, but he soon exceeded it, and remained for many years in an environment that was hugely harmful to him. The program specification also provided for individual psychological assessments on a monthly basis with psychiatric services provided as required; it was envisaged that anyone who required psychotropic medication would not ordinarily be housed in a control unit (p. 14). The response to this was to withhold psychotropic medicine rather than to move the prisoners to an environment where their treatment could continue uninterrupted, a perverse form of "compliance" described as follows:

> the BOP has placed incoming prisoners with an existing prescription for psychotropic medication in the Control Unit, where the BOP refuses to administer such medication. . . . The BOP has justified this in Orwellian fashion: it discontinued the prisoner's medication, thereby making the now non-medicated prisoner "eligible" for placement in the Control Unit. Then, when this newly "eligible" prisoner requested medication needed to treat his serious mental illness, he was told that BOP policy prohibits the administration of psychotropic medication to him so he should develop "coping skills" as a substitute for the medication being withheld. (*Cunningham v. Federal Bureau of Prisons* 2015: para. 59)

Reform

The *Cunningham* litigation had an impact. Even before the BOP settled, it began to make improvements, adding mental health programming, recruiting more psychologists and opening high-security units for mentally ill prisoners in USP Atlanta, Georgia, and USP Allenwood, Pennsylvania. When a settlement was looking likely, Binelli (2015) wrote: "Changes are very likely coming at the ADX, in no small part thanks to Powers's story. But it seemed entirely possible that he might not survive to see the outcome." As Rovner (2018: 513) summarized the process:

> After three years of negotiation, including 200 hours of formal mediation, the parties reached a resolution of the lawsuit. As counsel for the parties told [the judge] at the final fairness hearing: "By any measure, ADX is a different place than it was in 2011. . . . Nearly 100 mentally ill men have been transferred to other facilities . . . many staff members at ADX and

elsewhere within the BOP now understand mental illness better, and deal more humanely with inmates who struggle with mental health problems."

A settlement was approved on December 29, 2016. This applied to Powers and the other plaintiffs as well as to any other present or future inmates with serious mental illness. Some of the men who took the case were disappointed that they did not receive money damages and that no one was held accountable for the conditions in which they had been confined. Two experienced independent psychiatrists were appointed to monitor compliance with the settlement terms over a three-year period. The settlement included provisions regarding screening and diagnosis, healthcare delivery, suicide prevention, and improving conditions of confinement to reduce the risk of developing or exacerbating mental illness. Group therapy facilities and private counselling areas were created and psychotropic drugs were to be made available as required, regardless of where the individual was housed.

When men leave their cells for group therapy they are placed in individual cages in a converted gym, where they remain in shackles (District of Columbia Corrections Information Council 2018: 17). Up to five prisoners from general population units are allowed to attend these sessions, but control unit residents are separated by an empty cage and the number of participants is limited to three. The psychologist is positioned in front of the cages and two correctional officers remain in the room throughout. These cages are referred to, in BOP doublespeak, as "therapeutic modules."

Revised referral procedures were introduced and persons with serious mental illness were no longer to be placed at ADX Florence unless "extraordinary security needs are identified that cannot be managed elsewhere" and even then they would receive a level of treatment commensurate with their needs, including an individualized treatment plan (Federal Bureau of Prisons 2014b: 19). These "extraordinary security needs" were widely defined, existing:

> (1) when an inmate's communications are limited to prevent disclosure of classified information or to address a substantial risk that an inmate's communications could result in acts of terrorism, death, or serious bodily injury; (2) when an inmate is extremely dangerous and cannot be safely

housed in a less secure setting or a secure mental health unit; for example, when an inmate has committed serious assaults, murder, or escape while housed in secure environments and continues to pose a risk of engaging in such conduct; or (3) when an inmate or his crimes are of such notoriety that the inmate cannot be safely housed in a less secure environment with other inmates without a substantial risk of harm to him. (US Department of Justice 2016: 51)

Category 1 could embrace all of the prisoners under SAMs, meaning they would have to remain in ADX Florence even if they became seriously mentally ill. Category 2 mirrors the referral criteria for ADX Florence. Category 3 relates not to security needs as much as to the protection of vulnerable individuals.

According to the US Department of Justice (2016: 53): "Seriously mentally ill inmates who must remain at ADX due to extraordinary security issues have an individualized treatment program and are provided with at least 10, and as many as 20, hours of out-of-cell time per week, consistent with their individualized treatment plan." Less than three hours per day out of cell is still parsimonious by any reasonable standard. However, men whose needs are such that they are deemed to require psychiatric inpatient treatment are explicitly ruled out of placement in ADX Florence. Instead, they are located at one of the two new high-security mental health units. Would Jack Powers end up on the control unit today? Probably, as he was not seriously mentally ill when he was sent there. Would he unravel as much and stay as long? Unlikely, given the changes introduced as a result of *Cunningham*.

When integration is this low, regulation this high, legitimacy this thin, and compliance this coerced, prisoners will suffer. They will still try to connect—as a species we have evolved to be "obligatorily gregarious" (Cacioppo and Patrick 2008: 63)—but the barriers to doing so in a meaningful way are difficult to overcome. The prison's coordinates, as shown in figure 1.1, seem immutable. The notion of peer support that sustains a person is wildly fanciful in ADX Florence, no more than a carceral chimera. Those who manage to survive do so at a price. Extreme isolation acts to amplify distress. The atomized life is almost unbearable. The mad become madder and the fragile break. Thin bonds are stretched and snapped. This is unrelieved subjugation. The denial of opportunities to be sociable strikes at the very heart of personhood. Injury is added to the insult of isolation.

With characteristic acuity, the Irish writer Michael Harding (2019) observed: "It's not the mountains or the ocean that make us happy. It's not even the meaning we impose on it all. It's just the unexpected presence of other people in our little worlds that makes the difference." This never happens in ADX Florence. Even after the implementation of the reform package, it remained an environment where the conditions for pleasant spontaneity had been obliterated. This is not to gainsay the possibility of post-traumatic growth—Powers is a skilled writer and Silverstein came to define himself by his art—but a truly meaningful existence is a relational one.

The degree of in-cell confinement was greater in the H Blocks during the protest years than in the control unit at ADX Florence when Jack Powers was there (the IRA men did not have access to outside recreation or even a rudimentary gym); the conditions were more deplorable (the protestors were in unfurnished, excrement covered cells, with no clothing); and there was more physical brutality and degradation (some members of staff were recklessly rough during searches, cell extractions, and forced washing). But these deprivations only served to strengthen the bond among a group of men who saw their struggle as rooted in a principled opposition to the enemy's attempt to criminalize their actions. Many IRA men never joined the protest or lacked the fortitude to persist with it, but hundreds of their comrades withstood a degree of deprivation that often threatened to overwhelm. That they managed to do so says a great deal about the power of reinterpretation to make the unbearable bearable (O'Donnell 2014: 249–55). Besides, they had the passion and energy that goes with youth, the support of their families and communities, and were on the right side of history (as they saw it).

The prisoners in the H Blocks had much in common and this sustained them. Their counterparts in ADX Florence shared nothing apart from a remote location. They were not united in terms of their politics, they did not have supporters outside who were well-funded, experienced, and capable of generating political and public support. The harms they caused were universally seen as criminal in the US (whereas IRA operations resulting in death and misery received a significant measure of community support in Northern Ireland). This, together with traumatic backgrounds, histories of violence and disruption, and mental illness create a mix where common cause is unlikely to be found. When it is (e.g., through coordinated fasting), this is remarkable. The authorities were resolute in their imposition of relentless discipline on a group that was unlikely to unite in opposition.

During the decade of interest (2001 to 2011), although the BOP's own policies excluded the seriously mentally ill from ADX Florence, they remained there in plain sight, untreated, and in pain. There is an interesting parallel here with the Eastham Unit, where there was a prohibition on prisoners discharging a disciplinary role, yet they did so with official backing, unchallenged, and viciously. As examples of humbug in the penal realm these are difficult to beat. In each case it required legal action to force the authorities to acknowledge the gulf between policy and practice.

Running a Prison without the Prisoners' Consent

ADX Florence is run without the consent of the prisoners. This makes it exceptional among the captive societies examined in this book. It is the attempted—and largely successful—effacement of anything but the most denuded form of life. Figure 5.7 shows that the lines of control are unambiguous and relationships between prisoners are nonexistent. There is no intermediate level, nothing between the captives and captors to buffer (or, indeed, amplify) the latter group's effect. The psychological distance is wide even when the social distance is narrow. Such a state of affairs requires a high degree of enforcement of regulations that govern every aspect of the daily grind. This is a brutally simple set of human relations. It is a type of existence that is simultaneously disintegrative (among prisoners) and rigidly stratified (between prisoners and staff). The *Admission and Orientation Handbook* for ADX Florence that was distributed during my reference period extended to sixty-one closely typed pages (Federal Bureau of Prisons 2008). The *Handbook* contained a lengthy disciplinary code.

Table 5.4 shows a selection of illicit activities of varying degrees of severity. There was no such thing as "low," with the most minor matters being classified as "low moderate." A revised code (Federal Bureau of Prisons 2011b) substituted "low" for "low moderate" and removed the baffling Code 401 violation (possessing an unauthorized amount

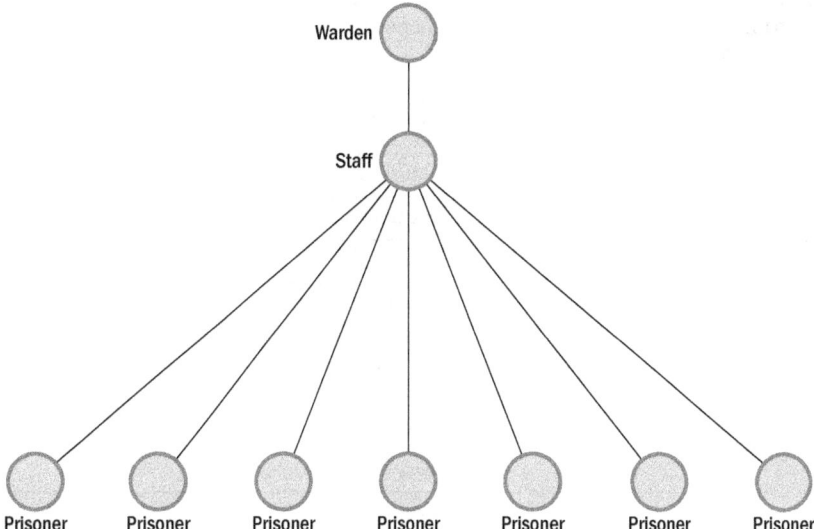
Figure 5.7. Authoritarian and Atomized.

of authorized clothing). Another change was that tattooing and self-mutilation (Code 405) were moved up a level in the hierarchy of seriousness and so was conducting a business (Code 408). Prisoners were sometimes charged with disciplinary infractions for damage caused to prison property during suicide attempts (e.g., tearing fabric to fashion a ligature, breaking a window to facilitate self-cutting). This is as absurd as it is horrific. The prohibition on martial arts (Code 220) extended to boxing, wrestling (alone! the mind boggles), and military drills and exercises unless supervised by staff. Attempting or planning was as serious as actually committing the offense. The associated sanctions ranged from forfeiting any prospect of early release, to disciplinary transfer or segregation, to monetary restitution, to loss of privileges such as commissary, recreation time, and access to personal property.

The *Handbook* exists within a complex framework of some four hundred policy documents (Federal Bureau of Prisons 2021c). These range from "Acceptance of Travel Funding from Outside Sources" to "Youth Corrections Act (YCA), Inmates," but there are none for "segregation," "solitary confinement," or "isolation," which, as previously noted, are not facets of imprisonment as far as the BOP is concerned. The rule book

TABLE 5.4. A Compendium of Unacceptable Conduct. Excerpted from Federal Bureau of Prisons (2008: Attachment D, Table 3)

Severity level	Code	Prohibited acts
Greatest	100	Killing
	101	Assault causing serious physical injury
	102	Escape from custody
	105	Rioting
	107	Hostage taking
	112	Drug use
High	201	Fighting
	205	Engaging in sexual acts
	207	Wearing a disguise or mask
	218	Damaging government property
	219	Stealing
	220	Demonstrating, practicing, or using martial arts
Moderate	300	Indecent exposure
	312	Insolence towards staff member
	313	Lying to staff member
	321	Interfering with count
	326	Possession of gambling paraphernalia
	330	Being unsanitary or untidy
Low moderate	401	Possessing unauthorized amount of authorized clothing
	402	Malingering, feigning illness
	404	Using abusive or obscene language
	405	Tattooing or self-mutilation
	408	Conducting a business
	409	Unauthorized physical contact (e.g., embracing)

was compendious, extending to pretty much every aspect of daily life. Discretion had been largely squeezed out and prisoner autonomy was hugely curtailed.

What is distinctive about ADX Florence is the lengths to which the authorities will go to narrow prisoners' identities. They are criminals, nothing else. This has become their master status. In Isir Bet, imprisoned men can simultaneously be weavers or farmers or cooks or shopkeepers. Sometimes they can achieve higher status and acquire greater wealth than was possible before their imprisonment. Contrastingly, it was an offense to run a business in ADX Florence. The men in the H Blocks could be poets or students or political activists, and some of them attained leadership positions and educational qualifications that may have eluded them had they remained at liberty. Men held in the Eastham Unit could earn reputations as hard workers or reckless gamblers or sexual predators. In ADX Florence, alone in their cells, they were monochrome men; all they could develop was their capacity to endure. This crushing of initiative and destruction of alternative identities is dehumanizing.

Even so, not everyone held there wished to move. According to CNA (2014: 129): "A majority . . . made it very clear that they wanted to remain in the ADX Florence and would commit a serious offense to ensure their ongoing housing in the facility. Several . . . said they would assault someone if they were told that they were going to be transferred to another Bureau facility. The reason given was their belief that the yards at the various USPs were exceedingly more dangerous and they knew that they would likely have to kill someone if transferred out of the ADX." The authors of this review interpreted the men's desire to stay put as "a tribute to the level of care the inmates are receiving" (p. 129). The report continued in a similar vein. "It should be noted that part of the desire for these inmates to remain at ADX is the unique and often close relationship these men have with the staff" (p. 130). And even more improbably: "This reluctance to leave ADX Florence may be related to privileges such as reading materials, television, and recreation activities afforded inmates at ADX and the professionalism of the security and program staff assigned there" (p. 130).

The impression given of comfort and care is at odds with the prisoner experience. How can a "close" relationship form with staff who strip you, ignore you, place you in chains, and keep you at arm's length? It might be dependent out of necessity because prisoners can do nothing for themselves and close on account of forced proximity but not in the sense of fellow feeling or empathy. Also, and more positively, it may reflect some easing of conditions that accompanied *Cunningham*. But it is a grim commentary on the violence that these men fear from their peers, and the limited conditions in the maximum-security facilities to which they might be transferred, that remaining in solitary confinement at ADX Florence was their preferred option. Being alone and alive was better than being in company and in jeopardy.

If people are willing to restrict their horizons to an area smaller than a standard parking space (see figure 5.2) for fear of the alternative, this is not a "tribute to the level of care" on offer but rather a condemnation of a penal system so stripped of meaning and opportunity that the life on offer at ADX Florence is seen as a sort of sanctuary. It also says something about how difficult it is for a man to return to company having been denied it for so long. When what was previously taken for granted becomes a source of confusion and crippling anxiety, a stable degree of misery may be preferable to risky uncertainty.

When prisoners in ADX Florence (usually H Unit) embark on hunger strikes they are ended with force feeding. They do not seem to be coordinated in advance but rather when others learn someone has begun to refuse food, this is their cue to join in. As an exercise in delegitimation this is brutally repressed. The costs of compliance are disregarded by the authorities who care not why it is given. Resigned to the unlikelihood that the worst of the worst will conform in the absence of the most onerous regulation they are indifferent as to the associated harms in human terms.

It is difficult to envisage what normative compliance would look like in ADX Florence, which has been designed to remove any opportunity for ordinary social intercourse. Ray Levasseur, a graduate of the institution, described the environment as a "proto-techno-fascist's architectural wetdream" (cited in Franzen 2004: 236). How could human beings who are confined (coffined, even) for all but a couple of hours each day to tiny and spartan living quarters ever consent to this treatment and feel morally obligated to comply with what was expected of them? ADX Florence has two design priorities. It was built to incorporate—rather than to bridge—a substantial legitimacy deficit and to negate attempts at delegitimation. It is a penological rarity, a prison intended to be run without the consent of its captive population.

Coda

As I have argued elsewhere, prolonged solitary confinement is chronically stressful and intrinsically inhumane. As such, it should not be tolerated (O'Donnell 2014). ADX Florence is a blot on the US penal landscape, an affront to human dignity, and a willful denial of the capacity of even the most apparently recalcitrant individuals to change. Built in an area contaminated by toxic waste it, in turn, pollutes the penal environment. The arguments for its continued existence are insubstantial, unpersuasive, and based on a picture of humanity (the worst of the worst) that has no place in a civilized society. It is better now than when Jack Powers had to endure it, but the sooner it joins the ranks of the many other failed and forgotten experiments in punishment the better. This is the kind of life that has nothing to recommend it.

6

Carceral Contours

Isir Bet was the only institution I studied where there was reasonably authentic alignment between official rhetoric and life on the ground. As the epigraphs for chapters 2 to 5 show, a Janus-faced penology was in evidence elsewhere. The Northern Ireland Office stated it would not recognize terrorist groupings, that prisoners were individual criminals and would be treated as such. The reality was IRA men living communally, wearing their own clothes, not doing prison work, and obeying their own leaders rather than the prison governor. The Texas Department of Corrections stated that the only assistance given by prisoners to staff was janitorial. The reality was that some among them (often the most violent) were appointed as a surrogate guard force. The official view of the Federal Bureau of Prisons is that solitary confinement does not exist. The reality is prolonged and painful isolation, treatment that is repugnant to the dignity of the person. One finding of this book therefore is that the language of imprisonment must be stripped of euphemism and hypocrisy if it is to be used with precision.

Revisiting Integration and Regulation

The four case studies that I describe are real examples rather than ideal types. (As conceded in chapter 1, the focus is on prisons for adult men. This book has an androcentric bias.) However, others evince similar arrangements, and all can be arranged along the two dimensions of integration and regulation of which the prisons under consideration represent the extreme combinations. The H Blocks were high on both, the Eastham Unit was low on both, Isir Bet was high on the former and low on the latter, and vice versa for ADX Florence.

ADX Florence was the only institution not characterized by regulatory pluralism. This singularity is one of the most striking things about it. Elsewhere, different sets of governance arrangements coexisted in relative harmony (i.e., Isir Bet, where the prisoners' elected representatives liaised with the institution's commander); jostled uncomfortably alongside each other (i.e., the Eastham Unit, where the prohibition on prisoners disciplining their peers was more honored in the breach and the BTs, as institutionalized snitches, violated the inmate code's prohibition on informing); or were at perpetual loggerheads (i.e., the H Blocks, where prisoners resisted and undermined the prison rules at every opportunity, preferring to live by their own charter). In the Eastham Unit and Isir Bet the system operated by/for/against the prisoners derived its authority from the administration it functioned beneath. Prisoners in the H Blocks lived by their own rules and when they sought guidance it was from the army council of the IRA rather than the Northern Ireland Prison Service.

The regulations in Isir Bet were difficult to wriggle free of but never became suffocatingly tight in Crewe's (2011) sense of an experience of imprisonment where power is exercised softly but grips the prisoner in so many ways that it is impossible to slough off. Bespoke arrangements that contain within them the possibility of further alteration are less painful than externally imposed and inflexible regulations. Life in the H Blocks could have been tight had the prison rules been taken seriously, but the prisoners rejected them. This rejection made their experience of imprisonment much heavier, in terms of hostile relationships with staff and poor conditions, and deeper, in terms of the prevailing level of security (using the concepts of weight and depth in the same way as King and McDermott 1995: 90). They fought against allowing the carceral experience to shape their identity or regulate their behavior, no matter the personal costs. Nonconforming IRA prisoners never willingly submitted to the prison's authority or internalized its value system. They did not enroll in offender management or cognitive behavioral programs, because they considered that their thinking was clear and their actions rational and not criminal (even if unambiguously unlawful and harmful).

The communal life on offer in the H Blocks was viewed by those who subscribed to it as superior to the official regulatory system, the legitimacy of which was not accepted beyond the obvious point that if IRA operatives saw themselves as POWs, then they had to accept the enemy's right to capture and contain them while the conflict continued. Those held in ADX Florence and the Eastham Unit protested against the official structures (and strictures) but could not emancipate themselves; the only respite was to cause sufficient self-injury to necessitate a (temporary) hospital transfer, or to fight for years, against substantial odds, through the courts. In Isir Bet there was no attempt to supplant the administration; what the prisoners devised and put in place was modeled on the kind of neighborhood self-government they were familiar with when at home, and it paralleled and intersected with the official system. The code specified matters deemed suitable for internal resolution and those that would be referred to the prison's commander.

There was nothing tight about the Eastham Unit, because the men imprisoned there had little involvement in the administration of their own sentences. ADX Florence was stifling for prisoners, not so much because they became entangled in their own sentence management but because their room for maneuver was so limited and the duration of stay so open-ended. Part of the pain of their imprisonment was the feeling of impotence about what they needed to do to move on to a less restrictive regime. They knew how to cause a deterioration in their situation but not how to ameliorate it. It is difficult to imagine a prison that is deeper (vast distance from family and community and level of restriction on movement and behavior; those on SAMs are almost completely cut off from developments inside and outside the prison), heavier (oppressive weight of regulations and poor relations with staff), and tighter (noncompliance results in an elongation of stay; mechanisms for the ventilation of grievances exist but are exhausting to pursue and the prospects of a successful application are slim) than ADX Florence.

There were shared meanings and behaviors among the prisoners in Isir Bet (whose interdependence was rooted in the need for self-sufficiency), the Eastham Unit (where it was understood that conflicts would be settled through force), and the H Blocks (where there was allegiance to a cause and opposition to a clearly defined enemy). ADX Florence was too atomized for its occupants to develop practices that could become embedded and be modeled by newcomers; there were few opportunities to create and nurture a unity of purpose. When people cannot communicate with ease it is difficult for them to arrive at mutual understandings (although the hunger strikes at ADX Florence showed that, with extreme patience, common purpose could occasionally be demonstrated via the choreography of individual decisions rather than the action of a group). The IRA men in the H Blocks deliberately located their struggle in the context of a fight for self-determination on the streets, and their educational and political journey within the prison influenced the direction of the peace process outside. New arrivals were inducted into a communal way of life and educated about its rationale and antecedents. The arrangements they developed did not so much reflect the lives they had left behind as much as they represented principles according to which they thought life ought to be lived.

Isir Bet mirrored the world outside. Its occupants lived, worked, studied, and worshiped at close quarters. They tried to get by and support their families financially. The Eastham Unit was a brutal, segregationist place where the reverberations of slavery continued to be felt; it took time for prisoners' rights to become seen as civil rights. ADX Florence was the outworking of a politics of fear and (in)difference. The *Cunningham* litigation certainly softened life for those with serious mental illness, but its ramifications were narrow; the prison remained cut off from wider concerns geographically, politically, and penologically. Compare it with Isir Bet in the middle of a teeming town. Or the H Blocks, a short ride from Belfast. The internal arrangements in some prisons sustained (Isir Bet) and even uplifted (H Blocks). In others they were endured (Eastham Unit) or threatened to obliterate (ADX Florence).

ADX Florence meets a minimalist definition of a society in that it has clear borders within which live adult men who share a history of criminality, are deemed to be among the worst of the worst, and whose dealings with staff and each other are strictly controlled and clearly patterned. It differs from other aggregations of prisoners in the paucity of opportunities to meet and engage. Whatever cursory interactions take place are one-dimensional, primarily involve staff members, and are based on hostility (at worst) or cool professionalism (at best). They are unleavened by contact with peers. This is life at its most desiccated.

Coping and adaptation were easier in highly integrated prisons where a degree of mutual support could be assumed and where there was scope for prisoners to sculpt their environment just as they were sculpted by it. In ADX Florence, where the interaction required for personhood was glaringly—and designedly—absent, life was so difficult that some disintegrated. In the Eastham Unit, while the material circumstances of confinement were better for BTs, they occupied an uneasy position and were continually alert to the possibility of attack from a disgruntled member of the general population (an attack that, it must be said, would almost certainly be repelled and then repaid in kind, and with interest).

The H Blocks are interesting because self-governance emerged despite a high level of staffing. Following the logic of governance theory (see chapter 1), there should be an inverse relationship between the number of staff and the emergence of inmate self-governance. But, as this book shows, this only explains circumstances where such arrangements emerge as a matter of necessity, not where they are created as a matter of policy. Coordination of activities was essential in Isir Bet to allow economic and domestic life to unfold predictably. In the H Blocks there was a fundamentally different imperative—governance was about identity (or, more specifically, resisting attempts at criminalization). In this way, the H Blocks charter was more of an aberration than the code that was disseminated at Isir Bet.

The story of the Eastham Unit and ADX Florence is of incarcerated men using the courts to force change upon a regulatory environment that was causing them pain. They had to seek relief externally. In Isir Bet the process to create an acceptable set of rules for living was an internal one, driven by the prisoners, but in cooperation with the prison's commander. In the H Blocks an entirely parallel way of living was devised, to the dismay of the authorities, who viewed the success of the commune as a mark of their failure to operate a normal prison regime. There is a gradient here from full-blooded engagement with the legal process (*Ruiz v. Estelle*, *Cunningham v. Federal Bureau of Prisons*), to the creation of local arrangements that had the backing of prison management (Isir Bet code), to the molding of a sub rosa set of rules (the Charter for Frelimo Communities was subversive both of the prison regime and the IRA's previous structures, which had been hierarchical and required unthinking obedience). To varying degrees the different prisoner societies shaped the rules governing their inhabitants' lives, most emphatically perhaps in Texas, where the results of the *Ruiz* litigation were felt right across the state. As a result of the decision in this case, a long-established form of life was abolished by decree and the prison's carceral geometry was redrawn, with movement along the axes of both integration and regulation.

After we have located a prison's coordinates according to the two primary scales (figure 1.1), we need to add to the mix the existence (or

TABLE 6.1. Describing Prison Life: A Three-Step Approach

	H Blocks	Eastham Unit	Isir Bet	ADX Florence
1. Plot the key coordinates				
Integration	High	Low	High	Low
Regulation	High	Low	Low	High
2. Add texture				
Legitimacy:				
Horizontal	✓	×	✓	×
Vertical	×	×	✓	✓
Basis of compliance	Absent	Manipulative	Normative	Coercive
3. Think about subsidiary factors				
Porosity	Medium	Low	High	Negligible
Autonomy	High	Low	High	Low
Room to roam (daytime)	Adequate	Limited	Ample	Minuscule
Status of prisoner:				
Official view	Terrorist	Penal subject	Offender	Worst of the worst
Self-conception	POW	Slave	Displaced citizen	Exile
Relations with staff	Non-existent	Brutal	Cordial	Distant
Written constitution	✓	×	✓	×
Bodily integrity	Secure	In jeopardy	Secure	Vulnerable
Threats to psyche	Low	Modest	Modest	Severe

otherwise) of the various levels of legitimacy to get a sense of how prisoners feel and fare. This, together with an exploration of the basis of compliance, is the second of three steps—summarized in table 6.1—that must be taken to describe life in any prison. This three-step approach unites the theoretical concerns raised in chapter 1 (steps 1 and 2) with the key empirical findings from the four case studies set out in chapters 2 to 5 (step 3).

Inserting Legitimacy

Beetham (1991: 3) posited: "Where power is acquired and exercised according to justifiable rules, and with evidence of consent, we call it rightful or legitimate." As proposed in chapter 1, we need to add horizontal (among prisoners) and vertical (between prisoners and officialdom) dimensions to complete our understanding. This allows us to conclude that while the communal life developed in the H Blocks was an abomination to the prison staff, for whom it flew in the face of official aims and objectives, it was legitimate in the prisoners' eyes. It was wrongful for one group and rightful for the other. In ADX Florence, consent was neither sought nor desired, so there was a built-in legitimacy deficit. The courts also found that the regime was illegitimate for those suffering from serious mental illness. For others it was legally unproblematic, no matter how degrading, so there was a thin shard of vertical legitimacy. There were occasions when prisoners withdrew their compliance, for example, by not eating voluntarily, and this delegitimated the regime.

Isir Bet came closest to a legitimate set of arrangements, viewed horizontally or vertically by prisoners. It was fluid and dialogic rather than stagnant and one-sided. As a result, its longevity is most likely. This is not to say that there will never be any upheaval but rather to predict that the solidity of the preexisting arrangements makes a return to orderly coexistence likely, in the event of an occasion of delegitimation. As proposed in chapter 1, this can be thought of as triple-ply legitimacy in that all three levels of Beetham's definition (see box 1.1) are clearly and meaningfully satisfied; this is the strongest and most durable configuration. The same durability characterized the H Blocks (viewed horizontally) once a period of volatility and an exodus of activists, including those affiliated with the League of Communist Republicans, had passed.

In the Eastham Unit, the exercise of power was at odds with stated declarations and the consent of the general prison population was not considered relevant so long as the BTs were prepared to act as the administration's agents. Such arrangements demonstrated a substantial legitimacy deficit. Furthermore, when the prisoners engaged in self-mutilation or work stoppages, they were providing evidence of delegitimation. Finally, when the courts found that the prisoners' treatment was unconstitutional, this showed that it was illegitimate. In other words, across all three of Beetham's levels, the Eastham Unit failed. There was not even a veneer of legitimacy.

It is apposite at this juncture to return to Beetham's (1991: 3) claim that all systems of power relations seek legitimation and that "societies will seek to subject it to justifiable rules, and the powerful themselves will seek to secure consent to their power from at least the most important among their subordinates." In the Eastham Unit, consent from the men selected to be BTs was enough, but when this "rotten crutch" (DiIulio 1987a: 210) was finally discarded there was a short-lived period of lethal chaos before legitimate power relations emerged. In ADX Florence this consent was never sought. In Isir Bet it operated at two levels. First, the prisoners' leaders were elected (and thereby accountable) and the charter they developed was discussed with, and ratified by, the overwhelming majority of those who would be bound by it. Second, the prisoners' chairman worked closely with the prison's commander to ensure a mutually acceptable modus vivendi. The negotiation of order was an open-ended process.

If the use of force is a proxy for the failure of authority, then the Eastham Unit failed perennially and Isir Bet seldom did. In the case of the H Blocks, yet again it is a matter of perspective. The prisoners did not use force to ensure compliance with the rules of the commune (although several expulsions took place). From time to time the staff did, in an attempt to uphold the prison rules of Northern Ireland, but this could not have reduced their standing in the eyes of the prisoners because they had none to begin with. In addition, it further undermined their claim to legitimacy; resorting to force was (ironically) a sign of weakness, because it was futile. In ADX Florence the threat of force undergirded every aspect of the institution's operation; it was omnipresent, and technology further reduced the quality of interpersonal relationships (which were poor to start with). There was no dynamic security in the sense of a connection between captor and captive built on mutual understanding and acceptance.

A key question is who controls discipline. In the H Blocks the prisoners won this battle and—astonishingly for a maximum-security prison—the punishment block was shut down. In ADX Florence it was emphatically the staff; prisoners had no role in supervising or sanctioning each other. Isir Bet and the Eastham Unit were hybrid affairs with prisoners policing and punishing their peers. In the latter institution, the staff were enthusiastic participants, but in the former they became involved only if a case was referred to them as per the provisions of the code.

In the H Blocks, the prison governor and his political masters in the Northern Ireland Office eventually accepted the de facto political status of the prisoners and communication was routed between the senior management and the camp staff. This was a pragmatic solution to a problem of legitimacy that could never be officially resolved so long as those imprisoned for republican activism were deemed to be criminals. IRA men could accept that as POWs there would have to be a forum for dialogue with the other side but only in a context where they retained a great deal of autonomy about the organization of their lives. The contrast with ADX Florence could hardly be greater. The most dangerous terrorists in Europe had carceral lives very different from the worst of the worst in the US.

Coercive power was unapologetically front and center in ADX Florence, vicarious in the Eastham Unit, pushed behind the scenes in Isir Bet, and strategically resisted in the H Blocks. This is quite a diversity of power relations. Where power was not seen as problematic by the authorities—ADX Florence and the Eastham Unit—it proved to be intensely so, and the courts eventually intervened.

In Isir Bet steps were taken to codify and constrain discretion. ADX Florence was the apotheosis of bureaucratic depersonalization, a literal iron cage where encounters were impersonal and formal with no meaningful scope—or indeed desire—to allow the give and take of normal human relations. There were minimal rights and few privileges. The H Blocks comprised two competing legally valid (in the eyes of those subordinate to them) regimes; the IRA rejected the official system in favor of its own, which was also heavily bureaucratic. Looking at the IRA side of the equation what we see is an attempt to displace traditional authority and unquestioning obedience with a set of arrangements more suitable for men who had been through intense suffering for whom pre-existing hierarchies made little sense, and who needed structures that were flatter, more inclusive, and more open (regarding membership, ideas, and critique).

At the Eastham Unit tradition was sufficient justification for the status quo: things were done this way because they had always been done this way. But as a highly discretionary setup it was inherently open to abuse. Indeed, how could it have been otherwise when the existence of a system of inmates exercising a disciplinary function was not officially acknowledged? In ADX Florence the personal was peripheral. But the staff were not completely detached emotionally, and an ecology of cruelty emerged. Even "neutral" rule enforcement is painful in ADX Florence because any vestige of humanity has been stripped away; there is nothing benign about consistent and dispassionate treatment in an environment where the possibility of meaningful human engagement has evaporated.

Members of highly integrated prison societies fare well. They do better if there is horizontal legitimacy, and best if there is vertical legitimacy to boot. Having thought about the prison's carceral geometry in terms of integration and regulation and having introduced the various components of legitimacy to the analysis, the next stage in understanding the texture of its social life is to reflect upon compliance.

Basis of Compliance

As outlined in chapter 1, it is difficult to ascertain whether abiding by the rules is truly normative, or results from fear of the consequences of noncompliance, or a calculation of where the balance of advantage is to be found, or unreflective conformity ("dull compulsion"), or learned helplessness. Acquiescence will often result from a combination of these factors, such as when values and self-interest overlap or when the cost-benefit ratio is taken for granted. Even in Isir Bet, obedience could not be assumed, so the consequences of noncompliance were codified and a body of order keepers was appointed to deal with any breaches. Self-interest was also a factor in Isir Bet as compliance meant access to paid employment and a more comfortable and hygienic environment.

Crewe (2009) distinguished four forms of social power. The first of these was coercion, which is "a provocative, inefficient, and illegitimate means of enforcing order" (p. 81). It is seldom applied in a sustained fashion, but ADX Florence shows that, on occasion, it can be. It may be undesirable and costly in human, financial, and organizational terms, but it has been a way of life at this institution since it opened. Chains, barriers, isolation, and physical restraints are the norm at ADX Florence. What are exceptional measures elsewhere have become routinized here. The second was manipulation or inducement. This characterized arrangements at the Eastham Unit, where internal markets were controlled by the BTs and prisoners were willing to oversee their peers for the associated perks. Power operates through (enlightened or benighted) self-interest; small rewards assume large significance when personal possessions and autonomy are limited. Third came habit, ritual, or fatalistic resignation. This was not exclusive to ADX Florence, where subjugation is inevitable and unavoidable, but is a characteristic of all prison regimes to a greater or lesser extent because the timetable and an unchanging routine scaffold the day and allow the prisoner to move forward without needing to give much serious consideration to the situation.

Fourth was normative compliance, based on shared values rather than coercion, incentives, or unthinking acceptance. Prisoners believe that the rules by which they live are issued by a legitimate authority with which they identify. They fall in line willingly, allowing individual priorities to be trumped by those of the collective. They comply because they believe this to be the correct thing to do rather than out of fear, the prospect of a reward, or thoughtless habit. (There are echoes here of the National Prison Association's fifteenth principle, which emphasized that "moral forces should be relied upon, with as little admixture of physical force as possible, and organized persuasion be made to take the place of coercive constraint"; see box 5.1). This was the situation in Isir Bet, where the prisoners drew up their own code for daily life with whose provisions the administration agreed.

The IRA prisoners in the H Blocks were entirely noncompliant. This allows a refinement of Crewe's analysis in that IRA members did not assign any (vertical) legitimacy to the state that guarded them and nor did they share its values or objectives. In other words, the grounds for normative compliance did not exist. They were willfully and persistently unamenable and could not be coerced or manipulated into toeing the line. However, their lives went smoothly because they subscribed to their own set of values and aims (horizontal legitimacy) that operated in parallel with official statements of purpose that were ascribed no penological significance.

There is some overlap, of course, as in return for inducements, BTs were prepared to use coercion. Prison authorities in Texas claimed that the BT system facilitated a safe and orderly existence, but the reality was that most prisoners were cowed into anxious submission with little in the way of normative compliance (and a large dollop of learned helplessness). In ADX Florence the authorities cared not whether there was normative compliance on the part of those who must endure the regime; legitimacy—apart from legal validity—was not a necessary element of the power relations they oversaw.

There was a constant struggle between the authorities and the IRA in the H Blocks to see whose version of legitimacy would triumph; this was an existential struggle with fatalities on both sides. IRA activists accepted that the role of the prison authorities was to keep them behind bars, but their identity as POWs meant their commitment was to subvert the regime and to escape. The legitimacy that they ascribed to their captors as enemy forces determined to crush them was rejected by an administration wedded to the notion that they were no more than common criminals.

In broad-brush terms, we could say that rule-following in the Eastham Unit was motivated by fear of the consequences of noncompliance within a scheme in which prisoner was pitted against prisoner; it was manipulative (with a strong undertow of coercion). In the early days of the H Blocks the institution's rules were ignored to the point of self-imposed nakedness, squalor, and starvation, but the charter was seen as a guide to right—and comradely—relations. In Isir Bet the code promoted normative compliance but there was a prudential element too; those who followed the rules had access to employment opportunities and a degree of collective comfort. In ADX Florence there was little scope to disobey the rules, and breaches (e.g., self-harm) were met with a rigid disciplinary response; this was unvarnished coercion. Everywhere, prisoners simply followed the routine, however harsh, often without too much soul-searching or reflection.

It should be noted that even brute force involves a transaction and a set of expectations. Hunger strikers in ADX Florence struggled mightily to begin a conversation because of the SAMs under which they lived. While resistance may be futile it can still be mounted. It is minimally dialogic, a whisper to a shout. Even against mighty odds, human agency is never fully extinguished.

Work in the area of international relations (e.g., Nye 2008) distinguishes between "hard" and "soft" forms of power. These concepts can be applied in the micropolitics of the carceral arena. Hard power embraces what Crewe described as coercion and manipulation. It was evident in the Eastham Unit (among prisoners and between staff and prisoners), in ADX Florence (between staff and prisoners; it was not really relevant among prisoners as there was so little interaction between them, although Jack Powers succumbed to the threats being made against him in his isolation cell), and in the H Blocks (unusually it was bidirectional, with staff violence against prisoners repaid by multiple killings outside, often cautionary).

Soft power—Crewe's normative compliance—can be seen in Isir Bet (among prisoners; it was not relevant between staff and prisoners as there was little in the way of daily interaction, although some of the guards carried guns, so the potential for lethal force existed) and the H Blocks (among prisoners). It supports rather than suffocates. The bases of soft power may wax, wane, and morph, but they are never far from the surface. When hard power is being exercised its hammer blows ring clear and its intent is unambiguous.

Crewe's final variant of social power—habit or resignation—may have roots that are hard (violence, threats, bribery) or soft (attraction, persuasion, wanting to do what others do) but, because of repetition, the behaviors are perpetuated without any continuing need for the basis of power to be made explicit. It is only in the event of a rupture that the underlying dynamics become clear.

In the Eastham Unit, armed BTs, handpicked for their brutality and rewarded for their exertions, oversaw and violently subdued their peers. They were an adjunct guard force rather than an element of prisoner self-governance and both the circumstances of their appointment and their modus operandi made it unlikely that they would inspire the loyalty and affection of their subordinates. By deciding not to provide adequate funding, the state of Texas in the 1970s was abrogating its responsibility and sending a strong signal about the low importance it placed on prisoner welfare.

In Isir Bet the prisoners selected their own cadre of order keepers, who policed by consent under an agreed-upon framework of rules. As volunteers from among the general population they were a long way from the BTs, who were appointed by staff without reference to prisoner preferences. The former lived among their peers rather than keeping a wary distance from them. They did not operate as a coercive unit. They did not carry weapons. Trust was reciprocal. They were allies rather than foes. While there were some modest material benefits (i.e., a monthly soap ration), the most important perk was the relative freedom of movement that went with the job and the opportunities that this generated for transmitting information and accumulating favors. It is noteworthy that while the BTs were supposed to not have a disciplinary function, the order keepers did, and kept a written record of infractions. Also, a punishment tariff was codified (see box 4.1).

Adherence was never perfect and there was always potential for order to fray. Some of the men on IRA wings in the H Blocks had, at best, a lukewarm commitment to the commune and the associated structures (political education, dialogue, and disputation), feeling they were temperamentally unsuited to the environment; all benefited, however. Some at Isir Bet were frustrated in their attempts to secure a workspace or resented some of the code's prohibitions, but they played along as to do otherwise would have been to their detriment. The BTs trod a fine line between being seen as institutional lackeys and powerful enforcers; other prisoners complied only when to do otherwise would place them at risk—their deference was insincere, a survival sham. Prisoners in ADX Florence had fewer options but—with some effort—they could reinterpret their surroundings and create a context for imaginative disengagement. The systems were well enough established in each of the four prisons to withstand occasional shocks, especially if they came from within.

Having considered integration and regulation (step 1), then legitimacy and compliance (step 2), the third and final step in the process of describing prison life is to ponder the subsidiary issues listed in table 6.1. In no particular order these comprise the degree of infiltration of the outside world (porosity), the quantum of residual autonomy, the status of the prisoner (both officially ascribed and self-identified), the nature of relations with staff, the existence (or not) of a written constitution, and threats to mind and body. These are discussed in turn throughout the remainder of the chapter.

Porosity

Prisoners in the H Blocks and Isir Bet were closely connected with the outside community. They remained part of it, albeit spatially displaced.

In ADX Florence and the Eastham Unit, partly for reasons of geography, these ties (which may already have been damaged by the behavior that led to incarceration) were more attenuated.

Visits at Isir Bet may have been infrequent for the individual whose family had to travel a great distance on foot, carrying supplies, and losing a day's income in the process. But at least when they arrived they could sit with their loved ones without the impediments of screens separating them or staff eavesdropping on their conversations. Guards checked the parcels of food, clothing, and other essentials being brought by visitors, but this was a cursory rummage or visual inspection rather than a thorough search. They were supposed to read outgoing correspondence, but this seldom happened as a prisoner who had a letter would simply hand it to his visitor. In any event, given low levels of literacy, writing was seldom the preferred mode of communication. Visits were not directly supervised by staff, but order keepers made sure that the hall did not get overcrowded, that people were notified when their visitors arrived, and that a sense of decorum was maintained given the presence of women and children.

Access to visits did not depend on sentence length or offense type; it was democratic—if a visitor arrived, the prisoner could socialize with them. The prison was a highly porous place. In addition, its inhabitants could keep up to date with news and current affairs via the televisions in their dormitories. They had no access to telephones unless they managed to smuggle one in and keep it charged and hidden, or a member of staff could be prevailed upon to hire out his or her cell phone for a brief call. If they could afford to pay the overtime rates for the accompanying guards, an occasional excursion to the local town was a possibility.

The men in the Eastham Unit could send and receive letters and avail of (non-contact and supervised) social visits at the weekend. However, the prison's rural location was an impediment to easy and regular access. Traveling there was awkward and expensive for anyone who did not have private transport and, like most of those who ended up incarcerated in the TDC, happened to be a city dweller. Some prisoners formed strong attachments with their lawyers (once or twice straying from the professional to the romantic) as they worked together to challenge the legality, and even constitutionality, of their treatment.

Visiting in the H Blocks was free-flowing in the sense that anyone could turn up, without booking or preclearance. They were searched and the process was carefully controlled, but community contacts were good. A message could be sent out during a morning visit and a reply received later the same day. Access to education was easy and prisoners could watch television and listen to the radio. They benefited from periods of furlough as their sentences progressed. It has been observed that some long-termers cut ties with loved ones to make doing time easier (O'Donnell 2014: 223–25). This was not the case in the H Blocks, where the prisoners saw themselves as defenders of communities that understood their actions and waited to welcome them home. Some of these men, who had pledged their lives to sever the links between Northern Ireland and the United Kingdom and who had caused massive loss of life in the process (figures 2.1 and 2.2), became politicians and community leaders upon release. It is difficult to imagine this happening (or even being contemplated) with men from ADX Florence who are restored to liberty.

In ADX Florence if an individual was not on the visitors' list completed upon arrival it was difficult to add their name afterward. Given the vast distances between prisoners and their homeplaces (table 5.2), and the lengths of their sentences (table 5.3), this had the inevitable—and predictable—effect of causing circles of support to contract. Admittedly it is difficult to create new friendships from behind bars, but it seems needlessly cruel to close off this possibility. ADX Florence was as impermeable as a prison could be while remaining within the law. The faint possibility of keeping community ties intact was even further reduced for those confined there under SAMs.

Literate individuals in ADX Florence could receive (and send) letters subject to the censor's approval, but they could be denied access to the original missive. The charm of a piece of correspondence lies not only in the written contents but in the paper chosen, the ink used, the imaginative possibilities of holding an object that had earlier been touched and folded (and maybe keened over or kissed) by someone special. A directive from the warden in December 2018 stipulated that, with effect from the following month, homemade greeting cards would be prohibited and commercial cards would be photocopied with the original withheld and the copy passed on to the intended recipient. Any correspondence with a scent of fragrance would be rejected as would any epistle not written on white paper and inserted in a white envelope. Anything written in crayon or containing stickers or glitter—the accessories beloved of children everywhere—would also be rejected (Matevousian 2018b).

Notwithstanding the need to take security seriously it is difficult to appreciate the threat posed by a love letter sprayed with a favorite perfume, or a card made by a child in school, inscribed in crayon, adorned with a sticker or two, and mailed in time for Father's Day to a parent who might never be seen again. One senses that a reaction of this magnitude would not occur unless the intended recipients were viewed as evil geniuses who could create havoc using the most apparently benign materials. Letters assume a greater importance at ADX Florence than elsewhere because the prison is so far from prisoners' families and telephone calls are strictly limited. Depersonalizing them in this way seems gratuitous, even spiteful.

Another aspect of porosity concerns how life in prison is penetrated by life on the street. For republican activists it was a continuation and their struggle was prosecuted simultaneously on each side of the wall. In Isir Bet, both were places where the entrepreneurial, wealthy, and lucky prospered, but there was little in the way of a safety net for the less fortunate. Isir Bet reflected the complex web of relationships outside, in terms of work, family, language, and faith tradition. Indeed, it is possible that the shared experience of imprisonment temporarily erased some of the intergroup differences (based on religious or ethnic identity, occupational status, or nature of offense, for example) that would result in mutual indifference or hostility outside. The Eastham Unit was violent and racist like Texas more generally, so those who managed outside were primed, in some way at least, for the magnification of inequality inside, although life on a prison farm would have taken some getting used to for urban men. In ADX Florence the discrepancy was greatest and there was no preparation for the stripped-back existence that awaited (except perhaps for the rare individual making a return visit or the men transferred from another supermax environment).

Isir Bet reflected the world outside and some external governance institutions continued to apply. Representatives of the country's largest bank visited twice each week so that cash could be deposited or withdrawn. Families brought food, a favorite dish offering a sensory reminder of home. Priests and pastors came in to lead services. There were cafés and shops (e.g., clothing, footwear, barbering). Prisoners worked on contracts (e.g., making fishing nets) or wove blankets and sold them on the open market. Tourists sometimes dropped by to purchase their wares, leaving with a range of overpriced wood carvings, scarves, and hats. Teachers ensured that students could follow the same school curriculum as their counterparts in the town outside. Artists brought materials and shared ideas and techniques. Dormitory members pooled their resources to take out satellite television subscriptions and watched the news together each evening. In other words, many of the usual modes of legal governance remained available. To a greater extent than elsewhere, the community came into the prison compound, and there was a degree of normalization and congested homeliness.

Autonomy

All prisons aim to prevent easy egress. Despite the exceptionally high level of security, the H Blocks failed spectacularly with a massive group escape in 1983 and a prisoner, disguised as a woman, departing with a contingent of visitors in 1997 (the same year a sophisticated tunnel was discovered). That the IRA men viewed themselves differently is seen in a disciplined adherence to periods of furlough—they always returned on time—that coexisted with their devotion to escaping. Prisoners fled from the Eastham Unit farm (including David Ruiz). There was an escape from Isir Bet between my first and second visits (unusually the man then broke back in at night so that he could remove the safe from another prisoner's shop). Since it opened in 1994, there has never been an escape from ADX Florence (other than through suicide).

Those confined in Isir Bet and the H Blocks were free to move about during the day, and to work and recreate. They were not reduced to weak, dependent creatures required to ask permission to do anything. With the exception of alcohol, drugs, tobacco, and cell phones, prisoners in Isir Bet had access to the same range of goods and services as would be available to them outside, if they happened to be in funds. There was plenty of residual autonomy. IRA men in the H Blocks during the 1990s wore their own clothing, kept their own possessions, decorated their cells, and could opt to relocate to a non-English-speaking wing. Considerable scope existed for placing their stamp upon the day.

Once again, the contrast with ADX Florence could hardly be greater. A bulletin issued in 2018 by the institution's acting warden announced that with immediate effect the commissary would no longer sell "Sugar Cubes, Tang, Skittles, Fusion Ice Tea, Jolly Ranchers, Honey and Milk Caramels" because these items had been used to make intoxicants (Klein 2018). Prisoners the world over have been inventive when it comes to brewing and distilling alcohol, but one wonders whether it is a proportionate response to deny the occupants of the most isolating prison in North America access to the occasional packet of candy, or sugar in their tea, because a few among them have identified a way to use these treats as the ingredients for hooch. Also, given the limited quantity of possessions allowed in cells, the frequency of searches, and the constant surveillance, it is difficult to imagine that this activity was being conducted on a large scale unbeknownst to staff. Again, not for a moment gainsaying the need to take security seriously, it is difficult to imagine that the guard force in ADX Florence would not be a match for a solitary prisoner who was inebriated on a cocktail of Jolly Ranchers and Tang.

The loss of autonomy was pronounced in the Eastham Unit, where prisoners had limited access to goods and services, wore uniform clothing, and were slaves to the prison work schedule. In ADX Florence the room for maneuver was virtually nonexistent; a man could choose not to avail of an exercise period and whether to lie, stand, sit, or pace in his tiny cell but, beyond this, choices were severely constrained.

Routine victimization, exploitation, and violence undermine social cohesion (Edgar et al. 2003), while mutual support, advocacy, and agreed-upon expectations boost consensus and community solidarity. Men in Isir Bet and the H Blocks felt safe. The potential for conflict was reduced and mechanisms for its resolution were in place. But in ADX Florence, where the physical security was extreme, they were anxious and conflict with staff was endemic. In the Eastham Unit predatory BTs were difficult to avoid and the less favored prisoners had to run the gauntlet of correctional staff and their more powerful peers.

In ADX Florence and the H Blocks, men were idle (by choice in the latter institution, where they refused to work on the basis that they were POWs rather than common criminals). In the Eastham Unit, they contributed to the prison's economy, but their field labor was involuntary and they never benefited financially or had any say as to how the profits they generated were spent. This was grim and unremitting penal servitude. (The Thirteenth Amendment to the US Constitution banned slavery and involuntary servitude except as punishment for crime.) Prisoners had limited choices about how to spend their meager personal resources in the prison's commissary.

The life that IRA men created for themselves in the H Blocks did not mirror what they left behind; it was more deliberately political and aspirational. They transformed their lives in prison with a view to transforming the political arena outside the prison. By dint of a sustained collective effort they controlled the narrative of their prison stories, their discipline and determination eventually winning the grudging acknowledgment of their captors. They emerged with renewed commitment to the struggle that had resulted in their incarceration but with the substitution of the ballot box for the bomb; politics had become war by other means.

The inhabitants of Isir Bet re-created the outside world within the prison in terms of economic structures (there were rich and poor) but minimized the extent of intergroup chafing and conflict with a written code containing a set of arrangements that paralleled the criminal justice system with its order keepers, tariff of sanctions, and appeal mechanism. The aim was to mimic outside life so that people could generate an income and pass their time productively.

In Texas the racially unjust world outside was magnified inside the prison. There were no beneficent lessons that could be exported. In ADX Florence, as so often, there was a complete disjuncture between then and now. The Alcatraz of the Rockies is penal force at its most exposed and most raw; there is nothing like it outside and no right-minded person would wish there to be. There is such an abrupt disjuncture with communal life that nothing can be taken away with profit and rebuilding an approximate life is a substantial task.

ADX Florence highlights the potentially obliterative power of the state just as Isir Bet shows its weaknesses. In the first, the prison is designed to reduce its occupants to automatons; their temporal and spatial horizons are welded in place. In the second, they are largely autonomous, even if temporarily deprived of their liberty; flung together they create a world that resembles what they are used to outside. The state is not wholly impotent in Isir Bet; it put the prisoners there and can decide to pardon or parole them.

This causes us to think differently about importation and deprivation theories of adjustment to prison life. The experience of the H Blocks shows how a new type of society can be created despite the potentially annihilating implications of the environment and the lack of a model of conduct to import. In such circumstances it may be more productive to think in terms of accumulation and exportation whereby a penal milieu creates a context that enables people to forge new identities that accompany them post-release. Staff in the H Blocks were likely to bring with them shared values and a common perspective (importation), and they were the ones crushed by the deprivations of the prison environment as evidenced by high levels of suicide, absenteeism, alcoholism, and family breakdown.

The BT system was the only indigenous form of governance: it could not be applied outside, being specific to the prison context, although the race-based gangs that were formed to replace the BTs soon extended to the outside world. BTs were not training for transformation (like IRA men) or simply trying to generate an income or learn a trade (like those in Isir Bet). Gangs differed from BTs in that they were not sponsored by the prison authorities. They did not act with the warden's imprimatur. This meant that they had a qualitatively different relationship with staff, who could neither assume a commonality of purpose nor turn a blind eye to abuses.

Security in Isir Bet depended on padlocked dormitory doors and direct monitoring of areas such as the main gate rather than cameras, scanners, and screens. This is not to suggest a completely low-tech environment—there were satellite televisions in the dormitories, after all—but the institution's residents were not living in an environment festooned with CCTV, sensors, and alarms.

Room to Roam

The convivial life in the compound at Isir Bet is far removed from the bleak isolation of the range at ADX Florence. But there is a role for agency in terms of engaging with spatial and temporal arrangements.

The design of the H Blocks created a major impediment to social interaction that the prisoners overcame by winning so many concessions that their doors remained unlocked, they personalized their living quarters (no one in ADX Florence had hung wallpaper in their cell), painted murals in the corridors, where they erected decorative arches (both to normalize the environment and to obstruct the surveillance cameras), and demarcated certain wings as Irish-language–only zones. In these ways, a high-security cellular environment became a place of color and movement.

Prisoners in the H Blocks accepted that unfettered access throughout the prison was never going to be possible but strove to maximize freedom of movement within the wing or block. They knew the importance of putting their own stamp on time. While food was delivered to the wings in accordance with the institutional schedule, they chose when to eat and with whom. They organized their days according to their own personal agendas, whether this comprised study, craftwork, or endless recreation.

In Isir Bet, once dormitory doors were unlocked in the morning their residents were spatially unconstrained within the compound's secure perimeter. This was a place of promiscuous mixing and remained so until evening lockup. If they were not attending school or eating the food served by the prison, they were temporally unconstrained and could work, socialize, and dine according to their personal preferences.

In ADX Florence, the timetable was rigid and controls on movement were tight. Prisoners experienced a phenomenal degree of spatial and temporal restriction. Phone calls and visits were brief and infrequent, and while exercise periods were regularly available, they were of short duration and spent in tightly confining spaces.

Life on the Eastham Unit was organized according to the demands of the farm or whatever job individuals were allocated within the institution. Any sense of freedom that might have accompanied the prospect of working outdoors was soon crushed by the backbreaking nature of the labor, the searing heat, the limited availability of breaks, and the impossibility of escaping without significant outside assistance. Once back inside, unless a BT, they walked along the corridor, staying between the line and the wall, until they reached their housing unit, from which they could not emerge without specific permission. When they rose and ate, where they worked and showered, with whom they socialized, all lay outside of their control.

There was little in the way of classification in the H Blocks other than men being assigned to a wing based on their acceptability to the faction in charge. There was not much variation in any event as most were serving long sentences for serious crimes that they considered to be politically motivated, and they were white, predominantly young and working-class, and overwhelmingly Roman Catholic. In Isir Bet, there were no white prisoners and dormitory allocation was based on sentence length (those on remand and recidivists were allocated to specific dormitories but could mingle with the others during the day). The Eastham Unit held older, recidivist offenders, with cell blocks and work parties segregated by race until the late 1970s. In ADX Florence classification was important in the sense that the prison was reserved for the worst of the worst, but the degree of isolation was such that once a man arrived there the need for careful differentiation between himself and his peers was obviated; everyone was segregated from everyone else.

Life is spatially constrained for prisoners everywhere and can be particularly intense in overcrowded dormitories or where there is multiple occupancy of a single cell. After lockup in Isir Bet, prisoners were confined to the space of a foam mattresses that measured thirty inches by seventy-one inches, a total area of 14.8 square feet. A cell in ADX Florence measured eighty-seven square feet (and there was a little more room in the sally port, which was not routinely accessible to the prisoner). The bed in an ADX Florence cell was a little wider (thirty-six inches) and around the same length as a mattress in Isir Bet. But these dimensions give a misleading sense of the degree of confinement as the dormitories in the latter place were unlocked all day and their occupants were free to wander within the compound or be escorted further afield if they were allocated to a job outside the prison (e.g., fetching water, working on the farm). The prisoner in ADX Florence has nowhere to roam and cannot even create more room in his cell by relocating the furniture as the bed and seat are concrete fixtures and a steel shower takes up another nine square feet, leaving a minuscule amount of unencumbered space. The dormitory dweller in Isir Bet may be cramped, even crushed, at night but during the day he can savor the open air and has opportunities to work and socialize that his counterpart in ADX Florence can only dream of in the trammels of his single cell.

The men incarcerated in the Eastham Unit had the worst of all worlds, occupying dormitories that were dangerously overfull cells that were unbearably congested. Judge Justice condemned the crowding in dormitories where the average space per person was 40 square feet (ranging from 17 to 60; *Ruiz v. Estelle* 1279). Things may have been tighter in Isir Bet, but at least when the dormitories were unlocked the Ethiopian prisoner had options; he was not forced to toil for no pay in the fields or indoor facilities such as workshops, laundries, and kitchens.

As for the cells, Justice severely criticized the practice of routinely accommodating two people in cells measuring five feet by nine feet, which was the usual size in Texas at the time (paras. 1277–78). This was twice as many people in half as much space as the person held at ADX Florence "enjoys." Sometimes three or more men were crammed into these small spaces, where they spent their time, cheek by jowl, between the barred door at the front and the sink and toilet at the back. The degree of discomfort they endured, especially in the sweltering summer heat, is difficult to comprehend. Ekland-Olson (1986: 391) described how a major building program undertaken in response to *Ruiz* resulted in an improvement in the average living space per person from (a stifling) 27.5 square feet in 1979 to (a still paltry) 35.2 square feet in 1984.

The prisoner in ADX Florence may have had a little more space— although a cell smaller than a standard parking bay is hardly roomy— but there was no one to share it with. The Eastham Unit and Isir Bet were socially dense and ADX Florence was socially sparse. In the H Blocks the cells were small (67.5 square feet) and lacked sanitary facilities, but from 1994 they were never locked and their occupants had access to handicrafts rooms, the canteen and ablutions area, and the outside yard, and could spend as much time out of cell as they wished.

Status of Prisoner and Relations with Staff

In none of the case study prisons were relationships with staff warm, personal, or interactive (except between some of the Eastham Unit guards and "their" BTs). Nor did they extend beyond the disciplinary realm. The prevailing narrative regarding the status of prisoners varied greatly.

The occupants of ADX Florence were characterized as a toxic version of humanity that must be securely contained, often until the end of their natural lives; they were socially dead. If they had supporters, these were individuals such as parents, children, or romantic partners, who might or might not be resident in the US. If they had the backing of a group (e.g., Al Qaeda or Gama'a Al-Islamiyya), its members were unlikely to make their presence known for fear of being arrested themselves. There was no domestic agitation specifically on their behalf (although they were potential beneficiaries of national campaigns against prolonged solitary confinement) and even if there had been, it is likely that few would have found it persuasive. The imperative was to hold them securely and to regulate every aspect of their lives.

The defects of total power can be seen in each institution. Staff required inmate allies in the Eastham Unit, where the degree of control was as impressive as it was pernicious and prisoners who did not count themselves among the staff's favorites realized that the only prospect of relief would come from external action via the courts. Relations with staff were cursory, brutal, and racially patterned, with most positions of power occupied by white correctional officers and white BTs. While they may have been thin on the ground the staff were no slouches when it came to meting out corporal punishment. Prisoners were slaves to the state during their incarceration and thrown back on their own (depleted) resources afterward. They excited little sympathy for the poor choices they had made and were seen as the authors of their own misfortune; they were society's jetsam.

In Isir Bet the numerical inferiority of the guards led to a minimalist approach outside of an emergency situation. Staff were largely indifferent to how their charges spent their days so long as they remained within the compound. Relations were generally superficial, informal, and cordial. There was no great antagonism. Prisoners lost their liberty, not their identities; they were displaced citizens.

ADX Florence had the (dubious) virtue of minimal deviation from the rule book, impartiality, relentless enforcement, and consistent outcomes; individual differences were entirely disregarded. But these "fair" procedures appear cruel in an environment that is so stripped back, where a kind word and human touch are so sorely absent, and where any freedom of movement is so tightly delimited. Impersonal treatment, when protracted, connotes a failure to recognize the inherent worth and dignity of the person. While no one has canvassed the prisoners' views it seems unlikely, from the fragments of available evidence, that they would describe their treatment as fair, their representation ("worst of the worst") as accurate or humane, the regulations as just, or the regime as much more than tenuously legitimate, even if the courts upheld its legal validity for those who were not seriously mentally ill.

These men were triply exiled: first, from their home communities, which were many miles away, then from other prisons in the Federal system (ADX Florence was one of a kind), and finally from other prisoners within the institution. This threefold exclusion was unique and was copper-fastened by cool relations with their captors. Staff maintained a distance from their charges (physically and psychologically) and contributed to the creation of a climate of mutual indifference that could slide into cruelty and neglect.

IRA supporters in the H Blocks rejected the view that they were terrorists in need of deradicalization, or "ordinary decent criminals" who required individualized rehabilitation, so that their future behavior would be in accordance with what the law permitted. Their self-identity was emphatically that of POW. They saw the prison struggle as another theater of war and orchestrated their activities accordingly. Their resistance was unflagging and staff were ignored, with any communication taking place via an established chain of command. Biddable they certainly were not. Although the staff were plentiful—outnumbering the prisoners—they were despised. They had nothing in common politically with the republicans they guarded, rarely shared their religious faith, and while there were no racial differences between the groups this was not surprising given the homogeneous nature of Northern Ireland's population at the time. Perceiving that management were unsupportive and the Northern Ireland Office was pursuing an alternative agenda, they felt impotent despite the manifold available resources.

The men in the H Blocks were viewed as the most dangerous and determined terrorists in Europe, whose actions undermined the integrity and security of Northern Ireland and rippled across Britain and further afield. This necessitated a penal strategy based on heavy regulation. Yet as circumstances changed so did the level of perceived threat and they were released without jeopardizing public safety; their lives were interrupted and then resumed.

BTs collaborated with staff on the warden's behalf. In Isir Bet the prisoners' leaders cooperated with the prison's commander, and even contributed to the prison's finances. Some of the prisoners managed to generate larger incomes than some of the custodial staff. In ADX Florence the prisoners' attitudes were largely irrelevant as their dealings with staff and each other were heavily barriered. In the H Blocks the prisoners did their best to ignore, confront, or condition the staff; few interactions were without an ulterior motive. This was the only institution where the prisoner body, as one, was deliberately at odds with the staff body. Elsewhere, the opposition was nonexistent, covert, individualized, or sporadic.

The boundaries between staff and prisoner roles were blurred in the Eastham Unit because the BTs assumed an oversight and disciplinary function on behalf of the administration. The division of labor was clear in Isir Bet, with staff taking charge of security and prisoners being responsible for order maintenance, but the two groups operated in tandem. In ADX Florence the roles were sharply defined and there was no overlap. In the H Blocks the prisoners imposed their own set of roles on top of those put in place by the system, which were effaced in the process.

Isir Bet was akin to a village where people were forced to reside with others, not of their choosing. They were detained but not under perpetual surveillance with a view to transforming their minds. Their treatment did not progress much beyond containment but with good access to education, work, recreation, and even an art studio. In the H Blocks, attempts at surveillance were undermined to such a degree that the prisoners could fill cells with rubble from a tunnel they were digging without staff noticing. In the Eastham Unit, the staff were not all-seeing, but they did not need to be as this function was delegated to the BTs. Even in ADX Florence the emphasis was not so much on disciplining the mind as the body; the men held there were tightly constrained spatially and their bodies were chained before they were permitted to leave their tiny living quarters. Sometimes they were tied down in their cells; they were trussed because they could not be trusted (figure 5.4 shows a bed with restraint points). As the *Cunningham* litigation revealed, the authorities cared little about the prisoners' minds and were content for them to decompensate so long as their bodies could be subdued.

Written Constitutions: Prescriptions and Proscriptions

The inmate code is like an unwritten constitution. Its tenets are well-known, seldom prison-specific, somewhat fluid, and often breached. At best, it was a loose guide to life in some US prisons—and on some city streets—at a time when the prison population was smaller and less varied in its makeup. Young men recognized the importance of self-reliance, not exploiting others, and not bringing their grievances to the authorities. The Charter for Frelimo Communities drawn up in the H Blocks and the Isir Bet code were created to deal specifically with the exigencies of incarceration and had few parallels outside, although the drafters of the former hoped that the transformation they strove for would become the blueprint for a remodeling of society more generally. The Charter for Frelimo Communities was a manifesto, a set of guiding principles rather than a rulebook for daily life. The Isir Bet code was more the latter and less the former. The one was *prescriptive* and the other *proscriptive*.

The existence of a written constitution should not be taken to imply that the prisoners were sovereign. How could they be, so long as they lived somewhere they were not free to leave, where perimeter security was maintained by armed guards? But the positions of authority in each system were open to all, and over time many served as block or wing OCs, or order keepers or dormitory heads, or members of one committee or another. Anyone who had the time, talent, and inclination would find a role to play. These roles were not reserved for the privileged (or exploitative) few, and this fluidity kept the legitimacy dialogue flowing. Also, their authority derived from their fellows; their power—subject to obvious spatial limitations—was from the people and it was by their peers that they would be called to account in the first instance should they overstep the mark or fail to discharge their duties. The authority conferred on one may at some stage be assumed by another. It was of, by, and for the many. (Loyalists and members of other republican groupings in the H Blocks did not have the same degree of engineered solidarity. The code in Isir Bet applied to everyone.)

Life in Isir Bet was precarious because of prisoners' need to generate an income to be able to live with dignity and to support a family outside. It was made more fretful by an uncertain legal process, the unsafety of some convictions, the disproportionate nature of some penalties, and a lack of clarity around sentence planning. The press of numbers was such that avoidance could not function effectively as an approach to conflict reduction. However, the potentially destabilizing effects of precarity were balanced by the orderly nature of daily life and the existence of shared priorities and agreed-upon standards of conduct. The predictability ushered in by the governance code acted as a sort of ballast during potentially turbulent times. Similarly, fear and brutality were so deeply rooted in the Eastham Unit that they created a predictable lifeworld where force and suspicion were the order of the day. As we have seen, the abolition of the BT system led to instability and an interlude of bloodletting.

Authority in the H Blocks was vested by the prisoners in the commune and the IRA camp staff, not in the Northern Ireland Prison Service. In Isir Bet, authority was vested in the prisoners' executive committee (who were accountable to their peers in that continuation in office required reelection) but could be transferred to the prison's commander and the code allowed for such an eventuality. The commander delegated responsibility to the prisoners, having taken time to review the code during the drafting phase; the NIPS did not play a similar role. If someone did not wish to live according to the precepts of the Charter for Frelimo Communities he could opt to transfer to another institution. (These transfers had mostly taken place by the time the charter was agreed to; indeed, the departure of a group of unreconstructed Marxist-Leninists was part of the stimulus for its creation.) Moving on was not an option in Isir Bet.

The Isir Bet code was formal, prosocial (rather than criminal), cooperative (rather than in conflict with the authorities), and comprehensive. It interfaced with—and had the approval of—the prison's commander, with whom the prisoners' leadership team liaised closely. An individual in Isir Bet could not disengage from the peers with whom he lived, ate, worked, played, and prayed. The code clarified the parameters of acceptable behavior, the order keepers policed them, and a complex committee structure was in place to ensure that daily life was as frictionless as it could be given the constraints of space and deep poverty. Prisoners could petition staff, but they were so few in number that it made sense to put their own extralegal governance structures in place. They applied to the executive committee if they wished to rent a workspace. They purchased supplies, worked on contracts, and made sales. If they were feeling flush, they played pool, bought meals prepared by another prisoner, and paid for laundry services. If funds were tight, they ate the *injera* offered by the prison and sought out opportunities to earn a few additional birr. There was a great deal of communication, negotiation, and to-ing and fro-ing among prisoners, carried out in a variety of languages in addition to the official Amharic. If anything characterized the institution it was a high level of carceral chatter.

In the H Blocks, the charter was formal, prosocial, disdainful of the prison rules, and comprehensive. There were more than twice as many staff in the H Blocks as there were prisoners (Her Majesty's Chief Inspector of Prisons for England and Wales 1998: 38, 154), so it was not a case of the latter group developing their own charter because they could not rely on the staff, but rather they developed their own charter because they had no time for the staff. In ADX Florence there was a similar imbalance in that when the men imprisoned there were out of their cells they were always outnumbered (and, indeed, physically restrained). Relationships were cool and distant at best and openly hostile and violent at worst. The weight of the rulebook and the oppressiveness of the regime meant that alternative arrangements could not take root, let alone flourish. In the Eastham Unit, the governance mechanisms were less explicit, although they were expressly sanctioned by the administration, and they were inherently exploitative. It was unlikely that prisoners would have turned to staff for support when the same staff oversaw their brutal daily grind; they could not have relied on them for any amelioration of treatment.

The process of drawing up a constitution like that in Isir Bet or the H Blocks seemed to promote solidarity and to unite prisoners around principles that eased life for the collective by regulating conduct and creating a predictable environment. Signing up to them legitimated the arrangements therein. In many ways these documents were guidebooks for conflict resolution. What was at issue was finding a way of life that was at ease with prisoners' sentiments and that promoted community harmony. The purpose was the ordering of daily life rather than the advancement of criminal goals. In Isir Bet it was to create some clarity around economic activity, access to a workspace and materials, working hours, and acceptable behavior in crowded dormitories.

Like in the H Blocks, the prisoners in Isir Bet reviewed their code periodically so that they did not lose sight of the rules that undergirded their lives. There was an induction process for newcomers and there were refresher sessions and occasional opportunities for revision. If there is a written constitution and a turnover of prisoners, such refreshers are necessary to ensure consistency of understanding and application. Norms need occasional restatement (and regular reinforcement) if they are to be internalized and to endure as guides to conduct. This became apparent in the H Blocks and Isir Bet in that when a new variety of carceral life had been created successfully, it was necessary to remind its beneficiaries of what had been sacrificed to obtain it (H Blocks) and what was necessary to promote companionable coexistence (Isir Bet).

All constitutions contain provisions to deal with breaches. In the H Blocks the ultimate sanction was expulsion from the commune and transfer to another institution. In Isir Bet, noncompliance could result in loss of access to a profitable workspace or a comfortable bed place. Punitive exercise drills were alternative sanctions and these took place in public so that everyone knew there had been a transgression and it was being responded to. An element of shaming accompanied the physical tiredness that ensued.

In the Eastham Unit the unwritten rule was that nonconformity met with beatings or perhaps allocation to a cell that was undesirable on account of its location or with whom it would be shared. In ADX Florence, prisoners could do nothing to discipline their peers even if they felt that an egregious violation of the inmate code, in whatever abridged version still applied, had been committed (although in the units where limited interaction was permitted there were some killings).

External shocks such as court decisions can lead to a sudden reordering of prisoner society, accompanied by turbulence, at least in the short term, whereas if the reordering occurs as a result of internal pressure—such as the development of written constitutions in Isir Bet and the H Blocks—this builds gradually and in a manageable way.

The inmate code is normative, couched at a high level of generality and necessarily imprecise. The Isir Bet code, by contrast, was a document that delineated key principles and expectations as well as the consequences of rule infringement. It was policed by a team of order keepers and had clear limits, with serious breaches being referred to the prison authorities. Furthermore, the prisoners signed up to it (literally) as opposed to "learning" the inmate code through osmosis. This was not a secret document like a gang constitution that is not intended to be seen by outsiders. I was given a typed and stamped copy; the drafters were proud of it, seeing what they had assembled as a humanitarian manifesto that promoted well-ordered community life. Prisoners were no longer bound by the code after release. This again distinguished it from the rules of some prison gangs, where disentanglement can be problematic. Similarly, the Charter for Frelimo Communities was the end product of much discussion and became an integral part of the socialization process for new arrivals at the H Blocks.

The danger that one group will exploit the absence of legal governance in order to control trade and dominate the vulnerable is reduced when the society agrees to its own (universal) rules and these rules promote stability. Such circumstances inhibit the emergence of a truculent minority who would have to work hard to defy what those with whom they share a carceral space have codified as legitimate. The more embedded the rules and the norms that they promulgate the more difficult it becomes for a challenger to emerge. The relationship between prisoner leaders and the rest of the population was symbiotic in Isir Bet and the II Blocks, parasitic in the Eastham Unit, and nonexistent in ADX Florence.

Predictability and endurability are key reasons for the development of written constitutions; they emerge in—and then reinforce—stable societies. They facilitate harmonious living and constrain capriciousness. The other advantages of predictability and routine are that they give structure to the day, and this helps to speed the passage of time (O'Donnell 2014: 183–88). Formal constitutions attempt to create new cultural conditions by specifying permissible conduct, coordinating expectations, promoting cooperation, and providing schedules of reward and punishment. They have the signal virtues of clarifying the coordinates of daily life and rendering it predictable. They promote legitimacy because the parameters of acceptable self-interest are made clear. Prisoners defer to the constitutional arrangements they put in place not because they are frightened of being punished for not doing so but because they feel it is the right and proper thing to do. Where there were no written constitutions—ADX Florence and the Eastham Unit—integration remained low and legitimacy was weak or nonexistent.

Bodily Integrity and Threats to Psyche

Life in the H Blocks during the 1990s was not about survival but about enduring and overcoming. (For some, during the protest years that preceded my decade of interest, the struggle involved relinquishing the right to survive through hunger striking.) Isir Bet in the 2010s was about keeping the family intact. The prisoners' needs for food, shelter, and medicine might have been better met than those of any dependents in the community. Life on the Eastham Unit in the 1970s was about maintaining bodily integrity; there was no real threat to the mind. The challenge for the person incarcerated at ADX Florence in the 2000s, especially on the control unit, was to keep his mind intact. The main corporeal threat came from staff use of force.

Prisoners at the Eastham Unit were routinely at risk from each other, and sexual violence was perpetrated by BTs who saw it as one of the spoils of office. This was not the case in the H Blocks (where rape was unheard of), or in Isir Bet (where there was the added consideration that sex between men is outlawed in Ethiopia), or in ADX Florence (where, even for a motivated predator, the opportunities simply did not exist). The threat from staff varied and was probably greatest at the Eastham Unit, where summary justice was meted out with impunity before the *Ruiz* reforms, and on occasions in the H Blocks (e.g., during the protest years in the 1970s and after a mass escape in 1983) but was not routine thereafter because of the ferocity of the IRA response. In the H Blocks the hardships were more physical than psychological; the opposite was the case in ADX Florence. One would expect Isir Bet to be less violent given the complexity of the society and the interdependence of its members.

Self-harm and suicide were alien to the highly integrated H Blocks and Isir Bet. There would be no tactical advantage for a prisoner in Ethiopia to maim himself to avoid work as he would only be depriving himself of an opportunity to generate an income. By contrast, in the Eastham Unit the body was attacked as a way of escaping a brutal work regime and in ADX Florence, assaults on the self were either a form of resistance, an expression of agency, a wail of despair, a symptom of psychosis, or the manifestation of a desire to escape from an atomized world where other prisoners could not be called upon for support. Some—but not all—of the men sent there had histories of mental illness, and environmental factors exercised a powerful effect. At least seven suicides were recorded in the first twenty years that the institution was in operation (*Cunningham v. Federal Bureau of Prisons* 2015: para. 97). All were by hanging. This is quite a lot of self-annihilation for such a small population.

All but one of the four case study prisons was characterized by the occasional descent into riotous behavior. The exception, of course, was ADX Florence. Collective pushback is impossible when people cannot gather and on those rare occasions when individuals coordinated their actions, they targeted themselves by refusing food. But such refusals were overcome with mighty force. Again, the totalizing effects of incarceration were most visible here. As well as heel stringing at the Eastham Unit, there was some coordinated opposition in the form of occasional work stoppages or disturbances. In the H Blocks the prisoners acted as one and the consequences of their intractability were all too often lethal, with pressure put on staff through campaigns of intimidation and murder and rallying public support for their stance. In Isir Bet, widespread frustration at what was seen as the government reneging on a promised amnesty led to arson, destruction, and death.

Sparks et al. (1996: 300) stated: "It is unavoidably true that the social order of the prison is imposed and enforced. Prisons, especially maximum security prisons, entail deprivations and compulsions considerably beyond those ordinarily found in advanced industrial societies. Their 'order,' to the extent that it exists at all, is neither spontaneous nor consensual." I think that this summation may be unduly emphatic. It certainly applies to ADX Florence and the Eastham Unit, but the form of order that evolved in Isir Bet was consensual and so were the arrangements in the H Blocks, when viewed horizontally, if not in the eyes of the staff whose role in order generation and maintenance became, over time, largely ceremonial.

Another pertinent difference relates to architecture (see figures 2.3, 3.2, 4.1, and 5.1). Decisions about where to locate a prison and how to construct it give insights into penal priorities, such as the degree to which the target population is seen as socially redundant, or the value placed on family and community ties. Buildings, and boundaries, are difficult to repurpose and can long outlive stated rationales. For example, it would be difficult to engineer a consensual, communal life in the control unit at ADX Florence and to retrofit Isir Bet as a cellular prison would require huge capital investment, a massive reduction in numbers, and an upscaling of the staff complement.

Dramatis Personae

The characters of the four men whose stories underpin this book were forged in traumatic circumstances. Nothing in their biographies suggested that they would triumph. Laurence McKeown was a schoolboy, politicized like many of those around him by the conflict engulfing Northern Ireland. David Ruiz was a recidivist offender, a product of the criminal justice state. Chalew Gebino was a despairing first-time prisoner. Jack Powers was a failed businessman who turned to bank robbery. All were transformed by their experience (although Powers and Ruiz could have died as a result of their persistent self-harm and, had his mother not intervened, McKeown's hunger strike would have reached its grim conclusion). All had prison experiences that could have overwhelmed but that they decided to use as springboards for action. They strived and they survived. Sometimes they thrived.

All left an important legacy, whether it was externally imposed changes resulting from successful litigation, or the internal stability generated by a written constitution. Their life stories reveal how ordinary men can become extraordinary in captivity, and how their example can inspire. They show that a rounded appreciation of prison life offers lessons for understanding human affairs more generally. They allow us to illuminate "the ways in which personal troubles are connected with public issues" (Mills 1959: 185). They bring biography into conversation with law and policy.

While it would be going too far to suggest that one person could be fully representative of the social world they inhabited, neither were their experiences unique. Ruiz was one of a cohort of writ writers in the Eastham Unit and his petition was joined with seven others in the litigation that bore his name. Powers was one of more than a dozen named plaintiffs in *Cunningham v. Federal Bureau of Prisons* (2015). McKeown was one of hundreds of nonconforming republican prisoners who came to view their incarceration as another site for their struggle, where they would strive to set the terms of engagement. After his election to office Chalew exercised his chairmanship with aplomb in close collaboration with a small executive team and a wide network of committees and other office holders.

Not everyone can succeed like this, but the fact that some do implies that others might. I do not for a moment wish to minimize the harms of confinement, but anyone who takes the time to get close to the prison experience will know that prisoners identify benefits among the burdens. If we are to be true to their accounts, we must accept them in the round; to do otherwise is to risk straying into caricature. Prisoners everywhere strive to master the art of living, and to not recognize this is to diminish their efforts. Imprisonment is destructive, expensive, overused, and unfairly targeted at groups that already groan under the weight of multiple layers of disadvantage. But it does not crush everyone in the same way and there are vital lessons to be drawn from modes of organization that protect and, occasionally, empower. It is necessary to acknowledge the variegated effects of the prison while simultaneously demanding that fewer people experience its rigors; appreciation should not be read as approbation.

McKeown completed a PhD after his release in 1992 and became an author and playwright. Ruiz died in custody in 2005. Chalew earned a pardon in 2018 on the strength of demonstrable self-improvement and the betterment of his peers. Powers ended his grueling prison journey in 2021 and published two books. Cruel places can be crucibles for character transformation just as they can cause a descent into despair and self-injury; sometimes one person can experience both, plummeting then soaring.

The prisons these four men spent so long in have been similarly transformed. All but one of the H Blocks has been demolished and the site lies idle, with no consensus as to how it should be used. Some believe it should be cleared entirely for fear that the remaining structure will become a monument to the glorification of terrorism. Others would prefer to find a way to incorporate it into the story of Northern

Ireland, holding that to raze it would be to efface an important part of the historical record. The litigation spearheaded by Ruiz and the other writ writers led to an overhaul not just of the Eastham Unit but of the Texas prison system in its entirety. Time will tell if Chalew's code is embedded deeply enough to survive leadership changes within the prison society and the planned relocation of the facility to a greenfield site. ADX Florence is still a harsh, unyielding, and inhumane place, but at least its managers have been forced to acknowledge, and respond to, the adverse mental health consequences that it generates with depressing predictability.

The Prison in Society

Prisons are usually unrepresentative of the societies within which they persist in terms of the gender, age, race, and social class of their occupants, who further stand apart with regard to low levels of educational attainment, poor mental health, adverse childhood experiences, and patterns of problematic drug and alcohol use. However, prisons' internal lives, including the level of violence they generate and the strategies of adaptation and resistance they evoke, derive from the society within which they are rooted. When the Troubles in Northern Ireland were at their peak (see figure 2.1), so was the turbulence in the prisons and the threat posed to staff. (Although as figure 3.7 shows, the levels of lethal violence in prisons and the community in Texas were not correlated.)

A prison's internal life encapsulates the values and priorities of the wider society in which it is embedded. Understanding the one sheds light on the other. To be properly understood and fully articulated, in other words, the prison world cannot be detached from the wider environment in which it has been fashioned (for a penetrating analysis of these shifting interrelationships as they played out in Stateville Penitentiary, Illinois, see Jacobs 1977). The political context shapes the vigor and direction of growth (what might be thought of as penal tropism). The best-resourced prisons are not necessarily the most orderly ones. The predictable, and generally harmonious, unfolding of daily life in Isir Bet was striking against a background of material poverty and dense overcrowding. The huge financial commitment to the H Blocks did not prevent escapes, murder, and the prisoners taking control.

Isir Bet reflected the outside world in the sense that there was a strong emphasis on organized religion, solidarity, and collectivism. A similar range of work opportunities existed. As in the community one could be a trader, weaver, carver, cook, barber, cleaner, or remain idle through choice or circumstance. There was a pronounced respect for elders and an acceptance that non-state actors played an important role in policing and dispute resolution. The H Blocks were another war zone, with casualties on both sides (hunger-striking republicans and murdered prison officers). The ghetto in Texas might have been characterized by powerful criminals operating a regime of fear and violence but, unlike the BTs, they were not put in place—and maintained there—by the authorities.

It is difficult to imagine that anything approximating ADX Florence could emerge in a society where prisoners had not been so thoroughly demonized and marginalized. It reflects the wider world but in a distorting mirror, expressing a moral view of how to deal with the criminal—and, more recently, terrorist—threat. The grotesque rush to execute as many of the occupants of federal death row as possible during the closing days of the Donald Trump administration is an extreme example of how some US residents are viewed as politically expendable (O'Donnell 2020, 2021b).

My purpose is primarily descriptive and it is not my intention to engage with debates about democratic theory. I am content to have set out what I believe to be the key dimensions of prison life, indicated how they might be mapped, and examined a series of permutations. Nevertheless, I have not always been able to refrain from making evaluative claims, such as those concerning the destruction of human potential that characterizes life at ADX Florence, the malign effects of the lack of legitimacy that defined the BT system at the Eastham Unit, and the buffering effects of integration in Isir Bet and the H Blocks.

The case studies offered in this book are fragments in a penal mosaic that, all too often, has tended to lack balance and vitality because of its overreliance on materials from the US and Britain. It is helpful on occasion to take stock and refocus the scholarly gaze rather than allowing the trend toward bewilderingly narrow specialization to blind us to the exciting possibilities offered by fresh fields of inquiry. The purpose of this book is to add another contour to a well-mapped research landscape and to suggest we seek out terra incognita rather than continuing to traverse paths that are already well-worn. A broader gaze is in the interests of theoretical elaboration as well as knowledge accumulation. We need to be prepared to revisit received understandings as we become aware of developments elsewhere. If accepted frameworks prove unfit for purpose they must be reconstituted or jettisoned.

I close with a trilogy of hopes.

First, I hope that I have managed to twist the penal kaleidoscope enough to cause the reader to question the validity of Sykes's assertion, cited in chapter 1, that custodial institutions share "basic similarities which . . . override the variations of time, place, and purpose." If Sykes had worked in a Southern state, rather than in New Jersey, power relations would not have had the same complexion; there would have been different prohibitions, norms, and pains; and claims of universality would surely have been more muted. If he had taken a comparative approach, who knows how the "society of captives" would have been theorized?

My second hope is that the three-step approach articulated in this chapter offers a template that might allow novel perspectives on environments that have lost their capacity to inspire on account of excessive viewing, as well as a route into new areas of inquiry. I would be pleased if what I have assembled prompts reflection, dialogue, and, dare I say it, dissent—that it offers a way of thinking about the organization of prison life that can be explored with profit in other contexts.

My third and final hope is that the pen portraits are stimulating. Where individuals find meaning and how they make sense of their experiences are at the heart of the human endeavor. Idiosyncrasy is not everything, but it is something. It is time to think more seriously about the particular. After all, punishment is about pain, and pain is personal.

ACKNOWLEDGMENTS

I accumulated many debts in many places during the research for this book and while it will take me many years (and much imagination) to discharge them, for now I hope it is enough to list those to whom I am beholden for their many courtesies, insights, critical commentaries, and practical assistance along the way.

Having dabbled for a while, I began to think seriously about the social lives of prison during a period as a senior visiting scholar at the Institute of Criminology in Cambridge University in Michaelmas Term 2018. It was a delight to return to the Institute thirty years after I had been a graduate student there, and I thank Ben Crewe and Alison Liebling for hosting my visit.

At University College Dublin, which has been my academic home for two decades, I am most obliged to Deirdre Healy, Vincent Hoban, Ciara Molloy, Aogán Mulcahy, Jane Nolan, Óran Ó Síocháin, and Otávio Vinhas.

Colleagues from other institutions were generous with their expertise and, for carving time out of their schedules to respond to queries or read chapters in various states of readiness, I am grateful to Cormac Behan, Piers Beirne, Mary Bosworth, Eamonn Carrabine, Ben Crewe, Ben Crouch, Rod Earle, Kimmett Edgar, Robert Fong, Joe Garrihy, Rosemary Gido, Craig Haney, Derek Jeffreys, Yvonne Jewkes, Seán McConville, Jill McCorkel, Kieran McEvoy, Fergus McNeill, Ruán O'Donnell, Eoin O'Sullivan, Keith Price, Bill Rolston, David Skarbek, and Justice Tankebe.

As a student of prison life, I still have much to learn and appreciate the patience and goodwill of those who have been willing to act as mentors and guides. Each of the prisons that features in this book has its own roll call of gratitude. For deepening my understanding, challenging my preconceptions, facilitating my site visits, and sharing their memories of bad times as well as good, I am indebted to the following people from the following places:

H Blocks, Northern Ireland: Harry Maguire, Tommy McKearney, Laurence McKeown, Jim McVeigh, Féilim Ó hAdhmaill, Deaglán Ó Mocháin, and Séanna Walsh.

Eastham Unit, Texas: Wayne Brewer, Kalli Dawson, Kenneth Hutto, Billy Lewis, Jeff Linderman, Tammie Mitchell, Donald Muniz, and Bill Stephens.

Isir Bet, Ethiopia: Amanuel Gebremichael, Alemu Kento, Chalew Gebino, Kilimpe Garbicha, Paddy Moran, Tesfamichael Yohannes, and Yohannes Ethiopia. The Irish Spiritan Province and FitzPatrick Family Foundation Research Fund provided financial support. Some of the material about Isir Bet draws liberally—with permission—from a previous journal article ("The Society of Captives in an Ethiopian Prison," *Prison Journal* 99: 267–84) and book chapter ("Ethiopian Notes," in *Sensory Penalities: Exploring the Senses in Spaces of Punishment and Social Control*, edited by Kate Herrity, Bethany E. Schmidt and Jason Warr, 203–16, Bingley: Emerald Publishing).

ADX Florence, Colorado: Jack Powers, Jane Powers, and Renée Silverstein.

Finally, my thanks to the team at NYU Press, who oversaw the book's evolution and production with flair and finesse, especially Ilene Kalish and Martin Coleman.

REFERENCES

60 Minutes. 2007. "Supermax: A Clean Version of Hell." CBS, October 14, www.cbsnews.com.

Abera, Semaw Ferede, and Kelemework Adane. 2017. "One-Fourth of the Prisoners Are Underweight in Northern Ethiopia: A Cross-Sectional Study." *BMC Public Health* 17: 449.

Abiye, Yonas. 2018. "Amnesty Bill Sparks Prison Riot." Reporter Ethiopia, July 28, www.thereporterethiopia.com.

African Child Policy Forum. 2007. *Children in Prisons and Detention Centres in Ethiopia: The Way Forward*. Addis Ababa: ACPF.

African Commission on Human and Peoples' Rights. 2012. "Resolution on the Human Rights Situation in the Democratic Republic of Ethiopia." 51st Session. April 18–May 2, 2012. Resolution 218. Banjul: ACHPR.

Alpert, Geoffrey P., Ben M. Crouch, and C. Ronald Huff. 1984. "Prison Reform by Judicial Decree: The Unintended Consequences of *Ruiz v. Estelle*." *Justice System Journal* 9: 291–305.

American Correctional Association. 2019. "Declaration of Principles." January 15, www.aca.org.

Amnesty International. 2014. *Entombed: Isolation in the US Federal Prison System*. London: Amnesty International.

Bacote, Michael. 2012. Letter to United States District Court, Denver, Colorado. Case 1:12-cv-01570-RPM-MEH Document 28. October 9.

Bacote v. Federal Bureau of Prisons. 2012. Case No. 1:12-cv-01570. Document 1. United States District Court, Colorado. June 18.

Beetham, David. 1991. *The Legitimation of Power*. Basingstoke: Macmillan.

———. 2013. "Revisiting Legitimacy, Twenty Years On." In *Legitimacy and Criminal Justice: An International Exploration*, edited by Justice Tankebe and Alison Liebling, 19–36. Oxford: Oxford University Press.

Bekele, Yeshtila Wondemeneh, and Darley Jose Kjosavik. 2016. "Decentralised Local Governance and Poverty Reduction in Post-1991 Ethiopia: A Political Economy Study." *Politics and Governance* 4 (4): 1–15.

Binelli, Mark. 2015. "This Place Is Not Designed for Humanity." *New York Times Magazine*, March 29, 37.

Blackburn, Ashley G., and Meredith Matthews. 2011. "Crime and Punishment in Ethiopia: A Country Profile." *International Journal of Comparative and Applied Criminal Justice* 35: 167–81.

Blue, Ethan. 2012. *Doing Time in the Depression: Everyday Life in Texas and California Prisons*. New York: New York University Press.

Bottoms, Anthony, and Justice Tankebe. 2012. "Beyond Procedural Justice: A Dialogic Approach to Legitimacy in Criminal Justice." *Journal of Criminal Law and Criminology* 102: 119–70.

Bradshaw, Phillip. 2016. *Prison Rape Elimination Act Audit Report*. Washington, DC: US Department of Justice.

Brand, Christo, with Barbara Jones. 2014. *Mandela: My Prisoner, My Friend*. New York: St. Martin's Press.

Buntman, Fran Lisa. 2003. *Robben Island and Prisoner Resistance to Apartheid*. New York: Cambridge University Press.

Cacioppo, John T., and William Patrick. 2008. *Loneliness: Human Nature and the Need for Social Connection*. New York: W.W. Norton.

Camp, George M., and Camille G. Camp. 1985. *Prison Gangs: Their Extent, Nature and Impact on Prisons*. Washington, DC: US Department of Justice.

Campbell, Brian. 1991. "Prison Publications: Expressions of Resistance." In *Éirí na Gealaí: Reflections on the Culture of Resistance in Long Kesh*, edited by Felim O'Hagan, 11–16. Belfast: Sinn Féin Department of Culture.

Campbell, Brian, Laurence McKeown, and Felim O'Hagan, eds. 1994. *Nor Meekly Serve My Time: The H Block Struggle 1976–1981*. Belfast: Beyond the Pale Publications.

Carrabine, Eamonn. 2005. "Prison Riots, Social Order and the Problem of Legitimacy." *British Journal of Criminology* 45: 896–913.

Carrington, Kerry, Russell Hogg, and Máximo Sozzo. 2016. "Southern Criminology." *British Journal of Criminology* 56: 1–20.

Center for Constitutional Rights and Lowenstein International Human Rights Clinic. 2017. *The Darkest Corner: Special Administrative Measures and Extreme Isolation in the Federal Bureau of Prisons*. New Haven, CT: Yale Law School.

Cepheus Research and Analytics. 2020. "Ethiopia's 2020–21 Budget." July 31, https://cepheuscapital.com.

Chase, Robert T. 2015. "Cell Taught, Self Taught: The Chicano Movement behind Bars—Urban Chicanos, Rural Prisons, and the Prisoners' Rights Movement." *Journal of Urban History* 41: 836–61.

———. 2020. *We Are Not Slaves: State Violence, Coerced Labor, and Prisoners' Rights in Postwar America*. Chapel Hill: University of North Carolina Press.

Clemmer, Donald. (1940) 1958. *The Prison Community*. Reprint. New York: Holt, Reinhart and Winston.

CNA. 2014. *Federal Bureau of Prisons: Special Housing Unit Review and Assessment*. Arlington, VA: CNA.

Cohen, Andrew. 2012. "Death, Yes, but Torture at Supermax?" *Atlantic*, June 4.

Coid, Jeremy W. 2001. "The Federal Administrative Maximum Penitentiary, Florence, Colorado." *Medicine, Science and the Law* 41: 287–97.

Cooley, Charles Horton. 1902. *Human Nature and the Social Order*. New York: Charles Scribner's Sons.

Corcoran, Mary S. 2006. *Out of Order: The Political Imprisonment of Women in Northern Ireland, 1972–1998.* Cullompton: Willan.

Correctional Leaders Association and Arthur Liman Center for Public Interest Law. 2020. *Time-in-Cell 2019: A Snapshot of Restrictive Housing Based on a Nationwide Survey of U.S. Prison Systems.* New Haven, CT: Yale Law School.

Crewe, Ben. 2009. *The Prisoner Society: Power, Adaptation, and Social Life in an English Prison.* Oxford: Oxford University Press.

———. 2011. "Depth, Weight, Tightness: Revisiting the Pains of Imprisonment." *Punishment & Society* 13: 509–29.

Crouch, Ben M., and James W. Marquart. 1989. *An Appeal to Justice: Litigated Reform of Texas Prisons.* Austin: University of Texas Press.

———. 1990. "Resolving the Paradox of Reform: Litigation, Prisoner Violence, and Perception of Risk." *Justice Quarterly* 7: 103–23.

Cunningham v. Federal Bureau of Prisons. 2013. Case No. 1:12-cv-01570-RPM-MEH. Document 67. United States District Court, Colorado. May 24.

Cunningham v. Federal Bureau of Prisons. 2015. Second Amended Complaint. Case No. 1:12-cv-01570-RPM-MEH. Document 274. United States District Court, Colorado. June 15.

Dagne, Behailu. 2013. *Implementing the Human Rights of Women Prisoners in Ethiopia: The Case of Bahir Dar City Prison.* Saarbrücken: LAP Lambert.

Dana, Jacqueline, and Seán McMonagle. 1997. "Deconstructing 'Criminalisation': The Politics of Collective Education in the H-Blocks." *Journal of Prisoners on Prisons* 8: 67–74.

Death Penalty Information Center. 2020. "Execution Database." Accessed March 9, 2020. https://deathpenaltyinfo.org.

Delgado, Bobby. 2007. *Gangs, Prison, Parole & The Politics behind Them.* Crown Oak Press.

DiIulio, John J. 1987a. *Governing Prisons: A Comparative Study of Correctional Management.* New York: Free Press.

———. 1987b. "Prison Discipline and Prison Reform." *Public Interest* 89: 71–90.

Di Nunzio, Marco. 2014. "Thugs, Spies and Vigilantes: Community Policing and Street Politics in Inner City Addis Ababa." *Africa* 84: 444–65.

District of Columbia Corrections Information Council. 2018. *USP Florence Administrative Maximum Security (ADX) Inspection Report and USP Florence-High Survey Report.* Washington, DC: Corrections Information Council.

Doerr-Zegers, Otto, Lawrence Hartmann, Elizabeth Lira, and Eugenia Weinstein. 1992. "Torture: Psychiatric Sequelae and Phenomenology." *Psychiatry* 55: 177–84.

Dowker, Fay, and Glenn Good. 1993. "The Proliferation of Control Unit Prisons in the United States." *Journal of Prisoners on Prisons* 4 (2): 95–110.

Edgar, Kimmett, and Ian O'Donnell. 1998. "Assault in Prison: The 'Victim's' Contribution." *British Journal of Criminology* 38: 635–50.

Edgar, Kimmett, Ian O'Donnell, and Carol Martin. (2003) 2012. *Prison Violence: The Dynamics of Conflict, Fear and Power.* Reprint. Abingdon: Routledge.

Ekland-Olson, Sheldon. 1986. "Crowding, Social Control, and Prison Violence: Evidence from the Post-*Ruiz* Years in Texas." *Law & Society Review* 20: 389–422.

Federal Bureau of Investigation. 2020. "Uniform Crime Reporting Statistics." Accessed June 18, 2020. www.fbi.gov.

Federal Bureau of Prisons. 2001. *Control Unit Programs*. Program Unit Statement 5212.07. Washington, DC: US Department of Justice.

———. 2008. *Admission and Orientation Handbook*. Florence, CO: United States Penitentiary Administrative Maximum Facility.

———. 2011a. *Visiting Procedures: Institution Supplement*. Florence, CO: United States Penitentiary Administrative Maximum Facility.

———. 2011b. *Inmate Discipline Program*. Program Unit Statement 5270.09. Washington, DC: US Department of Justice.

———. 2014a. *Visiting Procedures: Institution Supplement*. Florence, CO: United States Penitentiary Administrative Maximum Facility.

———. 2014b. *Treatment and Care of Inmates with Mental Illness*. Program Statement 5310.16. Washington, DC: US Department of Justice.

———. 2021a. *Female Offender Manual*. Program Statement 5200.07. Washington, DC: US Department of Justice.

———. 2021b. "Inmate Statistics: Restricted Housing." November 4, www.bop.gov.

———. 2021c. "BOP Policies." Accessed April 28, 2021. www.bop.gov.

Fong, Robert S. 1990. "The Organizational Structure of Prison Gangs: A Texas Case Study." *Federal Probation* 54: 36–43.

Franzen, Jonathan. 2004. *How to Be Alone*. London: HarperPerennial.

Freire, Paulo. (1970) 2017. *Pedagogy of the Oppressed*. Translated by Myra Bergman Ramos. Reprint. London: Penguin Classics.

Gates v. Collier. 1972. 349 F. Supp 881. United States District Court, Northern District of Mississippi.

Gebino, Chalew. 2021. *Hope Never Sinks: An Autobiography*. Unpublished typescript.

Gettinger, Stephen, and Kevin Krajick. 1978. "Are 'Building Tenders' the Key to Control?" *Corrections Magazine* 4 (March): 22–24.

Gormally, Brian, Kieran McEvoy, and David Wall. 1993. "Criminal Justice in a Divided Society: Northern Ireland Prisons." In *Crime and Justice: A Review of Research*, vol. 17, edited by Michael Tonry, 51–135. Chicago: University of Chicago Press.

Gulick, David B. 1984. "Crisis and Change in a Prison System: A Critical Analysis of Control Practices in the Texas Department of Corrections." Unpublished PhD thesis, Sam Houston State University, Texas.

Guutama, Ibsaa. 2003. *Prison of Conscience: Upper Compound Maa'ikalawii Ethiopian Terror Prison and Tradition*. Flushing, NY: Gubirmans.

Haney, Craig. 2008. "A Culture of Harm: Taming the Dynamics of Cruelty in Supermax Prisons." *Criminal Justice and Behavior* 35: 956–84.

Harding, Michael. 2019. "It's Not the Mountains or the Ocean That Make Us Happy." *Irish Times*, September 11, 11.

Her Majesty's Chief Inspector of Prisons for England and Wales. 1998. *HM Prison The Maze (Northern Ireland): Report of a Full Inspection 23 March–3 April 1998*. London: Home Office.
Holt v. Sarver. 1970. 309 F. Supp. 362. United States District Court, Eastern District of Arkansas.
Human Rights Watch. 2013. *"They Want a Confession." Torture and Ill-Treatment in Ethiopia's Maekelawi Police Station*. New York: HRW.
———. 2018. *"We Are Like the Dead." Torture and Other Human Rights Abuses in Jail Ogaden, Somali Regional State, Ethiopia*. New York: HRW.
Jackson, Bruce. 2009. *Pictures from a Drawer: Prison and the Art of Portraiture*. Philadelphia: Temple University Press.
Jackson, Paul, Demelash Kassaye, and Edward Shearon. 2019. "'I Fought the Law and the Law Won': Evidence on Policing Communities in Dire Dawa, Ethiopia." *British Journal of Criminology* 59: 126–43.
Jacobs, James B. 1977. *Stateville: The Penitentiary in Mass Society*. Chicago: University of Chicago Press.
Kemerer, Frank R. 1991. *William Wayne Justice: A Judicial Biography*. Austin: University of Texas Press.
King, Roy D., and Kathleen McDermott. 1995. *The State of Our Prisons*. Oxford: Oxford University Press.
Klein, P. 2018. "Removal of Commissary Items." ADX Florence Inmate Bulletin, March 15.
Lamar v. Coffield. 1972. 353 F. Supp 1081. United States District Court, Southern District of Texas.
League of Communist Republicans. 1988. "From Long Kesh to a Socialist Ireland." Unpublished typescript.
Liebling, Alison, with Helen Arnold. 2004. *Prisons and Their Moral Performance*. Oxford: Oxford University Press.
Longwell, Alan. 1998. "The Maze Community: A Study of the Interaction between Staff and Prisoners and the Redistribution of Power and Control." Unpublished MPhil thesis, Queen's University Belfast.
Mac Cormaic, Eoghan. 1991. "Séanadh Ceart Cultúrtha sa Jailtacht." In *Éirí na Gealaí: Reflections on the Culture of Resistance in Long Kesh*, edited by Felim O'Hagan, 17–19. Belfast: Sinn Féin Department of Culture.
Mac Giolla Chríost, Diarmait. 2012. *Jailtacht: The Irish Language, Symbolic Power and Political Violence in Northern Ireland, 1972–2008*. Cardiff: University of Wales Press.
Mac Ionnrachtaigh, Feargal. 2013. *Language, Resistance and Revival: Republican Prisoners and the Irish Language in the North of Ireland*. London: Pluto Press.
Marquart, James W., and Ben M. Crouch. 1984. "Coopting the Kept: Using Inmates for Social Control in a Southern Prison." *Justice Quarterly* 1: 491–509.
———. 1985. "Judicial Reform and Prisoner Control: The Impact of *Ruiz v. Estelle* on a Texas Penitentiary." *Law & Society Review* 19: 557–86.

Martin, Steve J., and Sheldon Ekland-Olson. 1987. *Texas Prisons: The Walls Came Tumbling Down*. Austin: Texas Monthly Press.

Maruna, Shadd, and Amanda Matravers. 2007. "N=1: Criminology and the Person." *Theoretical Criminology* 11: 427–42.

Matevousian, Andre. 2018a. "United States Penitentiary Administrative Maximum, Florence, CO. Commissary List." June 5.

———. 2018b. "Changes to Mail Procedures." FCC Florence Inmate Bulletin, December 3.

McConville, Seán. 2021. *Irish Political Prisoners 1960–2000: Braiding Rage and Sorrow*. Abingdon: Routledge.

McCoy, Alfred W. 2006. *A Question of Torture: CIA Interrogation, from the Cold War to the War on Terror*. New York: Metropolitan Books.

McEvoy, Kieran. 1999. "Prisoners, the Agreement, and the Political Character of the Northern Ireland Conflict." *Fordham International Law Journal* 22: 1539–76.

———. 2001. *Paramilitary Imprisonment in Northern Ireland: Resistance, Management, and Release*. Oxford: Oxford University Press.

McKane, William. 2008. *Unpretentious Valour: An Autobiography*. Dungannon: CR Print.

McKee, William. 2009. *Governor: Inside the Maze*. Dublin: Gill & Macmillan.

McKeown, Laurence. 1996. "Jailtacht / Gaeltacht." *Cascando: The National Student Literary Magazine* 5/6: 43–49.

———. 1998. "Unrepentant Fenian Bastards: The Social Construction of an Irish Republican Prisoner Community." Unpublished PhD thesis, Queen's University Belfast.

———. 2001. *Out of Time: Irish Republican Prisoners Long Kesh 1972–2000*. Belfast: Beyond the Pale Publications.

———. 2020. "From D102 to Paulo Freire: An Irish Journey." In *Degrees of Freedom: Prison Education at the Open University*, edited by Rod Earle and James Mehigan, 179–89. Bristol: Policy Press.

McNeill, Fergus, and Gwen Robinson. 2012. "Liquid Legitimacy and Community Sanctions." In *Legitimacy and Compliance in Criminal Justice*, edited by Adam Crawford and Anthea Hucklesby, 116–37. Abingdon: Routledge.

McWhorter, William L. 1981. *Inmate Society: Legs, Half-Pants and Gunmen. A Study of Prison Guards*. Saratoga, CA: Century Twenty One Publishing.

Mekonnen, Mihretab. 2012. *Rights of Children Living in Prison with their Mothers: Case Study in Southern Ethiopia*. Saarbrücken: LAP Lambert.

Mills, C. Wright. 1959. *The Sociological Imagination*. New York: Oxford University Press.

Moran, Dominique. 2015. *Carceral Geography: Spaces and Practices of Incarceration*. Farnham: Ashgate.

Murtagh, Tom. 2018. *The Maze Prison: A Hidden Story of Chaos, Anarchy and Politics*. Hampshire: Waterside Press.

Northern Ireland Office. 1989. *Report on the Work of the Northern Ireland Prison Service 1988/89.* Belfast: HMSO.
Nye, Joseph S. 2008. "Public Diplomacy and Soft Power." *Annals of the American Academy of Political and Social Science* 616: 94–109.
O'Donnell, Ian. 2004. "Prison Rape in Context." *British Journal of Criminology* 44: 241–55.
———. 2014. *Prisoners, Solitude, and Time.* Oxford: Oxford University Press.
———. 2016. "The Aims of Imprisonment." In *Handbook on Prisons*, 2nd ed., edited by Yvonne Jewkes, Jamie Bennett, and Ben Crewe, 39–54. Abingdon: Routledge.
———. 2018. "Psychological Survival in Isolation: Tussling with Time on Death Row." In *Living on Death Row: The Psychology of Waiting to Die*, edited by Hans Toch, James R. Acker, and Vincent Martin Bonventre, 193–211. Washington, DC: American Psychological Association.
———. 2019a. "The Society of Captives in an Ethiopian Prison." *Prison Journal* 99: 267–84.
———. 2019b. "The Art of Imprisonment." *Crime, Media, Culture* 15: 559–60.
———. 2020. "Time for Fresh Thinking on Capital Punishment." *Irish Examiner*, November 20, 9.
———. 2021a. "Ethiopian Notes." In *Sensory Penalities: Exploring the Senses in Spaces of Punishment and Social Control*, edited by Kate Herrity, Bethany E. Schmidt, and Jason Warr, 203–16. Bingley: Emerald Publishing.
———. 2021b. "Trump Pardons His Friends—He Must Show Clemency to Lisa Montgomery." *Irish Times*, January 7.
O'Donnell, Ian, and Eoin O'Sullivan. 2020. "Coercive Confinement: An Idea Whose Time Has Come?" *Incarceration: An International Journal of Imprisonment, Detention and Coercive Confinement* 1: 1–20.
Office of the Inspector General. 2017. *Review of the Federal Bureau of Prisons' Use of Restrictive Housing for Inmates with Mental Illness.* Washington, DC: US Department of Justice.
O'Hagan, Felim. 1991. "The Culture of Republican Wings: Individual and Collective Development." In *Éirí na Gealaí: Reflections on the Culture of Resistance in Long Kesh*, edited by Felim O'Hagan, 6–10. Belfast: Sinn Féin Department of Culture.
O'Hearn, Denis. 2009. "Repression and Solidary Cultures of Resistance: Irish Political Prisoners on Protest." *American Journal of Sociology* 115: 491–526.
Ó Mocháin, Deaglán. 2011. "Criminalization and the Post Hunger Strike Resistance of IRA Prisoners in the H-Blocks of Long Kesh—1981–2000." Unpublished PhD thesis, Queen's University Belfast.
O'Ruairc, Liam. 2001. "The League of Communist Republicans 1986–1991." Unpublished typescript.
Pelz, Mary E., James W. Marquart, and C. Terry Pelz. 1991. "Right-Wing Extremism in the Texas Prisons: The Rise and Fall of the Aryan Brotherhood of Texas." *Prison Journal* 71: 23–37.

Perkinson, Robert. 1994. "Shackled Justice: Florence Federal Penitentiary and the New Politics of Punishment." *Social Justice* 21 (3): 117–32.

———. 2010. *Texas Tough: The Rise of America's Prison Empire*. New York: Metropolitan Books.

Pew Research Center. 2007. *World Publics Welcome Global Trade—but Not Immigration: 47-Nation Pew Global Attitudes Survey*. Washington, DC: Pew Research Center.

Pickett, Carroll, with Carlton Stowers. 2002. *Within These Walls: Memoirs of a Death House Chaplain*. New York: St. Martin's Press.

Pitts, Edgar. 2020. "Waking Up on the Wrong Side of the Bed in the ADX Control Unit." *Minutes before Six*, October 15, https://minutesbeforesix.blogspot.com.

Powers, Jack. 2013. "Finally Out and Among the Living." *Colorado Independent*, November 28.

———. 2014. "Memo to Ross Todd re: Article about Ed Aro." April 29. Unpublished correspondence.

———. 2021a. *ADX Supermax: The Alcatraz of the Rockies*. Las Vegas: Good People Company.

———. 2021b. *The Manual Program: For Personal Growth*. Las Vegas: Good People Company.

Prendergast, Alan. 2007. "The Caged Life: Is Thomas Silverstein a Prisoner of His Own Deadly Past—Or the First in a New Wave of Locked-Down Lifers?" *Westword*, August 16.

Press, Aric. 1986. "Inside America's Toughest Prison." *Newsweek*, October 6, 46–61.

Ralph, Paige H., and James W. Marquart. 1991. "Gang Violence in Texas Prisons." *Prison Journal* 71: 38–49.

Reavis, Dick. 1985. "How They Ruined Our Prisons." *Texas Monthly* 13 (May): 152–59, 232–46.

Reinisch, Dieter. 2017. "Interview with Former Political Prisoner, Irish Republican Activist, and Playwright Laurence McKeown." *Studi Irlandesi: A Journal of Irish Studies* 7: 223–39.

Rolston, Bill. 2013. "Prison as a Liberated Zone: The Murals of Long Kesh, Northern Ireland." *State Crime* 2: 149–72.

Rolston, Bill, and Laurence McKeown. 2017. "Male Republican Prisoners in Northern Ireland: Resistance, Emotions and Homosociality." *State Crime* 6: 265–85.

Rovner, Laura. 2018. "On Litigating Constitutional Challenges to the Federal Supermax: Improving Conditions and Shining a Light." *Denver Law Review* 95: 457–517.

Ruiz, David. 2005. "Steel on Steel." *Texas Observer* 97 (December 2): 21.

Ruiz v. Estelle. 1980. 503 F. Supp. 1265. United States District Court, Southern District of Texas.

Ryder, Chris. 2000. *Inside the Maze: The Untold Story of the Northern Ireland Prison Service*. London: Methuen.

Sample, Albert R. 1984. *Racehoss: Big Emma's Boy*. Austin, TX: Eakin Press.

Schibbye, Martin, and Johan Persson. 2015. *438 Days*. Gothenburg: Offside Press.

Senbeta, Tesfaye Boresa. 2015. "Wrongful Convictions and the Quest for Remedies under the Ethiopian Criminal Justice System." Unpublished master's thesis, Addis Ababa University.

Sharoni, Simona. 2001. "Gendering Resistance within an Irish Republican Prisoner Community: A Conversation with Laurence McKeown." *International Feminist Journal of Politics* 2: 104–23.

Silverstein, Thomas. 2011. "Declaration." Exhibit 1. *Silverstein v. Federal Bureau of Prisons*. Civil Action No. 07–cv–02471–PAB–KMT, United States District Court, Colorado. April 2.

Silverstein v. Federal Bureau of Prisons. 2011. Civil Action No. 07-cv-02471-PAB-KMT. United States District Court, Colorado. April 2.

Skarbek, David B. 2014. *The Social Order of the Underworld: How Prison Gangs Govern the American Penal System*. New York: Oxford University Press.

———. 2016. "Covenants without the Sword? Comparing Prison Self-Governance Globally." *American Political Science Review* 110: 845–62.

———. 2020. *The Puzzle of Prison Order: Why Life behind Bars Varies around the World*. New York: Oxford University Press.

Sparks, Richard. 1994. "Can Prisons Be Legitimate? Penal Politics, Privatization, and the Timeliness of an Old Idea." *British Journal of Criminology* 34 (special issue): 14–28.

Sparks, Richard, and Anthony E. Bottoms. 1995. "Legitimacy and Order in Prisons." *British Journal of Sociology* 46: 45–62.

Sparks, Richard, Anthony E. Bottoms, and William Hay. 1996. *Prisons and the Problem of Order*. Oxford: Oxford University Press.

Special Rapporteur on Prisons and Conditions of Detention in Africa. 2004. *Report of the Mission to the to the Federal Democratic Republic of Ethiopia, 15–29 March 2004*. Banjul: African Commission on Human and Peoples' Rights.

Stahl, Aviva. 2019. "Gag Order." *Nation*, June 17–24, 12–19.

Sullivan, Kevin, K. 2016. "Re: Inmates of the Administrative Maximum United States Prison, Petition No. P-387-09, Response to Petition." Washington, DC: Permanent Representative of the United States of America to the Organization of American States.

Sutton, Malcolm. 2020. "An Index of Deaths from the Conflict in Northern Ireland." CAIN Archive. Accessed August 26, 2020. https://cain.ulster.ac.uk.

Sykes, Gresham. 1958. *The Society of Captives: A Study of a Maximum Security Prison*. Princeton, NJ: Princeton University Press.

Tertsakian, Carina. 2008. *Le Château: The Lives of Prisoners in Rwanda*. London: Arves Books.

Thatcher, Margaret. 1981. "Press Conference Ending Visit to Saudi Arabia." April 21, www.margaretthatcher.org.

Toch, Hans. 2001. "The Future of Supermax Confinement." *Prison Journal* 81: 376–88.

Toggia, Pietro. 2008. "The State of Emergency: Police and Carceral Regimes in Modern Ethiopia." *Journal of Developing Societies* 24: 107–24.

Tyler, Tom R., and Jonathan Jackson. 2013. "Future Challenges in the Study of Legitimacy and Criminal Justice." In *Legitimacy and Criminal Justice: An International Exploration*, edited by Justice Tankebe and Alison Liebling, 83–104. Oxford: Oxford University Press.

United Nations. 2014. *A Prison Evaluation Checklist for Post-Conflict Settings*. Vienna: United Nations Office on Drugs and Crime.

———. 2015. "Standard Minimum Rules for the Treatment of Prisoners (the Nelson Mandela Rules)." General Assembly resolution 70/175. Adopted December 17.

United Nations Committee against Torture. 2011. "Consideration of Reports Submitted by States Parties under Article 19 of the Convention against Torture and Other Cruel, Inhuman or Degrading Treatment or Punishment. Concluding Observations: Ethiopia." 45th Session. November 1–9, 2010. Geneva: UN.

US Department of Justice. 2016. *Report and Recommendations Concerning the Use of Restrictive Housing*. Washington, DC: US Department of Justice.

———. 2020. "Federal Prison System. FY2021 Budget Request at a Glance." www.justice.gov.

US Department of State. 2020. *Ethiopia 2019 Human Rights Report*. Washington, DC: Bureau of Democracy, Human Rights and Labor.

US Government Accountability Office. 2013. *Improvements Needed in Bureau of Prisons' Monitoring and Evaluation of Impact of Segregated Housing*. Washington, DC: United States Government Accountability Office.

Weber, Max. 1968. *Economy and Society: An Outline of Interpretive Sociology*. Edited by Guenther Roth and Claus Wittich. Vol. 3. New York: Bedminster Press.

Weldeyohannes, Behailu T. 2017. "Reforming Prison Policy to Improve Women-Specific Health and Sanitary Care Conditions of Prisons in Ethiopia." *William & Mary Journal of Women and the Law* 24: 101–26.

Whalen, Lachlan. 2007. *Contemporary Irish Republican Prison Writing: Writing and Resistance*. New York: Palgrave Macmillan.

Williams, Eric, J. 2011. *The Big House in a Small Town: Prisons, Communities, and Economics in Rural America*. Santa Barbara, CA: Praeger.

Wines, Enoch Cobb, ed. 1871. *Transactions of the National Congress on Penitentiary and Reformatory Discipline, Held at Cincinnati, Ohio, 12–18 October 1870*. Albany, NY: Argus Company.

World Bank. 2021. "World Bank Open Data." Accessed November 3, 2021. https://data.worldbank.org.

Yilma, Kassahun M., and Julian V. Roberts. 2019. "Out of Africa: Exploring the Ethiopian Sentencing Guidelines." *Criminal Law Forum* 30: 309–37.

INDEX

AB. *See* Aryan Brotherhood
Abouhalima, Mahmud, 192
ACA. *See* American Correctional Association
Administrative Maximum Facility Florence (ADX Florence), xii, 176, 195–96, 205, 227; *Admission and Orientation Handbook* for, 214–15, 216; cells at, 177–78; coercion demonstrated at, 229; without consent, 18, 20, 214–18, 215, 216; contact limited at, 198–99; criminalization emphasized by, 216, 257; *Cunningham v. Federal Bureau of Prisons* exposing, 202; dignity denied at, 190, 193, 207, 219; Eastham Unit compared with, 222; H Blocks contrasted with, 185–86, 201–2, 213, 228, 238; hunger striking at, 218; Isir Bet compared with, 166–68, 223, 239–43; without legitimacy, 18; letters censored at, 235–36; Marion replaced by, 173; Perkinson describing, 175; population differentiating, 174, *175*; power as asymmetric at, 20–21; prisoners with mental illness at, 209–12, 214; Range 13 at, 177, 180–83, *182*, 193, 196; recreation yard at, *181*; regulation as singular at, 220–21; rules enforced at, 9–10, 244–45; safety at, 217; SHU at, 29, 174, 177, 180, 183, 186; society reflected by, 4–5; solitary confinement at, 3, 171; SSU at, 177, 190–94, 218; step-down units at, 174, 177; Sullivan describing, 188; terrorists at, 190–91. *See also* control unit, at ADX Florence; Powers, John Jay "Jack"
administrative segregation, Ruiz in, 28, 98, 125; restoration of order with, 118–20, 123
Admission and Orientation Handbook, for ADX Florence, 171, 214–15, *216*
ADX Florence. *See* Administrative Maximum Facility Florence
ADX Supermax (Powers), 204–5
Africa, prisons in, 166–67
African Child Policy Forum, 142
Ahmed, Abiy, 169
Ainsworth, Butch, 100–101, 103–4
Alcatraz, USP, 173
Allenwood, USP, 210
aloneness, prisoners coping with, *197*, 200
Alpert, Geoffrey P., 107
American Correctional Association (ACA), 172–73, 179
Amnesty International, *177*, 183
anguish, in prison, 141, 208–9
architectural arrangements: at ADX Florence, 175–76, *179*, *181*, *182*; at Eastham Unit, 86–87; at H Blocks, 30–40, *70*, *80*; at Isir Bet, *134*, 165
Ard Fheis (annual party conference), Sinn Féin, 64–65
Arkansas, inmate trusty system in, 126
artwork, depicting culture of H Blocks, 76, *77*
Aryan Brotherhood (AB), 115–18, 203–4
Aryan Brotherhood of Texas (gang), 115–18

Atlanta, USP, 181, 210
The Audacity of Hope (Obama), 193
Austin Chronicle (newspaper), obituary of Ruiz in, 98
authority, 247–48; of BTs, 25, 95, 103, 113; charismatic, 4, 144, 146; politics diluting, 51; power contrasted with, 25; rational-legal, 9, 146–47; rules requiring, 146–47; traditional, 117, 124, 156, 228; use of force demonstrating failure of, 189, 227. *See also* guards, of prisons; legitimacy, of authority; staff, of prison
autonomy, of prisoners, 9, 63, 111, 168, 237–40
Averill, Liam, 72
Ayyad, Nidal, 192

Bacote v. Federal Bureau of Prisons, 200. See also *Cunningham v. Federal Bureau of Prisons*
Baxter, David, 208
beds, in dormitories, 135, 242–43
Beetham, David, 19–20, 225–27; on levels of legitimacy, *14*, 14–15, 26–27, 70
Berlin Wall, fall of, 65
Beto, George, 85–86, 97
Big Sandy, USP, 193
Binelli, Mark, 204, 210
Blackburn, Ashley G., 156
blanket protest, *34*, 35, 39, 42–43, 74, 81
Blue, Ethan, 95
Boal, Augusto (theorist), 65
bodies, of prisoners, 82–83, 252–54
bookkeepers, at Eastham Unit, 87–89, *88*, 106
BOP. *See* Federal Bureau of Prisons
Bottoms, Anthony, 19, 20–21, 51
Brand, Christo, 144
British Army, Northern Ireland and, 22, 34, 40
BTs. *See* building tenders
budget, of BOP, 166

building tenders (BTs), xii, 17, 83; authority of, 25, 95, 103, 113; with bookkeepers, 88–89, 106; coercion by, 8, 93, 116, 230–31; consent and, 226–27; cost reduced by, 89–90; at Eastham Unit, 3, 26; exploitation by, 3, 88, 90, 113, 125; gangs contrasted with, 8, 113–15, 118, 120, 240; guards working with, 92; head and rank-and-file, 85, *88*; homicide of, 121; integration compromised by, 95; Justice on, 98–99; leaders as, 90; noncompliance without, 15–16, 112; order keepers contrasted with, 232–33; perks for, 93–94; Pickett accepting, 104–5; population contrasted with, 94; power of, 8, 226; prisoners without, 124; racial breakdown of, 89; *Ruiz v. Estelle* and, 96–97, 103; as runners or strikers or hitmen, 86, *88*; sexual violence by, 94, 252; solidarity damaged by, 91, 95; staff relying on, 105, 110, 244; support service inmates replacing, 106–7; TDC denying existence of, 100, 102; Texas prisons relying on, 126; uniforms identifying, 92–93; violence without, 116–17; weapons allowed to, 8, 101, 103
Buntman, Fran Lisa, 81
bureaucracy: of dormitories, *153*; prisons influenced by, 228; Weber on, 146–47. *See also* governance, of prison

cages, prisoners in group therapy in, 211
calls, on phone from prisoners, 185, 191, 234
camp, Long Kesh, 31, *34*, 35, 60
Campbell, Brian, 39, 76
cannabis, expulsions from communes for, 59
The Captive Voice (An Glór Gafa), 76–78, *77*
carceral geometry, 13, 169, 224, 229
Carrabine, Eamonn, 23–25

case study method, xii–xiii, 2, 4, 5–6, 27, 220, 257
Catholic mission, Isir Bet improved by, 139
cells, prison: at ADX Florence, 177–78; multiple occupants in single, 242–43; parking space compared with, *179*, 218, 243; prisoners impacted by, 199; Range 13 differentiated by, 181–83, *182*
Center for Constitutional Rights and Lowenstein International Human Rights Clinic, 190–92
Central Intelligence Agency (CIA), 194–95
chairman, at Isir Bet, 135, *136*; Chalew as, 28, 128, 143–45, 151–52, 160; commander with, 161; of dormitories, 152–53
Chalew Gebino, vii, *136*, 254–57; as chairman, 28, 128, 143–45, 151–52, 160; code by, 6, 145, 157; pen portrait of, 143–45; violence without, 169
charter, of prison: by IRA prisoners, 7–8, 16–17; McKeown architecting, 31–32; republicans reviewing, 55; sexual orientation protected by, 57, 59; staff ignored by, 249
Charter for Frelimo Communities (IRA document), 55, *57*, *58*, 64, 247, 251
Chase, Robert T., 29, 92–93, 96, 105, 107, 114
children, with mothers in prison, 140–42
CIA. *See* Central Intelligence Agency
classification, of prisoners, 242
code, of prison, 12–14, 142, 144, 156; by Chalew, 6, 145, 157; discipline dealt with by, 147–48; dress, 185; gangs implementing, 11; on hygiene, 149; of Isir Bet, 3–4, 64, 248–52; legitimacy in, 143, 154–55; number of order keepers reduced by, 157; offenses and sanctions in, *150*; personality contrasted with, 146; prisoners assenting to, 145; on regulation, 127. *See also* charter, of prison; Charter for Frelimo Communities

coercion, 22, 228; ADX Florence demonstrating, 229; by BTs, 8, 93, 116, 230–31; compliance compared with, 160–61, 230; dull compulsion contrasted with, 23, 124. *See also* exploitation, in prisons
Coid, Jeremy W., 199
coiste. *See* committee, of H Blocks
Colorado Independent (newspaper), 208
commander, at Isir Bet, 15, 161–62
Commercial Bank of Ethiopia, 129
committee, of H Blocks (*coiste*), 60–61
communes, at H Blocks, 55, 65–66, 227, 248, 250; evolution of, 50, 63; expulsions from, 59; role allocation in, 44; solidarity at, 66; weekly pay shared at, 49
The Communist Manifesto (Marx and Engels), request for Irish language edition of, 79
community: building an integrated, 47–51; communication depended on by, 58; H Blocks in contact with, 185, 235; initiative of individual harnessed by, 61; Irish language extending, 81; prisoners connected with, 233; republicans sharing, 47–48
compliance, 22, 66–67, 154, 169, 225, *225*; basis of, 229–33; Carrabine on, 25; coercion compared with, 160–61, 230; conformity reflected by, 23–24; without consent, 218; fear maintaining, 95; through force, 227; legitimacy compared with, 160–61, 212–13, 233; monotony and, 24–25; normative, 23, 26–27, 160, 218, 229–32; power and, 116; prudential, 23, 160, 231; regulation without, 112–13. *See also* noncompliance
compulsory jail history program, by IRA, 63–64
conditioning, of staff, 66–73
conduct, BOP listing unacceptable, *216*
confinement, literature of, 76–81, *77*, *80*

Congress 86 (magazine), 46, 79
consent, *14*, 225, 232, 253; ADX Florence without, 18, 20, 214–18, *215*, *216*; BTs and, 226–27; compliance without, 218; election demonstrating, 18; legitimacy requiring, 14–15, 225–26
Constitution, United States, 102–3, 105–6, 126, 239
constitutions, by prisoners, 9, 163, 247–52
contact: ADX Florence limiting, 198–99; among prisoners, 186; control unit restricting, 183; religion demanding, 187; SAMs restricting, 191–92; Silverstein without, 181; with staff, 186–87, 196–97; visits without, 180
control unit, at ADX Florence, 177, 180, 210; contact restricted in, 183; medication discontinued in, 210; Powers describing, 203; Range 13 differentiated from, 181–82; recreation yard for, *181*
Cooley, Charles Horton, 171
Corrections Magazine, 100
courts, customary and religious, 155–56
Crewe, Ben, 221, 229–30, 232
criminalization: ADX Florence emphasized by, 216, 257; IRA prisoners rejecting, 51, 66, 228; politics contrasted with, 3, 54; POWs resisting, 60; support contrasted with, 213–14
Crouch, Ben M., 85–88, 91–94, 112, 120, 123–24, 126; on gangs, 118
Crumlin Road Gaol, 32
cumann. *See* political party branch
Cummins Prison Farm, 126
Cunningham v. Federal Bureau of Prisons, 200–201, 203, 207, 223, 246–47, 255; ADX Florence exposed in, 202; BOP impacted by, 210–11; mental illness shown in, 208–9
custodial institutions, similarities of, 1, 258

Dagne, Behailu, 141
Dáil Éireann. *See* Irish parliament
Dana, Jacqueline, 48–49
deaths: in dormitories, 158; IRA causing, 36, *37*, 52; of Mayberry, 96; in Prison Officers' Association, 52; relating to conflict in Northern Ireland, 35–36, *36*, *37*. *See also* homicide; murder
defoqa. *See* person who sleeps on ground, of dormitories
delegitimation, within prison, 14, *17*, 25, 47, 116–17, 169, 218, 226
Delgado, Bobby, 83, 91–93, 103
desegregation, of Texas prisons, 115
dignity: after death, 207; legitimacy and, 16; procedural fairness and, 26; social life with, 139; solitary confinement incompatible with, 171, 220; suffering in absence of, 193
DiIulio, John J., 90, 106, 111
discipline, in prison: *Admission and Orientation Handbook* on, 214–15, 216; code dealing with, 147–48; control of, 227; hierarchical, 42; hostility contrasted with, *172*; in TDC, 82
discretion, 9, 21, 111, 146, 202
District of Columbia Corrections Information Council, 177–78, 180, 185
Doerr-Zegers, Otto, 195–96
dormitories, at Isir Bet, *134*, 136, *137*; allocation to, 132–33; beds in, *135*; bureaucracy of, *153*; chairman of, 152–53; crowding of, 242–43; death in, 158; Eastham Unit compared with, 243; noise in, 141; person who sleeps on ground of, 159; rules required by, 146; without toilet, 135; UN standards contrasted with, 132–33
Dowker, Fay, 174
dress code, for visits, 131, 185
dull compulsion, prisoners experiencing, 23–25, 117, 124, 229

Eastham Unit, 82–83, *84*, 85, *87*, 99; ADX Florence compared with, 222; autonomy at, 238; bookkeepers at, 87–89, *88*, 106; BTs at, 3, 26; cities far from, 90; design of, 86; DiIulio on, 111; guards at, 106–7; homicide in, 113; inducement characterizing, 229–30; Justice criticizing, 243; labor at, 238–39, 241–42; legitimacy of, 125; porosity influencing, 236; slavery contrasted with, 4, 82, 91, 223, 238–39; staff at, 252; tradition influencing, 228–29; turnkeys at, 86–87, *88*, 93, 106, 126; visits to, 234; weapons in, 94. *See also* building tenders; Ruiz, David; *Ruiz v. Estelle*

Echo (newspaper), 116

education, in prison, 149; conventional, 65; Frelimo Documents and, 54–60, *57–58*; IRA prisoners denied, 43; Isir Bet offering, 138–39; McKeown on, 33; on politics, 49–50, 54–60, 63; republicans evolved by, 50

Eighth Amendment, United States Constitution, 126

Ekland-Olson, Sheldon, 104, 111, 113–14, 117, 243

election, of leaders of prisoners, 15, 18, 151

employment, of prisoners, 136–37

escape, by prisoners, 28, 63, 72, 143, 168, 237

Estelle, W. J., 100, 105. *See also Ruiz v. Estelle*

Ethiopia, xi, 127, 129, 166–69; homosexuality condemned in, 164; rights in, 140; Sharia law recognized by, 155

Ethiopian prisons: politics and, 16, 139; prisons in Rwanda compared with, 170; Special Rapporteur on Prisons and Conditions of Detention in Africa on, 167; torture and ill-treatment in, 140. *See also* Isir Bet (pseudonym)

executive committee, at Isir Bet, 145, 149, 160–62. *See also* chairman, at Isir Bet

exercise, by prisoners, 40, 179–80, 188

exploitation, in prisons, 238; by BTs, 3, 88, 90, 113, 125; of labor, 82, 125–26; of perceived weakness, 71–76; rules reducing, 251; of staff, 107, 110

families, of prisoners, 131, 163–64, 180, 185

Federal Bureau of Investigation (FBI), 191–92

Federal Bureau of Prisons (BOP), 16, 20, 173, 189, 209, 214; budget of, 166; *Cunningham v. Federal Bureau of Prisons* impacting, 210–11; on rights, 171; solitary confinement not recognized by, 102, 187, 215–16, 220; unacceptable conduct listed by, *216*. *See also* Administrative Maximum Facility Florence

Federal Medical Center Carswell, 29

Felons' Club (Belfast), 76

Fiaich, Tomás Ó, *34*

Fong, Robert S., 114, 117

food, in prison, *131*, 131–32, 159, 164, 238

food companion (*mequres*), 159

force, failure of authority demonstrated by use of, 189, 227

force feeding, of prisoners, 193, 218

four-pointing, of prisoners, 182, 190

Francisco, Jonathan, 209

freedom of movement, and prisoners, 165, 167, 237–38, 241

Freire, Paulo, 5, 43–44

Frelimo Documents: committee in, 60–61; education and, 54–60, *57–58*; IRA concealed in, 54–55. *See also* Charter for Frelimo Communities

Frente de Libertação de Moçambique (Frelimo), 54–61, *57–58*

Gaeltacht of the lark, at H Blocks (*Gaeltacht na Fuiseoige*), 79–81

gangs, in prison: BTs contrasted with, 8, 113–15, 120, 240; code implemented by, 11; Crouch and Marquart on, 118; homicide by, 117; *Ruiz v. Estelle* influencing, 107–8. *See also specific gangs*
Gates v. Collier, 126
gender, in prison, 29–30, 140–42, 164
Gettinger, Stephen, 100
Global North, prisons in, 1, 166, 168
Global South, prisons in, 1, 5
An Glór Gafa. See *The Captive Voice*
God, prisoners and, 132, 144, 209
Good, Glenn, 174
Good Friday Agreement, release of prisoners expedited by, 50
Gormally, Brian, 33, 69
governance, of prison, 251; extralegal, 10–11, 114; integration required for, 12; self-, 9, 156, 224, 232; theory of, 10–12, 114, 224. *See also* charter, of prison; Charter for Frelimo Communities; code, of prison
governor, leaders meeting with, 33, 35
group therapy, prisoners in cages in, 211
guards, of prisons: BTs working with, 92; at Eastham Unit, 106–7; prisoners in Mississippi as, 126; without snitches, 110; turnkeys working with, 86–87; violence by, 91–92, 111
Gulick, David B., 96, 116
Guutama, Ibsaa, 139–40

habit, prisoners influencing, 229–30, 232
Harding, Michael, 213
H Blocks, 3, 9, 36–38, *40*, 241, 248; ADX Florence contrasted with, 185–86, 201–2, 213, 228, 238; *Ard Fheis* voted at by, 64–65; artwork depicting culture of, 76, *77*; chronology of carceral conflict at, *34–35*; closure of, 74; committee of, 60–61; community in contact with, 185, 235; composition of, *39*; without conformity, 39; escape from, 63, 72; Gaeltacht of the lark at, 79–81; legitimacy at, 17–18, 231; McKee on, 67–68; murals in, 60; no wash protests at, 32, *34*, 35, 39, 42–43, 78; no work protests at, 35; OC of, 41, 44, 51, 68, 73; as political and aspirational, 239; power in, 7; Ramaphosa visiting, 74; rules rejected at, 221; staff at, 224; transformation of, 255–56; violence at, 53. *See also* communes, at H Blocks; Her Majesty's Prison Maze; IRA prisoners; Long Kesh camp; McKeown, Laurence
heel stringing, 82, 109, 206, 253
Her Majesty's Chief Inspector of Prisons for England and Wales, 35, 52–53, 59–60, 72–73
Her Majesty's Prison Maghaberry (HMP Maghaberry), 46–47, 55, 76
Her Majesty's Prison Maze (HMP Maze), 31, *34*, 53, 60, 73
hierarchy, in prisons, 91; committee contrasting, 61; discipline based on, 42; of force, 85–90, *87*, *88*, *89*
HMP Maghaberry. See Her Majesty's Prison Maghaberry
HMP Maze. See Her Majesty's Prison Maze
Holt v. Sarver, 126
homicide: by Aryan Brotherhood of Texas, 117–18; of BTs, 121; in Eastham Unit, 113; by gangs, 117; population contrasted with, 124; in Texas, 118, *118*; in Texas prisons, 119, *121*, 121–22. *See also* murder
homosexuality, condemned in Ethiopia, 164
Hood, Robert, 174
hope: evanescence of, 169; inculcation of, 172; indefatigability of, 205; trilogy of, 258
House Bill 1056, Texas prisons impacted by, 82, 100
Human Rights Watch, 177

hunger striking, by prisoners, 32, *34*, 37–38, 43, 83, 218; Stahl on, 193–94
hygiene, code on, 149

identity: disintegration of, 195; reinforcement of, 171, 198
illegitimacy, within prison, *14*, 15–17, 116, 226, 229
income, of prisoners, 137–38, *138*, *159*, 160, 248
individualized treatment plan, mental illness requiring, 212
inducement, Eastham Unit characterized by, 229–30
INLA. *See* Irish National Liberation Army
inmates. *See* prisoners
inmate trusty system, in Arkansas, 126
institutions, similarities of custodial, 1, 258
integration, 2, 225; BTs compromising, 95; definition of, 5; governance requiring, 12; regulation contrasted with, xi–xii, 7–10, *8*, 48, 83, 125, 169, 192–93, 212–13, 220–25, 233. *See also* solidarity
IRA Army Council, 41, *41*, 60, 221
IRA prisoners, 70; autonomy demonstrated by, 237–38; charter by, 7–8, 16–17; communal decision making by, 44; concessions won by, 69; conditioning by, 67; criminalization rejected by, 51, 66, 228; daytime lockup ended by, 68; education denied to, 43; Irish language learned by, 76–81, *77*, *80*; legitimacy contested by, 12, 21–22, 81, 221; noncompliance by, 230; ODCs differentiated from, 34, 48, 245; politics uniting, 28, 47–48, 239; power tilted by, 73; as POWs, 228, 245; prisoners at Isir Bet compared with, 76–77; reading lists for, 61, *62*; release of qualifying, 74; rules changed for, 3; society influenced by, 73; special category status of, *34*, 35, 37–38, 60; tunnel dug by, 71–72. *See also* McKeown, Laurence

Iris Bheag. *See* Little magazine
Irish language, IRA prisoners learning, 76–81, *77*, *80*
Irish National Liberation Army (INLA), 44, 59, 72
Irish parliament (*Dáil Éireann*), Sinn Féin in, 45
Irish Penal Reform Trust, xi
Irish Republican Army (IRA), 32, 38–39, 45, 59, 72, 78; Army Council of, 41, *41*, 60, 221; deaths caused by, 36, *37*, 52; Freire contrasted with, 44; Frelimo Documents concealing, 54–55; new consensus, 42–44, 48–49, 64–66; perseverance of, 9, 48, 74, 236; volunteers suspended by, 41–42. *See also* Charter for Frelimo Communities; IRA prisoners
Irish Times (newspaper), contact with columnist of, 79
Isir Bet (pseudonym), 8–9, 127–28, *165*, 226–27, 244; ADX Florence compared with, 166–67, 168, 223, 239–43; Catholic mission improving, 139; Charter for Frelimo Communities differentiated from code of, 64, 247; code of, 3–4, 248–52; commander at, 161–62; education offered at, 138–39; executive committee at, 145, 149, 160–62; freedom of movement at, 237–38; IRA prisoners compared with prisoners at, 76–77; leaders at, 15; legitimacy at, 16; neighborhoods compared with, 152; noncompliance at, 250; outside world mirrored by, 223, 236–37, 239, 257; painters at, 164–65; politics influencing, 168–69; poverty influencing, 161; protests at, 168; resources allocated at, *159*, 159–63, *162*; roles at, *151*; safety at, 157–58; security at, 240; sign on gate of, 128, *130*; structure and organization of, *151*, 151–54, *153*; without sufficient staff, 161–62; surveillance lacked at, 246;

Isir Bet (*cont.*)
    as village within town, *129*; violence avoided by, 158–59; visits at, 234. *See also* chairman, at Isir Bet; Chalew Gebino; dormitories, at Isir Bet; order keepers, at Isir Bet
isolation, xi, 176–77, 191; Powers impacted by, 208; self splintered by, 171; Silverstein in, 181, 196; technology deepening, 199. *See also* solitary confinement

Jackson, Bruce, 126
Jackson, Paul, 156
Jacobs, James B., 4, 256
Journal of Prisoners on Prisons, 78
Justice, William Wayne, 96, 101, 104, 108–9, 113; on BTs, 98–99; Eastham Unit criticized by, 243; as hate figure, 104; TDC admonished by, 102–3, 105–6

kebeles. *See* neighborhoods
the Kesh. *See* Long Kesh camp
Krajick, Kevin, 100

labor, 89, *89*; at Eastham Unit, 238–39, 241–42; exploitation of, 82, 125–26; slavery contrasted with, 82, 239; staff and, 155
Lamar v. Coffield, 115
language, prisoners learning Irish, 76–81, *77*, *80*
LCR. *See* League of Communist Republicans
leaders, of prisoners: as BTs, 90; election of, 15, 18; governor meeting with, 33, 35; at Isir Bet, 15; power of, 22; punishment block replaced by, 68–69. *See also* chairman, at Isir Bet
League of Communist Republicans (LCR), 45–47, 55, 79, 117, 226. *See also* Congress 86
learned helplessness, dull compulsion differentiating, 24

Leggett, Jaison, 209
legitimacy, of authority, 12–13, 116–18, 174, 225, 227–28; ADX Florence without, 18; Beetham on levels of, *14*, 14–15, 26–27, 70; in code, 143, 154–55; compliance compared with, 160–61, 212–13, 233; consent required for, 14–15, 225–26; deficit in, *14*, 15, 17, 25, 47, 116, 218, 226; dialogic, 19, 226; of Eastham Unit, 125; at H Blocks, 17–18, 231; horizontal and vertical, 17–19, 120, 145, 208, 226, 229; IRA prisoners contesting, 12, 21–22, 81, 221; at Isir Bet, 16; liquid, 19; politics challenging, 81; of power, *14*, 20; prisoners and staff disagreeing on, 26; of rules, 229–30; self-, 51; single-ply, 18–20, 208; staff and, 21, 26; triple-ply, 16, 70, 226; violence undermining, 23
letters, ADX Florence censoring, 235–36; H Blocks censoring, 71
Levasseur, Ray, 218
Linderman, Garrett, 174
literature, of confinement, 76–81, *77*, *80*
Little magazine (*Iris Bheag*), by Sinn Féin, 78
location, of prison, 21, 174, 201–2, 234, 253–54
lockdown, by TDC, 123
Long Kesh camp (the Kesh), 31, *34*, *35*, 60
Longwell, Alan, 54, 67, 71–72
loyalist (Irish politics), *37*, 38, *39*, 72

Mac Cormaic, Eoghan, 79–81
Mac Giolla Chríost, Diarmait, 79
Maghaberry, HMP. *See* Her Majesty's Prison Maghaberry
Mandela: My Prisoner, My Friend (Brand), 144
The Manual Program (Powers), 204
Marion, USP, 173, 181
marketplace, prison, *162*
Marquart, James W., 85–88, 91–94, 112, 120, 123–24, 126; on gangs, 118

Martin, Steve J., 104, 111
Martin chain, 180, 186, 189
Marxism, 45–46, 61
Matthews, Meredith, 156
Mayberry, Harvey, 96
Maze, HMP. *See* Her Majesty's Prison Maze
McEvoy, Kieran, 51, 52, 71
MCFP. *See* Medical Center for Federal Prisoners
McKane, William, 37–38, 50, 72
McKearney, Tommy, 45–47
McKee, William, 67–68
McKeown, Laurence, vii, 5, 28, 55, 56, 254–56; charter architected by, 31–32; on education, 33; Freire influencing, 5, 43; no wash protests joined by, 32; pen portrait of, 32–33; Powers compared with, 201–2; on republicans and change, 41–42
McMonagle, Seán, 48–49
McNeill, Fergus, 19
meaning, search for, 8, 63, 213, 218, 222–23, 258
Medical Center for Federal Prisoners (MCFP), 205–7
medication, for prisoners, 207, 210
Mekonnen, Mihretab, 141–42, 163, 164
men, contrasted with women in prison, 140–41
mental illness: *Cunningham v. Federal Bureau of Prisons* showing, 208; individualized treatment plan required for, 212; of Powers, 205; prisoners at ADX Florence with, 208–12, 214. *See also* self-mutilation
mequres. *See* food companion
Mexican Mafia (gang), 117
militias, order keepers contrasted with, 155
Mississippi, prisoners as guards in, 126
monotony, of prison, 1–2, 24–25
Moran, Paddy, xi, 127

mothers, with children in prison, 140–42
movement, prisoners and freedom of, 165, 167, 237–38, 241
Mowlam, Mo, 74
murder: Powers impacted by, 28, 204; of prisoners, 123; of prison officers, 53–54; safety contrasted with, 108; in Texas prisons, 25, 107–8, *108*
Murtagh, Tom, 54, 66, 69
Music from the Blocks (album), 78
Muslims, prisoners as, 104, 132, 187, 190, 194

National Prison Association, confidence of, 172, *172*, 230
neighborhoods (*kebeles*), Isir Bet compared with, 152
Newsweek (magazine), 83, *84*
New York Times Magazine, 179
NIO. *See* Northern Ireland Office
NIPS. *See* Northern Ireland Prison Service
no-human-contact order, 181, 198
noise, in dormitories, 141
noncompliance, 24–25, 229; without BTs, 15–16, 112; by IRA prisoners, 230; at Isir Bet, 250; rules contrasted with, 231
Nor Meekly Serve My Time (published oral history), 78
Northern Ireland: deaths related to conflict in, 35–36, *36*, *37*; peace process in, 74; Troubles in, 35, 60, 156, 256. *See also* H Blocks; Irish Republican Army
Northern Ireland Assembly, 74
Northern Ireland Office (NIO), 31, *41*, 51, 73, 220, 228; NIPS contrasted with, 69
Northern Ireland Prison Service (NIPS), 15, 31, 54, 69, 70, 248; staff not supported by, 52–53; statement of aims for, 31, 39
no touch torture, CIA recognizing, 194–95
no wash protests, at H Blocks, 32, *34*, 35, 39, 42–43, 78

no work protests, at H Blocks, *35*
Nugent, Kieran, *34*

Obama, Barack, 193
OC. *See* Officer Commanding, of H Blocks
ODCs. *See* ordinary decent criminals
Officer Commanding (OC), of H Blocks, 41, 44, 51, 68, 73
Ó Mocháin, Deaglán, 59–61, 63
Open University, 33, 54, 65
opponents, prisons housing political, 139–40
order keepers, at Isir Bet, 154, 156; BTs contrasting, 232–33; code reducing number of, 157; militias contrasted with, 155
ordinary decent criminals (ODCs), IRA prisoners differentiated from, *34*, 48, 245
O'Ruairc, Liam, 45, 47, 55

painters, at Isir Bet, 164–65
parking space, cells compared with, *179*, 218, 243
pay, communes sharing weekly, 49
peace process, in Northern Ireland, 35, 50, 74, 223
Pedagogy of the Oppressed (Freire), 43
Pelz, Mary E., 115, 118
penal practice, rhetoric contrasted with, 27–28, 128, 173, 220
pen portraits, 5–6, 28, 32–33, 97–98, 143–45, 203–5
perceived weakness, exploitation of, 71–76
Perkinson, Robert, 82, 91, 94–95, 97, 175, 199
person who sleeps on ground, of dormitories (*defoqa*), 159
Philokalia (religious text), 204
phone calls, from prisoners, 185, *198*
Pickett, Carroll, 98, 104–5
Pitts, Edgar, 182

political party branch (*cumann*), of Sinn Féin, 64–65
politics, *31*, 64–66, 116; authority diluted by, 51; criminalization contrasted with, 3, 54; education on, 49–50, 54–60, 63; Ethiopian prisons and, 139–40; IRA prisoners united by, 28, 47–48, 239; Irish, *37*, 38, *39*, 72, 74; Isir Bet influenced by, 168–69; LCR objecting to, 45–46; legitimacy challenged by, 81. *See also* republicans; Sinn Féin
population, of prison, 128; ADX Florence differentiated by, 174, *175*; BTs contrasted with, 94; homicide contrasted with, 124; race among staff compared to, 89
porosity, of prisons, 74, 81, 163, 233–37
Portlaoise Prison, 36
postcard, from spokesperson of prisoners, 74, *75*
post-traumatic stress disorder (PTSD), 203–4, *206*
poverty: Isir Bet influenced by, 161; prisoners informed by, 167–68; purpose and, 136–40, *137*, *138*
power, 7, 19, 91; as asymmetric at ADX Florence, 20–21; authority contrasted with, 25; of BTs, 8, 226; compliance and, 116; Crewe on social, 229–30; hard and soft, 231–32; IRA prisoners tilting, 73; of leaders, 22; legitimacy of, *14*, 20; NIO lacking, 51; possibility of reprisals diffusing, 21; staff realizing, 125
Powers, John Jay "Jack," vii, 6, 29, 173, 183, *184*, 254–56; control unit described by, 203; isolation impacting, 208; McKeown compared with, 201–2; mental illness of, 205; murder impacting, 28, 204; pen portrait of, 203–5; self-mutilation by, 82, 204, 207–8; timetable of trauma of, *206*
POWs. *See* prisoners of war
Press, Aric, 83

prison. *See specific topics*
prisoners, 106–7, 148, 242; at ADX Florence with mental illness, 209–12, 214; aloneness coped with by, 200; autonomy of, 9, 63, 111, 168, 237–40; bodies of, 82–83, 252–54; without BTs, 124; cells impacting, 199; code assented to by, 145; communication among, 192; community connected with, 233; constitutions written by, 9, 247–52; contact among, 186; in danger if leaving ADX Florence, 217; dull compulsion experienced by, 23–25, 117, 229; employment of, 136–37; escape by, 28, 72, 143, 168, 237; exercise by, 179–80; external shocks reordering, 250; force feeding of, 193, 218; four-pointing of, 182, 190; freedom of movement and, 165, 167, 237–38, 241; God and, 132, 144, 209; Good Friday Agreement expediting release of, 50; in group therapy in cages, 211; as guards in Mississippi, 126; habit influencing, 229–30, 232; hunger striking by, 32, *34*, 37–38, 43, 83, 218; income of, 137–38, *138*, *159*, 160, 248; Irish language learned by, 76–81, *77*, *80*; at Isir Bet compared with IRA prisoners, 76–77; killing other prisoners, *108*, *121*; legacy of, 254; legitimacy disagreed on by staff and, 26; medication for, 207, 210; murder of, 123; Murtagh describing, 54; as Muslims, 104, 132, 187, 190, 194; offenses committed by, 47, 133, *175*; phone calls from, 185, 191, 234; postcard from spokesperson of, 74, *75*; poverty informing, 167–68; religion of, 132, 187; restrained during visits, 185; rhetoric contrasted with life of, 27–28, 128, 173, 220; riotous behavior of, 253; *Ruiz v. Estelle* impacting, 116, 120; shared meanings and behaviors among, 222–23; staff contrasted with, 66–71, 105, 112, *121*, 122, 189–90, *215*, 243–46; with televisions, 141, 178, 234; trade among, 161–62, *162*; violence among, 113; women as, 29–30, 140–42, 164. *See also* Chalew Gebino; consent; criminalization; IRA prisoners; isolation; labor; leaders, of prisoners; McKeown, Laurence; mental illness; population, of prison; Powers, John Jay "Jack"; protests; rights, of prisoners; Ruiz, David; safety, perception of; Silverstein, Thomas
Prisoners, Solitude, and Time (O'Donnell), xi
prisoners of war (POWs), 17, 31, 63–64, 72, 221, 231; criminalization resisted by, 60; IRA prisoners as, *34*, 228, 245; Sands as, 75
Prison Officers' Association, deaths in, 52
protests: blanket, *34*, 35, 39, 42–43, 74, 81; Campbell on, 39; at Isir Bet, 168; no wash, 32, *34*, 35, 39, 42–43, 78; no work, 35; solidarity forged by, 43; on SSU, 193–94
psyche, threats to, 252–54
psychologists, weapons brandished by, 202
PTSD. *See* post traumatic stress disorder
punishment block, closure of, 68–69

Qur'an, 194

race, among staff compared to population, 89
racial desegregation, of Texas prisons, 115
racism, in prisons, 10, 15, 89, 115, 118, 239
Ramaphosa, Cyril, 74
Range 13, at ADX Florence, 177, 180–83, *182*, 193, 196
rape: absence of, 158; as control strategy, 94; by Robertson, 101
rational-legal authority, 9, 146–47
reading lists, for IRA prisoners, 61, 62
Reavis, Dick, 96, 104

recreation yard, at ADX Florence, 180, *181*; at H Blocks, 56, 68
recruitment, of staff, 104
regulation, 2, 11, 225; code on, 127; without compliance, 112–13; definition of, 5; integration contrasted with, xi–xii, 7–10, *8*, 48, 83, 125, 169, 192–93, 212–13, 220–25, 233; as singular at ADX Florence, 220–21; terrorists requiring, 245. *See also* rules
religion, of prisoners, 132, 187
rent, executive committee of Isir Bet charging, 160
republicans (Irish politics), 21–22, 38, 39, 63–64, 156; charter reviewed by, 55; community shared by, 47–48; education evolving, 50; Good Friday Agreement influencing, 50; McKeown on, 41–42; prison uniforms refused by, 32; solidarity acted in by, 67, 73; staff undermined by, 37. See also *The Captive Voice*; IRA prisoners; Irish Republican Army; League of Communist Republicans; McKeown, Laurence
resistance, body as site of, 82–83, 252–53
resources, allocated at Isir Bet, *159*, 159–63, *162*
rhetoric, penal practice contrasted with, 27–28, 128, 173, 220
rights, of prisoners: BOP on, 171; Charter for Frelimo Communities guaranteeing, *57*; in Ethiopia, 140
Robben Island, prison on, 81
Roberts, Julian V., 167
Robertson, Charlie, 100, *101*
Robinson, Gwen, 19
Rovner, Laura, 188, 210–11
Ruiz, David, vii, 5–6, *99*, 104, 254–57; in administrative segregation, 28, 98, 125; obituary in *Austin Chronicle* of, 98; pen portrait of, 97–98; self-mutilation by, 96

Ruiz v. Estelle, 29, 99–102, 114, 119, 243; BTs and, 96–97, 103; carceral geometry redrawn by, 224; expectations of prisoners raised by, 116; gangs influenced by, 107–8; prisoners impacted by, 116, 120; rules after, 124; staff demoralized by, 107, 109, 111. *See also* Justice, William Wayne
rules: ADX Florence enforcing, 9–10, 244–45; authority required by, 146–47; exploitation reduced by, 251; designed for individuals, 73; H Blocks rejecting, 221; IRA prisoners changing, 3; legitimacy of, 229–30; noncompliance contrasted with, 231; after *Ruiz v. Estelle*, 124; staff not enforcing, 51–53
Ryder, Chris, 34, 50, 71–72, 79

safety, perception of, 238; at ADX Florence, 217; at Eastham Unit, 108; at H Blocks, 53; at Isir Bet, 157–58; violence contrasted with, 119–20
Salameh, Mohammad, 193
Sample, Albert R., 98
SAMs. *See* special administrative measures
Sands, Bobby, 34, 74–75, 79
Scairt Amach. See Shout out
self, Silverstein maintaining sense of, 171, 198
self-mutilation, 97, 205–6, *206*, 252–53; as communication, 82–83; by Powers, 82, 204, 207–8; by Ruiz, 96; violence avoided with, 109
sexual orientation, charter protecting, *57*, 59
sexual violence, by BTs, 94, 103, 252
Sharia law, Ethiopia recognizing, 155
Shelby, David, 209
Shout out (*Scairt Amach*), 78
SHU. *See* special housing unit, at ADX Florence

INDEX | 283

Silverstein, Thomas, 213; drawing by, *197*; epic duration of solitary confinement of, 181; without human contact, 181, 198; isolation, 180, 196; sense of self maintained by, 198

Silverstein v. Federal Bureau of Prisons, 194

Sinn Féin (political wing of IRA), 45, 64–65, 78, 64–65

Skarbek, David B., 10–13

slavery, prisons contrasted with, 20, 82, 91, 223, 238, 239

snitches, BTs as, 90–92, 110

SNNPR. *See* Southern Nations, Nationalities, and Peoples' Region

social networks: at ADX Florence, 215; at Eastham Unit, 88; at H Blocks, 41; at Isir Bet, 151

society, 223; ADX Florence reflecting, 4–5; IRA prisoners influencing, 73; prison in, 256–58; Texas prisons reflecting, 116

society of captives, prison as, 1, 29, 258

solidarity, 238; BTs damaging, 91, 95; at communes, 66; constitutions promoting, 249–50; protests forging, 43; republicans acting in, 67, 73

solitary confinement, 28, 97; at ADX Florence, 3, 171; BOP not recognizing, 102, 187, 215–16, 220; on death row, 200; downward trend in, 176–77; as intrinsically inhumane, 171, 218–19; without medication, 207; SAMs intensify, 192–93; of Silverstein, 180–81; Sullivan denying, 187–88

"Something in the Air" (McKeown), 33

Southern Nations, Nationalities, and Peoples' Region (SNNPR), xi, 128, 141, 152, 163

Sparks, Richard, 2, 13–14, 20–22, 253

special administrative measures (SAMs), 212, 222, 231, 235; contact restricted by, 191–92; on Muslims, 190; solitary confinement intensified by, 192–93

special category status, of IRA prisoners, *34, 35*, 37–38, 60

special housing unit (SHU), at ADX Florence, 29, 174, 177, 180, 183, 186

special master, office of, 103, 107

Special Rapporteur on Prisons and Conditions of Detention in Africa, 139, 167, 168

Special Rapporteur on Torture and Other Cruel, Inhuman or Degrading Treatment or Punishment, 177

special security unit (SSU), at ADX Florence, 177, 190–94, 218

The Spirit of Freedom (artist unknown), 75

spokesperson, of prisoners, 74, 75

SSU. *See* special security unit, at ADX Florence

staff, of prison, 41, 70, 91; BTs relied on by, 105, 110, 244; charter ignoring, 249; conditioning of, 66–73, *70*; contact with, 186–87, 196–97; at Eastham Unit, 252; exploitation of, 107, 110; at H Blocks, 224; as homogeneous, 109; Isir Bet without sufficient, 161–62; labor and, 155; legitimacy and, 21, 26; NIPS not supporting, 52–53; power realized by, 125; prisoners contrasted with, 66–71, 105, 112, *121*, 122, 189–90, 215, 243–46; psychologists aligning with, 202; race among population compared to, 89; ratio of, to prisoners, 88, 105, 161, 190, 249; recruitment of, 104; republicans undermining, 37; *Ruiz v. Estelle* demoralizing, 107, 109, 111; rules not enforced by, 51–53; suicide by, 53; TDC boosting, 123; during Troubles, 256; uniform of, 129–31; violence and, 52, 189; visits without, 163; weapons carried by, 189. *See also* guards, of prisons

Stahl, Aviva, 191–92, 193–94

Stateville Penitentiary, 256

"Steel on Steel" (Ruiz), 98

step-down units, at ADX Florence, 174, 177
suicide, prisons and, 53, 207, 215, 252–53
Sullivan, Kevin K., 178, 187–88
supermax, prison as, xi, xii, 236. *See also* Administrative Maximum Facility Florence
support service inmates, BTs replaced by, 106–7
survival, psychological, 91, 167; seven Rs of, 200
Sykes, Gresham, 1, 10, 258

Tankebe, Justice, 19, 51
tattooing, 148, 204, 215
TDC. *See* Texas Department of Corrections
technology, isolation deepened by, 199
Teilifís na Gaeilge (Irish television service), 80
televisions, prisoners with, 141, 178, 234
terrorists, prisons with, 190–91, 245
Tertsakian, Carina, 169
Texas Department of Corrections (TDC), 85–86, 95, 111; discipline in, 82; existence of BTs denied by, 100, 102; Justice admonishing, 102–3, 105–6; lockdown ordered by, 123
Texas Observer (magazine), 98
Texas Prison Rodeo, 82
Texas prisons, 82; BTs relied on by, 126; budget of, 104; Constitution violated by, 102–3, 105–6; homicide in, 118, *118*, 119, *121*, 121–22; House Bill 1056 impacting, 100; murder in, 25, 107–8, *108*; racial desegregation of, 115; society reflected by, 116; violence in, 120–22; war years, 117–20. *See also* Eastham Unit
Texas Syndicate (gang), 114, 117
Thatcher, Margaret, 66
therapeutic modules, cages as, 211
Thirteenth Amendment, United States Constitution, 239
Toch, Hans, 190

toilet, dormitories without, 135
torture, CIA recognizing no touch, 194–95
Tough with a Knife, Hell with a Writ (Ruiz), 98
trade, among prisoners, 161–62, *162*
trauma, of Powers, *206*
Troubles, in Northern Ireland, 35, 60, 156, 256
Trump, Donald, killing spree, 257
Tucson, USP, 206
tunnel, IRA prisoners digging, 71–72
turnkeys, at Eastham Unit, 86–87, 97, 100, 106

UN. *See* United Nations
unacceptable conduct, BOP listing, *216*
uniforms, at prison: BTs identified by, 92–93; republicans refusing, 32, *34*; of staff, 129–31; wide sartorial range of, 130–32
unionist (Irish politics), 74
United Nations (UN), dormitories contrasted with standards of, 132–33, 177
United States Constitution, 102–3, 105–6, 126, 239
United States Penitentiary (USP): Alcatraz, 173; Allenwood, 210; Atlanta, 181, 210; Big Sandy, 193; Marion, 173, 181; Tucson, 206
"Unrepentant Fenian Bastards" (McKeown), 33
use of force, failure of authority demonstrated by, 189, 227
USP. *See* United States Penitentiary

Vega, Jose, 207
violence: of Ainsworth, 100–101; among prisoners, 113; without BTs, 116–17; without Chalew, 169; compliance maintained with fear of, 95; by guards, 91–92, 111; at H Blocks, 53; Isir Bet avoiding, 158–59; legitimacy undermined by, 23; Pelz describing, 118;

PTSD and, 204; safety contrasted with, 119–20; self-mutilation avoiding, 109; sexual, 94, 103, 252; staff and, 52, 189; in Texas prisons, 120–22. *See also* homicide; murder; self-mutilation

visits, to prison: without contact, 180; distance limiting, 201; dress code for, 131, 185; to Eastham Unit, 234; families challenged by, 163–64; at Isir Bet, 234; prisoners restrained during, 185; without staff, 163

vocabulary, prison-specific, 158–59

water, prison struggling to provide, 132, 139

weakness, exploitation of perceived, 71–76

weapons: BTs allowed, 8, 101, 103; in Eastham Unit, 94; in Isir Bet, staves discarded, 157; psychologist brandishing, 202; staff carrying, 189

Weber, Max, 146–47

weekly pay, communes sharing, 49

Weldeyohannes, Behailu T., 132

women, as prisoners, 29–30, 140–42, 164

worst of the worst, 5, 20, 26, 178, 218

Wright, Billy "King Rat," 72

writ writer, Ruiz as, 28, 97–98, 254

Yilma, Kassahun M., 167

ABOUT THE AUTHOR

IAN O'DONNELL is Professor of Criminology at University College Dublin. In recent books he examined how prisoners deal with the temporal dimension of their lives (*Prisoners, Solitude, and Time*) and analyzed clemency in death penalty cases (*Justice, Mercy, and Caprice*). He is a Member of the Royal Irish Academy and an adjunct fellow of Linacre College, Oxford.

www.ingramcontent.com/pod-product-compliance
Lightning Source LLC
Chambersburg PA
CBHW020247030426
42336CB00010B/648